Mike Holt's

UNDERSTANDING THE NATIONAL ELECTRICAL CODE® WORKBOOK

Articles 90 - 480

 Mike Holt Enterprises
MikeHolt.com • 888.632.2633

BASED ON THE
2023 NEC®

NOTICE TO THE READER

The text and commentary in this book is the author's interpretation of the 2023 Edition of NFPA 70®, *National Electrical Code*®. It shall not be considered an endorsement of or the official position of the NFPA® or any of its committees, nor relied upon as a formal interpretation of the meaning or intent of any specific provision or provisions of the 2023 edition of NFPA 70, *National Electrical Code*.

The publisher does not warrant or guarantee any of the products described herein or perform any independent analysis in connection with any of the product information contained herein. The publisher does not assume, and expressly disclaims, any obligation to obtain and include information other than that provided to it by the manufacturer.

The reader is expressly warned to consider and adopt all safety precautions and applicable federal, state, and local laws and regulations. By following the instructions contained herein, the reader willingly assumes all risks in connection with such instructions.

Mike Holt Enterprises disclaims liability for any personal injury, property or other damages of any nature whatsoever, whether special, indirect, consequential or compensatory, directly or indirectly resulting from the use of this material. The reader is responsible for relying on his or her personal independent judgment in determining safety and appropriate actions in all circumstances.

The publisher makes no representation or warranties of any kind, including but not limited to, the warranties of fitness for particular purpose or merchantability, nor are any such representations implied with respect to the material set forth herein, and the publisher takes no responsibility with respect to such material. The publisher shall not be liable for any special, consequential, or exemplary damages resulting, in whole or part, from the reader's use of, or reliance upon, this material.

Mike Holt's Guide to Understanding the National Electrical Code® Workbook, Articles 90-480, based on the 2023 NEC®

First Printing: February 2023
Author: Mike Holt
Cover Design: Bryan Burch
Layout Design and Typesetting: Cathleen Kwas
COPYRIGHT © 2023 Charles Michael Holt
ISBN 978-1-950431-76-2

All rights reserved. No part of this work covered by the copyright hereon may be reproduced or used in any form or by any means graphic, electronic, or mechanical, including photocopying, recording, taping, or information storage and retrieval systems without the written permission of the publisher.

For more information, or to request permission to use material from this text, e-mail Info@MikeHolt.com.

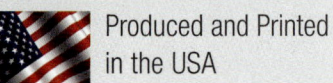 Produced and Printed in the USA

 This logo is a registered trademark of Mike Holt Enterprises, Inc.

 NEC®, NFPA 70®, NFPA 70E® and *National Electrical Code*® are registered trademarks of the National Fire Protection Association.

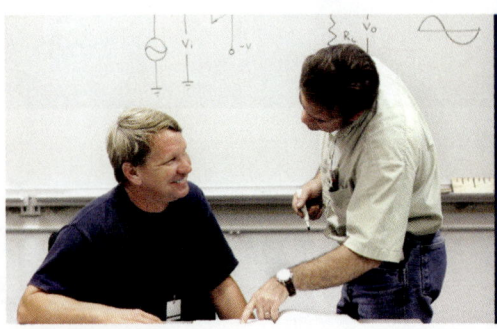

Are you an Instructor?

You can request a review copy of this or other Mike Holt Publications:

888.632.2633 • Training@MikeHolt.com

Download a sample PDF of all our publications by visiting MikeHolt.com/Instructors

I dedicate this book to the
Lord Jesus Christ, *my mentor and teacher.*
Proverbs 16:3

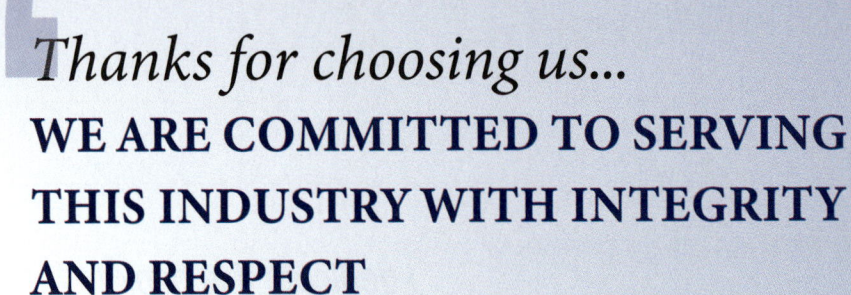

"*Thanks for choosing us...*
WE ARE COMMITTED TO SERVING THIS INDUSTRY WITH INTEGRITY AND RESPECT

Since 1975, we have worked hard to develop products that get results, and to help individuals in their pursuit of success in this exciting industry.

From the very beginning we have been committed to the idea that customers come first. Everyone on my team will do everything they possibly can to help you succeed. I want you to know that we value you and are honored that you have chosen us to be your partner in training.

You are the future of this industry and we know that it is you who will make the difference in the years to come. My goal is to share with you everything that I know and to encourage you to pursue your education on a continuous basis. I hope that not only will you learn theory, *Code*, calculations, or how to pass an exam, but that in the process, you will become the expert in the field and the person others know to trust.

To put it simply, we genuinely care about your success and will do everything that we can to help you take your skills to the next level!

We are happy to partner with you on your educational journey.

God bless and much success,

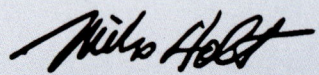

TABLE OF CONTENTS

About This Textbook vii

Additional Products to Help You Learn ix

How to Use the *National Electrical Code* 1

Article 90—Introduction to the *National Electrical Code* 7

CHAPTER 1—GENERAL RULES 11

Article 100—Definitions 13

Article 110—General Requirements for Electrical Installations 27

CHAPTER 2—WIRING AND PROTECTION 35

Article 200—Use and Identification of Grounded Conductors 37

Article 210—Branch Circuits 39

Article 215—Feeders 51

Article 220—Branch-Circuit, Feeder, and Service Load Calculations 53

Article 225—Outside Branch Circuits and Feeders 59

Article 230—Services 65

Article 240—Overcurrent Protection 73

Article 242—Overvoltage Protection 79

Article 250—Grounding and Bonding 81

CHAPTER 3—WIRING METHODS AND MATERIALS 101

Article 300—General Requirements for Wiring Methods and Materials 105

Article 310—Conductors for General Wiring 113

Article 312—Cabinets, Cutout Boxes, and Meter Socket Enclosures 119

Article 314—Boxes, Conduit Bodies, and Handhole Enclosures 123

Article 320—Armored Cable (Type AC) 131

Article 330—Metal-Clad Cable (Type MC) 135

Article 334—Nonmetallic-Sheathed Cable (Type NM) 139

Article 336—Power and Control Tray Cable (Type TC) 143

Article 338—Service-Entrance Cable (Types SE and USE) 145

Article 340—Underground Feeder and Branch-Circuit Cable (Type UF) 147

Article 342—Intermediate Metal Conduit (IMC) 149

Article 344—Rigid Metal Conduit (RMC) 153

Article 348—Flexible Metal Conduit (FMC) 157

Article 350—Liquidtight Flexible Metal Conduit (LFMC) 159

Article 352—Rigid Polyvinyl Chloride Conduit (PVC) ... 161

Table of Contents

Article 356—Liquidtight Flexible Nonmetallic Conduit (LFNC) 165

Article 358—Electrical Metallic Tubing (EMT) 169

Article 362—Electrical Nonmetallic Tubing (ENT) 171

Article 376—Metal Wireways 175

Article 380—Multioutlet Assemblies 179

Article 386—Surface Metal Raceways 181

Article 392—Cable Trays 183

CHAPTER 4—EQUIPMENT FOR GENERAL USE 187

Article 400—Flexible Cords 189

Article 402—Fixture Wires 191

Article 404—Switches 193

Article 406—Receptacles, Attachment Plugs, and Flanged Inlets 197

Article 408—Switchboards and Panelboards 203

Article 410—Luminaires 207

Article 411—Low-Voltage Lighting 213

Article 422—Appliances 215

Article 424—Fixed Electric Space-Heating Equipment 219

Article 430—Motor Circuits, Controllers, and Adjustable-Speed Drives 221

Article 440—Air-Conditioning Equipment 227

Article 445—Generators 229

Article 450—Transformers 231

Article 480—Stationary Standby Batteries 233

Final Exam A—Straight Order 235

Final Exam B—Random Order 245

About the Author 257

About the Illustrator 258

About the Mike Holt Team 259

ABOUT THIS TEXTBOOK

Mike Holt's Understanding the National Electrical Code Workbook, Articles 90-480, based on the 2023 NEC

This workbook was designed to complement *Mike Holt's Illustrated Guide to Understanding the National Electrical Code, Volume 1, based on the 2023 NEC* textbook and contains over 1,500 *NEC®* practice questions that are in *Code* order. It also includes two final exams, one in straight order and one in random order, with a total of 200 questions. These questions will test your knowledge and comprehension of the material covered in Mike Holt's related textbook, and in the *NEC*.

The *National Electrical Code®* establishes the general requirements for safe electrical installations in Article 90 and Chapters 1 through 4 which apply to all installations, unless modified in Articles 5 through 8 of the *Code*. The scope of the Chapters 1 through 4 covers definitions and general requirements, wiring and protection, wiring methods and materials, and equipment for general use. Rules for service and feeder calculations are also covered.

The Scope of This Workbook

The questions in this workbook are drawn from the sections of the *NEC* (Article 90 and Chapters 1-4) covered in *Mike Holt's Illustrated Guide to Understanding the NEC, Volume 1*. The questions in this book are based on the following conditions:

1. Power Systems and Voltage. All power-supply systems are assumed to be one of the following nominal voltages or "voltage class", unless identified otherwise:

- 2-wire, single-phase, 120V
- 3-wire, single-phase, 120/240V
- 4-wire, three-phase, 120/240V Delta High-Leg
- 4-wire, three-phase, 208Y/120V or 480Y/277V Wye

2. Electrical Calculations. Unless the question or example specifies three-phase, they're based on a single-phase power supply. In addition, all amperage calculations are rounded to the nearest whole number in accordance with Section 220.5(B).

3. Conductor Material/Insulation. The conductor material and insulation are copper THWN-2, unless otherwise indicated.

4. Conductor Sizing.

Circuits Rated 100A or Less. Conductors are sized to the 60°C column of Table 310.16 [110.14(C)(1)(a)(2)]. Where equipment is listed and identified for use with conductors having at least a 75°C temperature rating, the conductors can be sized to the 75°C column of Table 310.16 [110.14(C)(1)(a)(3)].

Circuits Rated Over 100A. Conductors are sized to the 75°C column of Table 310.16 [110.14(C)(1)(b)(2)].

5. Overcurrent Protective Device. The term "overcurrent protective device" refers to a molded-case circuit breaker, unless specified otherwise. Where a fuse is specified, it's a single-element type fuse, also known as a "onetime fuse," unless the text specifies otherwise.

How to Use This Workbook

You will need to use the 2023 *National Electrical Code* as a reference to ensure you answer questions correctly and to improve your ability to navigate the *Code* book.

This workbook is meant to be a practice tool to test your knowledge and retention of the *NEC* rules. There is no "pass" or "fail," only practice, review, and learning.

If you find yourself unable to answer the questions, or if you are not familiar with the material being reviewed, we recommend that you get a copy of *Mike Holt's Illustrated Guide to Understanding the National Electrical Code, Volume 1, based on the 2023* textbook and its video program.

Visit MikeHolt.com/Code.

About This Textbook

Answer Keys

If you ordered your product directly from Mike Holt Enterprises, your digital answer key can be found in your online account at Mike Holt Enterprises. Go to MikeHolt.com/MyAccount and log in to your account, or create one if you haven't already done so. If you are not currently a Mike Holt customer, you can access an answer key at MikeHolt.com/MyAK23UN1WB, or by scanning this QR code.

Technical Questions

As you progress through this workbook, you might find yourself feeling confused by the questions or not know where to find the answers. Don't become frustrated, and don't get down on yourself. Remember, the *National Electrical Code* is a complex document and it takes time to learn the *Code* rules. We recommend you review the explanations and examples in Mike's *Understanding the National Electrical Code, Volume 1* textbook, and refer to the *Code* book in order to understand the information. You may also find it helpful to discuss your questions with instructors, co-workers, other students, or your supervisor—they might have a perspective that will help you understand more clearly. If you are still confused, visit MikeHolt.com/Forum, and post your question on the free *Code* Forum, which is a moderated community of electrical professionals.

Textbook Errors and Corrections

We're committed to providing you the finest product with the fewest errors and take great care to ensure our textbooks are correct. But we're realistic and know that errors might be found after printing. If you believe that there's an error of any kind (typographical, grammatical, technical, etc.) in this book or in the Answer Key, please visit MikeHolt.com/Corrections and complete the online Correction Form.

ADDITIONAL PRODUCTS TO HELP YOU LEARN

Understanding the NEC Complete Training Library

Do you want a comprehensive understanding of the *Code*? Then you need Mike's Understanding the *NEC* Complete Training Library. This program takes you step-by-step through the *NEC*, in *Code* order with detailed illustrations, great practice questions, and in-depth video analysis. This library is perfect for engineers, electricians, contractors, and electrical inspectors.

PROGRAM INCLUDES:

Understanding the National Electrical Code—Volume 1 Textbook
- *General Requirements videos*
- *Wiring and Protection videos*
- *Wiring Methods and Materials videos*
- *Equipment for General Use videos*

Understanding the National Electrical Code—Volume 2 Textbook
- *Special Occupancies videos*
- *Special Equipment videos*
- *Special Conditions and Communications Systems videos*

Bonding and Grounding Textbook
- *Bonding and Grounding videos*

Understanding the National Electrical Code Workbook (Articles 90–480)

Digital answer keys

Plus! A digital version of each textbook

Product Code: [23UNDLIBMM]

To order call 888.632.2633 and mention that you already have the Workbook, so our team can price your product accordingly.

Understanding the National Electrical Code, based on the 2023 NEC, Volume 1 and 2 textbooks

This product is a combination of Mike's best-selling illustrated textbooks in one great package. Mike's ability to clarify the meaning of the *Code* with his straightforward, concise writing style, along with his full-color detailed instructional graphics, is the reason that these books continue to grow in popularity.

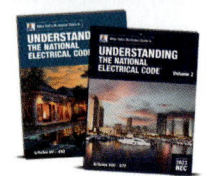

PACKAGE INCLUDES:

Understanding the National Electrical Code—Volume 1 Textbook

Understanding the National Electrical Code—Volume 2 Textbook

Digital answer keys

Product Code: [23UND12]

To order, visit MikeHolt.com/Code.

Additional Products to Help You Learn

Understanding Electrical Theory, for *NEC* Applications Video Program

Whether you're a first-year apprentice still struggling to understand the difference between a volt or ampere, or a veteran journeyman trying to sharpen your troubleshooting skills, this product has something for you. Once you know the principles behind how electricity works, you will be ready to correctly apply the rules in the *National Electrical Code* to the work you do every day.

This video program will take you on a journey that begins with the physics behind how electricity works all the way through topics and concepts that are relevant to everyone working in the electrical industry.

PROGRAM INCLUDES:

Understanding Electrical Theory for NEC Applications Textbook
- *Electrical Theory videos*

Digital answer keys

Plus! A digital version of the textbook

Product Code: [THLIBMM]

To order, visit MikeHolt.com/Theory.

HOW TO USE THE *NATIONAL ELECTRICAL CODE*

The original *NEC* document was developed in 1897 as a result of the united efforts of various insurance, electrical, architectural, and other cooperative interests. The National Fire Protection Association (NFPA) has sponsored the *National Electrical Code* since 1911.

The purpose of the *Code* is the practical safeguarding of persons and property from hazards arising from the use of electricity. It isn't intended as a design specification or an instruction manual for untrained persons. It is, in fact, a standard that contains the minimum requirements for an electrical installation that's essentially free from hazard. Learning to understand and use the *Code* is critical to you working safely; whether you're training to become an electrician, or are already an electrician, electrical contractor, inspector, engineer, designer, or instructor.

The *NEC* was written for qualified persons; those who understand electrical terms, theory, safety procedures, and electrical trade practices. Learning to use the *Code* is a lengthy process and can be frustrating if you don't approach it the right way. First, you'll need to understand electrical theory and if you don't have theory as a background when you get into the *NEC*, you're going to struggle. Take one step back if necessary and learn electrical theory. You must also understand the concepts and terms in the *Code* and know grammar and punctuation in order to understand the complex structure of the rules and their intended purpose(s). The *NEC* is written in a formal outline which many of us haven't seen or used since high school or college so it's important for you to pay particular attention to this format. Our goal for the next few pages is to give you some guidelines and suggestions on using your *Code* book to help you understand that standard, and assist you in what you're trying to accomplish and, ultimately, your personal success as an electrical professional!

Language Considerations for the *NEC*

Terms and Concepts

The *NEC* contains many technical terms, and it's crucial for *Code* users to understand their meanings and applications. If you don't understand a term used in a rule, it will be impossible to properly apply the *NEC* requirement. Article 100 defines those that are used generally in two or more articles throughout the *Code*; for example, the term "Dwelling Unit" is found in many articles. If you don't know the *NEC* definition for a "dwelling unit" you can't properly identify its *Code* requirements. Another example worth mentioning is the term "Outlet." For many people it has always meant a receptacle—not so in the *NEC*!

Article 100 contains the definitions of terms used throughout the *Code*. Where a definition is unique to a specific article, the article number is indicated at the end of the definition in parenthesis (xxx). For example, the definition of "Pool" is specific to Article 680 and ends with (680) because it applies ONLY to that article. Definitions of standard terms, such as volt, voltage drop, ampere, impedance, and resistance are not contained in Article 100. If the *NEC* does not define a term, then a dictionary or building code acceptable to the authority having jurisdiction should be consulted.

Small Words, Grammar, and Punctuation

Technical words aren't the only ones that require close attention. Even simple words can make a big difference to the application of a rule. Is there a comma? Does it use "or," "and," "other than," "greater than," or "smaller than"? The word "or" can imply alternate choices for wiring methods. A word like "or" gives us choices while the word "and" can mean an additional requirement must be met.

An example of the important role small words play in the *NEC* is found in 110.26(C)(2), where it says equipment containing overcurrent, switching, "or" control devices that are 1,200A or more "and" over 6 ft wide require a means of egress at each end of the working space. In this section, the word "or" clarifies that equipment containing any of the three types of devices listed must follow this rule. The word "and" clarifies that 110.26(C)(2) only applies if the equipment is both 1,200A or more and over 6 ft wide.

NEC Style and Layout | How to Use the *National Electrical Code*

Grammar and punctuation play an important role in establishing the meaning of a rule. The location of a comma can dramatically change the requirement of a rule such as in 250.28(A), where it says a main bonding jumper shall be a wire, bus, screw, or similar suitable conductor. If the comma between "bus" and "screw" was removed, only a "bus screw" could be used. That comma makes a big change in the requirements of the rule.

Slang Terms or Technical Jargon

Trade-related professionals in different areas of the country often use local "slang" terms that aren't shared by all. This can make it difficult to communicate if it isn't clear what the meaning of those slang terms are. Use the proper terms by finding out what their definitions and applications are before you use them. For example, the term "pigtail" is often used to describe the short piece of conductor used to connect a device to a splice, but a "pigtail" is also used for a rubberized light socket with pre-terminated conductors. Although the term is the same, the meaning is very different and could cause confusion. The words "splice" and "tap" are examples of terms often interchanged in the field but are two entirely different things! The uniformity and consistency of the terminology used in the *Code*, makes it so everyone says and means the same thing regardless of geographical location.

NEC Style and Layout

It's important to understand the structure and writing style of the *Code* if you want to use it effectively. The *National Electrical Code* is organized using twelve major components.

1. Table of Contents
2. Chapters—Chapters 1 through 9 (major categories)
3. Articles—Chapter subdivisions that cover specific subjects
4. Parts—Divisions used to organize article subject matter
5. Sections—Divisions used to further organize article subject matter
6. Tables and Figures—Represent the mandatory requirements of a rule
7. Exceptions—Alternatives to the main *Code* rule
8. Informational Notes—Explanatory material for a specific rule (not a requirement)
9. Tables—Applicable as referenced in the *NEC*
10. Annexes—Additional explanatory information such as tables and references (not a requirement)
11. Index
12. Changes to the *Code* from the previous edition

1. Table of Contents. The Table of Contents displays the layout of the chapters, articles, and parts as well as the page numbers. It's an excellent resource and should be referred to periodically to observe the interrelationship of the various *NEC* components. When attempting to locate the rules for a specific situation, knowledgeable *Code* users often go first to the Table of Contents to quickly find the specific *NEC* rule that applies.

2. Chapters. There are nine chapters, each of which is divided into articles. The articles fall into one of four groupings: General Requirements (Chapters 1 through 4), Specific Requirements (Chapters 5 through 7), Communications Systems (Chapter 8), and Tables (Chapter 9).

Chapter 1—General
Chapter 2—Wiring and Protection
Chapter 3—Wiring Methods and Materials
Chapter 4—Equipment for General Use
Chapter 5—Special Occupancies
Chapter 6—Special Equipment
Chapter 7—Special Conditions
Chapter 8—Communications Systems (Telephone, Data, Satellite, Cable TV, and Broadband)
Chapter 9—Tables–Conductor and Raceway Specifications

3. Articles. The *NEC* contains approximately 160 articles, each of which covers a specific subject. It begins with Article 90, the introduction to the *Code* which contains the purpose of the *NEC*, what is covered and isn't covered, along with how the *Code* is arranged. It also gives information on enforcement, how mandatory and permissive rules are written, and how explanatory material is included. Article 90 also includes information on formal interpretations, examination of equipment for safety, wiring planning, and information about formatting units of measurement. Here are some other examples of articles you'll find in the *NEC*:

Article 110—General Requirements for Electrical Installations
Article 250—Grounding and Bonding
Article 300—General Requirements for Wiring Methods and Materials
Article 430—Motors, Motor Circuits, and Motor Controllers
Article 500—Hazardous (Classified) Locations
Article 680—Swimming Pools, Fountains, and Similar Installations
Article 725—Class 2 and Class 3 Power-Limited Circuits
Article 800—General Requirements for Communications Systems

4. Parts. Larger articles are subdivided into parts. Because the parts of a *Code* article aren't included in the section numbers, we tend to forget to what "part" an *NEC* rule is relating. For example, Table 110.34(A) contains working space clearances for electrical equipment. If we aren't careful, we might think this table applies to all electrical installations, but Table 110.34(A) is in Part III, which only contains requirements for "Over 1,000 Volts, Nominal" installations. The rules for working clearances for electrical equipment for systems 1,000V, nominal, or less are contained in Table 110.26(A)(1), which is in Part II—1,000 Volts, Nominal, or Less.

5. Sections. Each *NEC* rule is called a "*Code* Section." A *Code* section may be broken down into subdivisions; first level subdivision will be in parentheses like (A), (B),..., the next will be second level subdivisions in parentheses like (1), (2),..., and third level subdivisions in lowercase letters such as (a), (b), and so on.

For example, the rule requiring all receptacles in a dwelling unit bathroom to be GFCI protected is contained in Section 210.8(A)(1) which is in Chapter 2, Article 210, Section 8, first level subdivision (A), and second level subdivision (1).

Note: According to the *NEC Style Manual*, first and second level subdivisions are required to have titles. A title for a third level subdivision is permitted but not required.

Many in the industry incorrectly use the term "Article" when referring to a *Code* section. For example, they say "Article 210.8," when they should say "Section 210.8." Section numbers in this textbook are shown without the word "Section," unless they're at the beginning of a sentence. For example, Section 210.8(A) is shown as simply 210.8(A).

6. Tables and Figures. Many *NEC* requirements are contained within tables, which are lists of *Code* rules placed in a systematic arrangement. The titles of the tables are extremely important; you must read them carefully in order to understand the contents, applications, and limitations of each one. Notes are often provided in or below a table; be sure to read them as well since they're also part of the requirement. For example, Note 1 for Table 300.5(A) explains how to measure the cover when burying cables and raceways and Note 5 explains what to do if solid rock is encountered.

7. Exceptions. Exceptions are *NEC* requirements or permissions that provide an alternative method to a specific rule. There are two types of exceptions—mandatory and permissive. When a rule has several exceptions, those exceptions with mandatory requirements are listed before the permissive exceptions.

Mandatory Exceptions. A mandatory exception uses the words "shall" or "shall not." The word "shall" in an exception means that if you're using the exception, you're required to do it in a specific way. The phrase "shall not" means it isn't permitted.

Permissive Exceptions. A permissive exception uses words such as "shall be permitted," which means it's acceptable (but not mandatory) to do it in this way.

8. Informational Notes. An Informational Note contains explanatory material intended to clarify a rule or give assistance, but it isn't a *Code* requirement.

9. Tables. Chapter 9 consists of tables applicable as referenced in the *NEC*. They're used to calculate raceway sizing, conductor fill, the radius of raceway bends, and conductor voltage drop.

10. Informative Annexes. Annexes aren't a part of the *Code* requirements and are included for informational purposes only.

Annex A.	Product Safety Standards
Annex B.	Application Information for Ampacity Calculation
Annex C.	Conduit, Tubing, and Cable Tray Fill Tables for Conductors and Fixture Wires of the Same Size
Annex D.	Examples
Annex E.	Types of Construction
Annex F.	Availability and Reliability for Critical Operations Power Systems (COPS), and Development and Implementation of Functional Performance Tests (FPTs) for Critical Operations Power Systems
Annex G.	Supervisory Control and Data Acquisition (SCADA)
Annex H.	Administration and Enforcement
Annex I.	Recommended Tightening Torque Tables from UL Standard 486A-486B
Annex J.	ADA Standards for Accessible Design
Annex K.	Use of Medical Electrical Equipment in Dwellings and Residential Board-and-Care Occupancies

11. Index. The Index at the back of the *NEC* is helpful in locating a specific rule using pertinent keywords to assist in your search.

12. Changes to the *Code*. Changes in the *NEC* are indicated as follows:

- Rules that were changed since the previous edition are identified by shading the revised text.
- New rules aren't shaded like a change, instead they have a shaded "N" in the margin to the left of the section number.
- Relocated rules are treated like new rules with a shaded "N" in the left margin by the section number.

- ▸ Deleted rules are indicated by a bullet symbol " • " located in the left margin where the rule was in the previous edition. Unlike older editions the bullet symbol is only used where one or more complete paragraphs have been deleted.
- ▸ A "Δ" represents partial text deletions and or figure/table revisions somewhere in the text. There's no specific indication of which word, group of words, or a sentence was deleted.

How to Locate a Specific Requirement

How to go about finding what you're looking for in the *Code* book depends, to some degree, on your experience with the *NEC*. Experts typically know the requirements so well that they just go to the correct rule. Very experienced people might only need the Table of Contents to locate the requirement for which they're looking. On the other hand, average users should use all the tools at their disposal, including the Table of Contents, the Index, and the search feature on electronic versions of the *Code* book.

Let's work through a simple example: What *NEC* rule specifies the maximum number of disconnects permitted for a service?

Using the Table of Contents. If you're an experienced *Code* user, you might use the Table of Contents. You'll know Article 230 applies to "Services," and because this article is so large, it's divided up into multiple parts (eight parts to be exact). With this knowledge, you can quickly go to the Table of Contents and see it lists the Service Equipment Disconnecting Means requirements in Part VI.

> **Author's Comment:**
> ▸ The number "70" precedes all page numbers in this standard because the *NEC* is NFPA Standard Number 70.

Using the Index. If you use the Index (which lists subjects in alphabetical order) to look up the term "service disconnect," you'll see there's no listing. If you try "disconnecting means," then "services," you'll find that the Index indicates the rule is in Article 230, Part VI. Because the *NEC* doesn't give a page number in the Index, you'll need to use the Table of Contents to find it, or flip through the *Code* book to Article 230, then continue to flip through pages until you find Part VI.

Many people complain that the *NEC* only confuses them by taking them in circles. Once you gain experience in using the *Code* and deepen your understanding of words, terms, principles, and practices, you'll find it much easier to understand and use than you originally thought.

With enough exposure in the use of the *NEC*, you'll discover that some words and terms are often specific to certain articles. The word "solar" for example will immediately send experienced *Code* book users to Article 690—Solar Photovoltaic (PV) Systems. The word "marina" suggests what you seek might be in Article 555. There are times when a main article will send you to a specific requirement in another one in which compliance is required in which case it will say (for example), "in accordance with 230.xx." Don't think of these situations as a "circle," but rather a map directing you to exactly where you need to be.

Customizing Your *Code* Book

One way to increase your comfort level with your *Code* book is to customize it to meet your needs. You can do this by highlighting and underlining important *NEC* requirements. Preprinted adhesive tabs are also an excellent aid to quickly find important articles and sections that are regularly referenced. However, understand that if you're using your *Code* book to prepare to take an exam, some exam centers don't allow markings of any type. For more information about tabs for your *Code* book, visit MikeHolt.com/Tabs.

Highlighting. As you read through or find answers to your questions, be sure you highlight those requirements in the *NEC* that are the most important or relevant to you. Use one color, like yellow, for general interest and a different one for important requirements you want to find quickly. Be sure to highlight terms in the Index and the Table of Contents as you use them.

Underlining. Underline or circle key words and phrases in the *Code* with a red or blue pen (not a lead pencil) using a short ruler or other straightedge to keep lines straight and neat. This is a very handy way to make important requirements stand out. A short ruler or other straightedge also comes in handy for locating the correct information in a table.

Interpretations

Industry professionals often enjoy the challenge of discussing, and at times debating, the *Code* requirements. These types of discussions are important to the process of better understanding the *NEC* requirements and applications. However, if you decide you're going to participate in one of these discussions, don't spout out what you think without having the actual *Code* book in your hand. The professional way of discussing a requirement is by referring to a specific

section rather than talking in vague generalities. This will help everyone involved clearly understand the point and become better educated. In fact, you may become so well educated about the *NEC* that you might even decide to participate in the change process and help to make it even better!

Become Involved in the *NEC* Process

The actual process of changing the *Code* takes about two years and involves hundreds of individuals trying to make the *NEC* as current and accurate as possible. As you advance in your studies and understanding of the *Code*, you might begin to find it very interesting, enjoy it more, and realize that you can also be a part of the process. Rather than sitting back and allowing others to take the lead, you can participate by making proposals and being a part of its development. For the 2023 cycle, there were over 4,000 Public Inputs and 1,956 Public Comments. This resulted in several new articles and a wide array of revised rules to keep the *NEC* up to date with new technologies and pave the way to a safer and more efficient electrical future.

Here's how the process works:

STEP 1—Public Input Stage

Public Input. The revision cycle begins with the acceptance of Public Input (PI) which is the public notice asking for anyone interested to submit input on an existing standard or a committee-approved new draft standard. Following the closing date, the committee conducts a First Draft Meeting to respond to all Public Inputs.

First Draft Meeting. At the First Draft (FD) Meeting, the Technical Committee considers and provides a response to all Public Input. The Technical Committee may use the input to develop First Revisions to the standard. The First Draft documents consist of the initial meeting consensus of the committee by simple majority. However, the final position of the Technical Committee must be established by a ballot which follows.

Committee Ballot on First Draft. The First Draft developed at the First Draft Meeting is balloted. In order to appear in the First Draft, a revision must be approved by at least two-thirds of the Technical Committee.

First Draft Report Posted. First revisions which pass ballot are ultimately compiled and published as the First Draft Report on the document's NFPA web page. This report serves as documentation for the Input Stage and is published for review and comment. The public may review the First Draft Report to determine whether to submit Public Comments on the First Draft.

STEP 2—Public Comment Stage

Public Comment. Once the First Draft Report becomes available, there's a Public Comment period during which anyone can submit a Public Comment on the First Draft. After the Public Comment closing date, the Technical Committee conducts/holds their Second Draft Meeting.

Second Draft Meeting. After the Public Comment closing date, if Public Comments are received or the committee has additional proposed revisions, a Second Draft Meeting is held. At the Second Draft Meeting, the Technical Committee reviews the First Draft and may make additional revisions to the draft Standard. All Public Comments are considered, and the Technical Committee provides an action and response to each Public Comment. These actions result in the Second Draft.

Committee Ballot on Second Draft. The Second Revisions developed at the Second Draft Meeting are balloted. To appear in the Second Draft, a revision must be approved by at least two-thirds of the Technical Committee.

Second Draft Report Posted. Second Revisions which pass ballot are ultimately compiled and published as the Second Draft Report on the document's NFPA website. This report serves as documentation of the Comment Stage and is published for public review.

Once published, the public can review the Second Draft Report to decide whether to submit a Notice of Intent to Make a Motion (NITMAM) for further consideration.

STEP 3—NFPA Technical Meeting (Tech Session)

Following completion of the Public Input and Public Comment stages, there's further opportunity for debate and discussion of issues through the NFPA Technical Meeting that takes place at the NFPA Conference & Expo®. These motions are attempts to change the resulting final Standard from the committee's recommendations published as the Second Draft.

STEP 4—Council Appeals and Issuance of Standard

Issuance of Standards. When the Standards Council convenes to issue an NFPA standard, it also hears any related appeals. Appeals are an important part of assuring that all NFPA rules have been followed and that due process and fairness have continued throughout the standards development process. The Standards Council considers appeals based on the written record and by conducting live hearings during which all interested parties can participate. Appeals are decided on the entire record of the process, as well as all submissions and statements presented.

After deciding all appeals related to a standard, the Standards Council, if appropriate, proceeds to issue the Standard as an official NFPA Standard. The decision of the Standards Council is final subject only to limited review by the NFPA Board of Directors. The new NFPA standard becomes effective twenty days following the Standards Council's action of issuance.

Temporary Interim Amendment—(TIA)

Sometimes, a change to the *NEC* is of an emergency nature. Perhaps an editing mistake was made that can affect an electrical installation to the extent it may create a hazard. Maybe an occurrence in the field created a condition that needs to be addressed immediately and can't wait for the normal *Code* cycle and next edition of the standard. When these circumstances warrant it, a TIA or "Temporary Interim Amendment" can be submitted for consideration.

The NFPA defines a TIA as, "tentative because it has not been processed through the entire standards-making procedures. It is interim because it is effective only between editions of the standard. A TIA automatically becomes a Public Input of the proponent for the next edition of the standard; as such, it then is subject to all of the procedures of the standards-making process."

> **Author's Comment:**
>
> ▸ Proposals, comments, and TIAs can be submitted for consideration online at the NFPA website, www.nfpa.org. From the homepage, look for "Codes & Standards," then find "Standards Development," and click on "How the Process Works." If you'd like to see something changed in the *Code*, you're encouraged to participate in the process.

ARTICLE 90
INTRODUCTION TO THE *NATIONAL ELECTRICAL CODE*

Introduction to Article 90—Introduction to the *National Electrical Code*

Article 90 describes the purpose of the *NEC*, when it applies, when it does not, who enforces the *Code*, and the arrangement of the different chapters. Although the information is valuable, this article contains no actual requirements. It only serves to provide the reader with the scope of the *National Electrical Code*.

This article stands alone outside of the chapter structure of the rest of the *Code* and has no parts because it contains no requirements. Take the time to become familiar with all nine sections of Article 90 before you begin your journey through the *NEC*. Doing so will help you better understand when and how to apply the *Code*.

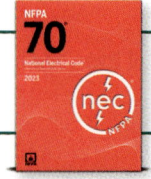

Please use the 2023 *Code* book to answer the following questions.

1. Article _____ covers use and application, arrangement, and enforcement of the *National Electrical Code*.

    (a) 90
    (b) 110
    (c) 200
    (d) 300

2. The purpose of the *NEC* is for _____.

    (a) it to be used as a design manual
    (b) use as an instruction guide for untrained persons
    (c) the practical safeguarding of persons and property
    (d) interacting with inspectors

3. Compliance with the *Code* and proper maintenance result in an installation that is _____.

    (a) essentially free from hazard
    (b) not necessarily efficient or convenient
    (c) not necessarily adequate for good service or future expansion
    (d) all of these

4. Electrical hazards often occur because the initial _____ did not provide for increases in the use of electricity.

    (a) inspection
    (b) owner
    (c) wiring
    (d) builder

5. The *NEC* covers the installation and removal of _____.

    (a) electrical conductors, equipment, and raceways
    (b) signaling and communications conductors, equipment, and raceways
    (c) optical fiber cables
    (d) all of these

6. Installations supplying _____ power to ships and watercraft in marinas and boatyards are covered by the NEC.

   (a) shore
   (b) primary
   (c) secondary
   (d) auxiliary

7. Installations used to export electric power from vehicles to premises wiring or for _____ current flow is covered by the NEC.

   (a) emergency
   (b) primary
   (c) bidirectional
   (d) secondary

8. The NEC does not cover installations in _____.

   (a) ships and watercraft
   (b) mobile homes
   (c) recreational vehicles
   (d) any of these

9. The Code does not cover underground mine installations, or self-propelled mobile surface _____ machinery and its attendant electrical trailing cable.

   (a) paving
   (b) mining
   (c) harvesting
   (d) excavating

10. Installations of communications equipment under the exclusive control of communications utilities located outdoors or in building spaces used exclusively for such installations _____ covered by the NEC.

    (a) are
    (b) are sometimes
    (c) are not
    (d) may be

11. The Code does not cover installations under the exclusive control of an electric utility such as _____.

    (a) service drops or service laterals
    (b) electric utility office buildings
    (c) electric utility warehouses
    (d) electric utility garages

12. Chapters 1, 2, 3, and 4 of the NEC apply _____.

    (a) generally to all electrical installations
    (b) only to special occupancies and conditions
    (c) only to special equipment and material
    (d) all of these

13. Chapters 5, 6, and 7 of the NEC apply to _____ and may supplement or modify the requirements contained in Chapters 1 through 7.

    (a) special occupancies
    (b) special equipment
    (c) special conditions
    (d) all of these

14. Chapter 8 covers _____ systems and is not subject to the requirements of Chapters 1 through 7 unless specifically referenced in Chapter 8.

    (a) communications
    (b) fire alarm
    (c) emergency standby
    (d) sustainable energy

15. Annexes are not part of the requirements of this Code but are included for _____ purposes only.

    (a) informational
    (b) reference
    (c) supplemental enforcement
    (d) educational

16. The enforcement of the NEC is the responsibility of the authority having jurisdiction, who is responsible for _____.

    (a) making interpretations of rules
    (b) approval of equipment and materials
    (c) granting special permission
    (d) all of these

17. By special permission, the authority having jurisdiction may waive NEC requirements or approve alternative methods where equivalent _____ can be achieved and maintained.

    (a) safety
    (b) workmanship
    (c) installations
    (d) job progress

18. If the *Code* requires new products that may not yet be available at the time the *NEC* is adopted, the _____ can allow products that comply with the most recent previous edition of the *Code* adopted by the jurisdiction.

    (a) electrical engineer
    (b) master electrician
    (c) authority having jurisdiction
    (d) none of these

19. In the *NEC*, the word(s) "_____" indicate a mandatory requirement.

    (a) shall
    (b) shall not
    (c) shall be permitted
    (d) shall or shall not

20. When the *Code* uses "_____," it indicates the actions are allowed but not required.

    (a) shall or shall not
    (b) shall not be permitted
    (c) shall be permitted
    (d) none of these

21. Explanatory material, such as references to other standards, references to related sections of this *Code*, or information related to a *Code* rule, is included in this *Code* in the form of _____.

    (a) Informational Notes
    (b) footnotes
    (c) table notes
    (d) italicized text

22. Nonmandatory information relative to the use of the *NEC* is provided in informative annexes and are _____.

    (a) included for information purposes only
    (b) not enforceable requirements of the *Code*
    (c) enforceable as a requirement of the *Code*
    (d) included for information purposes only and are not enforceable requirements of the *Code*

23. Except to detect alterations or damage, qualified electrical testing laboratory listed factory-installed _____ wiring of equipment does not need to be inspected for *NEC* compliance at the time of installation.

    (a) external
    (b) associated
    (c) internal
    (d) all of these

Notes

CHAPTER 1

GENERAL RULES

Introduction to Chapter 1—General Rules

Chapter 1 of the *NEC* is divided into two articles. The first contains the definitions of important terms used throughout the *Code*, and the second provides the general requirements for all electrical installations. The definitions and rules in this chapter apply to all electrical installations covered by the *NEC*.

Chapter 1 is often overlooked because the rules are very broad and do not clearly apply to specific situations. Be sure you understand the rules, concepts, definitions, and requirements in Chapter 1 as doing so will make a difficult rule(s) much easier to apply. Chapter 1 articles covered by this material are:

▶ **Article 100—Definitions.** Article 100 contains the definitions essential to the application of this *Code*. Where terms are not defined in Article 100, the *NEC Style Manual* directs us to use *Webster's Collegiate Dictionary*, or to consult with the authority having jurisdiction.

▶ **Article 110—General Requirements for Electrical Installations.** This article covers the general requirements for the examination and approval, installation and use, and access to spaces around electrical equipment.

Notes

ARTICLE 100 DEFINITIONS

Introduction to Article 100—Definitions

Have you ever had a conversation with someone only to discover that what you meant and what they understood were completely different? This often happens when people have different interpretations of the words being used, and that is why the definitions of key *NEC* terms are located at the beginning of the *Code*. Definitions used out of context are a leading cause of misinterpretations of rules by people such as electricians, engineers, and inspectors. Because the *NEC* exists to protect people and property, it is important to be able to convey and comprehend the language used. Review and reference Article 100 whenever there is a possibility of an inaccurate (or incorrect) definition of a term being used in a rule.

Please use the 2023 *Code* book to answer the following questions.

1. Capable of being removed or exposed without damaging the building structure or finish or not permanently closed in or blocked by the structure, other electrical equipment, other building systems, or finish of the building refers to _____.

    (a) wiring methods that are accessible
    (b) equipment that is accessible
    (c) being readily accessible
    (d) being serviceable

2. Capable of being reached quickly for operation, renewal, or inspections without climbing over or under obstructions, removing obstacles, resorting to portable ladders, or the use of tools (other than keys) is known as "_____."

    (a) accessible (as applied to equipment)
    (b) accessible (as applied to wiring methods)
    (c) accessible, readily (readily accessible)
    (d) all of these

3. The maximum current, in amperes, that a conductor can carry continuously under the conditions of use without exceeding its temperature rating is known as its "_____."

    (a) short-circuit rating
    (b) ground-fault rating
    (c) ampacity
    (d) all of these

4. An appliance is utilization equipment, generally other than _____, that is fastened in place, stationary, or portable, and normally built in a standardized size or type. Examples of appliances are ranges, ovens, cooktops, refrigerators, drinking water coolers, and beverage dispensers.

    (a) industrial
    (b) commercial
    (c) residential
    (d) institutional

Article 100 | Definitions

5. "_____" means acceptable to the authority having jurisdiction.
   (a) Identified
   (b) Listed
   (c) Approved
   (d) Labeled

6. An arc-fault circuit interrupter is a device intended to de-energize the circuit when a(an) _____ is detected.
   (a) overcurrent condition
   (b) arc fault
   (c) ground fault
   (d) harmonic fundamental

7. A device that, when inserted in a receptacle, establishes a connection between the conductors of the attached flexible cord and the conductors connected permanently to the receptacle is known as a(an) "_____."
   (a) attachment plug
   (b) plug cap
   (c) plug
   (d) any of these

8. In many circumstances, the _____ or his or her designated agent assumes the role of the authority having jurisdiction.
   (a) property owner
   (b) developer
   (c) general contractor
   (d) insurance underwriter

9. A "_____" is an area including a sink with one or more of the following: a toilet, urinal, tub, shower, bidet, or similar plumbing fixtures.
   (a) suite
   (b) bathroom
   (c) rest area
   (d) all of these

10. "Bonded" is defined as _____ to establish electrical continuity and conductivity.
    (a) isolated
    (b) guarded
    (c) connected
    (d) separated

11. The connection between two or more portions of the equipment grounding conductor is the definition of a(an) "_____."
    (a) system bonding jumper
    (b) main bonding jumper
    (c) equipment ground-fault jumper
    (d) equipment bonding jumper

12. The connection between the grounded circuit conductor and the equipment grounding conductor, or the supply-side bonding jumper, or both, at the service is the "_____ bonding jumper."
    (a) main
    (b) system
    (c) equipment
    (d) circuit

13. A conductor installed on the supply side of a service or within a service equipment enclosure, or for a separately derived system, to ensure the required electrical conductivity between metal parts required to be electrically connected is known as the "_____."
    (a) supply-side bonding jumper
    (b) ungrounded conductor
    (c) electrical supply source
    (d) grounding electrode conductor

14. The connection between the grounded circuit conductor and the supply-side bonding jumper or equipment grounding conductor, or both, at a _____ is called a "system bonding jumper."
    (a) service disconnect
    (b) separately derived system
    (c) motor control center
    (d) separate building or structure disconnect

15. The circuit conductors between the final overcurrent device protecting the circuit and the outlet(s) are known as "_____ conductors."
    (a) feeder
    (b) branch-circuit
    (c) home run
    (d) main circuit

16. A "_____" consists of two or more ungrounded conductors that have a voltage between them, and a neutral conductor that has equal voltage between it and each ungrounded conductor of the circuit and that is connected to the neutral conductor of the system.

    (a) multi-phase branch circuit
    (b) three-phase lighting supply circuit
    (c) poly-phase branch circuit
    (d) multiwire branch circuit

17. The *NEC* defines a(an) "_____" as a structure that stands alone or that is separated from adjoining structures by fire walls.

    (a) unit
    (b) apartment
    (c) building
    (d) utility

18. An enclosure designed for either surface mounting or flush mounting provided with a frame in which a door(s) can be hung is called a(an) "_____."

    (a) electrical housing
    (b) outlet box
    (c) cutout box
    (d) cabinet

19. A cable tray system is a unit or assembly of units or sections and associated fittings forming a _____ system used to securely fasten or support cables and raceways.

    (a) structural
    (b) flexible
    (c) movable
    (d) secure

20. Type _____ cable is a fabricated assembly of insulated conductors in a flexible interlocked metallic armor.

    (a) AC
    (b) TC
    (c) NM
    (d) MA

21. Type _____ cable is a cable with insulated conductors within an overall nonmetallic jacket.

    (a) AC
    (b) MC
    (c) NM
    (d) TC

22. Type _____ cable is a factory assembly of two or more insulated conductors, with or without associated bare or covered grounding conductors, under a nonmetallic jacket.

    (a) NM
    (b) TC
    (c) SE
    (d) UF

23. A(An) "_____" is a single conductor or multiconductor cable provided with an overall covering, primarily used for services.

    (a) service entrance cable
    (b) underground feeder cable
    (c) tray cable
    (d) nonmetallic sheath cable

24. Type _____ is a service-entrance cable, identified for underground use, having a moisture-resistant covering, but not required to have a flame-retardant covering.

    (a) SE
    (b) NM
    (c) UF
    (d) USE

25. Type _____ cable is a factory assembly of one or more insulated conductors with an integral or an overall covering of nonmetallic material suitable for direct burial in the earth.

    (a) NM
    (b) UF
    (c) SE
    (d) TC

26. A "circuit breaker" is a device designed to open and close a circuit by nonautomatic means and to _____ the circuit automatically on a predetermined overcurrent without damage to itself when properly applied within its rating.

    (a) energize
    (b) reset
    (c) connect
    (d) open

Article 100 | Definitions

27. A(An) _____ circuit breaker is a qualifying term indicating that there is a delay purposely introduced in the tripping action of the circuit breaker, and the delay decreases as the magnitude of the current increases.

    (a) adverse time
    (b) inverse time
    (c) time delay
    (d) timed unit

28. A _____ is an area within a clothes closet in which combustible materials can be kept.

    (a) hazardous (classified) location
    (b) working space
    (c) closet
    (d) clothes closet storage space

29. Wires are considered _____ if rendered inaccessible by the structure or finish of the building.

    (a) inaccessible
    (b) concealed
    (c) hidden
    (d) enclosed

30. A separate portion of a conduit or tubing system that provides access through a removable cover(s) to the interior of the system at a junction of two or more sections of the system or at a terminal point of the system defines the term "_____."

    (a) junction box
    (b) accessible raceway
    (c) conduit body
    (d) cutout box

31. _____ is a raceway of circular cross section made of a helically wound, formed, interlocked metal strip.

    (a) Type MC cable
    (b) Type AC cable
    (c) LFMC
    (d) FMC

32. _____ is a raceway of circular cross section having an outer liquidtight, nonmetallic, sunlight-resistant jacket over an inner flexible metal core.

    (a) FMC
    (b) LFNMC
    (c) LFMC
    (d) Vinyl-Clad Type MC

33. A rigid nonmetallic raceway of circular cross section, with integral or associated couplings, connectors, and fittings for the installation of electrical conductors and cables describes _____.

    (a) ENT
    (b) RMC
    (c) IMC
    (d) PVC

34. A "continuous load" is a load where the maximum current is expected to continue for _____ hour(s) or more.

    (a) ½
    (b) 1
    (c) 2
    (d) 3

35. A "_____" is a device or group of devices that govern, in some predetermined manner, the electric power delivered to the apparatus to which it is connected.

    (a) relay
    (b) breaker
    (c) transformer
    (d) controller

36. Any switch or device that is normally used to start and stop a motor by making and breaking the motor circuit current is the definition of a(an) "_____."

    (a) motor controller
    (b) start-stop station
    (c) disconnect
    (d) emergency disconnect

37. A cord set is a length of _____ cord having an attachment plug at one end and a cord connector at the other end.

    (a) heavy duty
    (b) hard usage
    (c) flexible
    (d) light duty

38. A flexible cord is defined as _____ or more flexible insulated conductors enclosed in a flexible covering.

    (a) two
    (b) three
    (c) four
    (d) five

39. A counter or countertop is a fixed or stationary surface typically intended for _____.

    (a) food preparation
    (b) serving
    (c) laundering
    (d) any of these

40. "_____" is defined as the ratio of the maximum demand of a system, or part of a system, to the total connected load of a system or the part of the system under consideration.

    (a) Load
    (b) Demand factor
    (c) Minimum load
    (d) Calculated factor

41. A unit of an electrical system, other than a conductor, which carries or controls electric energy as its principal function is known as a(an) "_____."

    (a) raceway
    (b) fitting
    (c) device
    (d) enclosure

42. A(An) _____ is a device, or group of devices, by which the conductors of a circuit can be disconnected from their source of supply.

    (a) feeder
    (b) enclosure
    (c) disconnecting means
    (d) conductor interrupter

43. A dormitory unit is a building or a space in a building in which group sleeping accommodations are provided for more than _____ persons who are not members of the same family in one room, or a series of closely associated rooms, under joint occupancy and single management, with or without meals, but without individual cooking facilities.

    (a) 6
    (b) 10
    (c) 12
    (d) 16

44. A _____ is a single unit that provides complete and independent living facilities for one or more persons, including permanent provisions for living, sleeping, cooking, and sanitation.

    (a) one-family dwelling
    (b) two-family dwelling
    (c) dwelling unit
    (d) multifamily dwelling

45. A building that contains three or more dwelling units is called a "_____."

    (a) one-family dwelling
    (b) two-family dwelling
    (c) dwelling unit
    (d) multifamily dwelling

46. A fixed, stationary, or portable self-contained, electrically operated and/or electrically illuminated utilization equipment with words or symbols designed to convey information or attract attention is the definition of _____.

    (a) an electric sign
    (b) equipment
    (c) appliances
    (d) exit lighting

47. An automotive-type vehicle for on-road use, such as _____, primarily powered by an electric motor that draws current from a rechargeable storage battery, fuel cell, photovoltaic array, or other source of electric current defines an electric vehicle.

    (a) passenger automobiles
    (b) buses, trucks, and vans
    (c) neighborhood electric vehicles and electric motorcycles
    (d) all of these

48. Off-road, self-propelled electric vehicles, such as _____ are not considered electric vehicles.

    (a) industrial trucks, hoists, and lifts
    (b) golf carts and airline ground support equipment
    (c) tractors and boats
    (d) all of these

Article 100 | Definitions

49. "Likely to become energized" is defined as conductive material that could become energized because of _____ or electrical spacing.

    (a) improper installation
    (b) poor maintenance
    (c) the failure of electrical insulation
    (d) power surges

50. A(An) _____ is a system consisting of a monitor(s), communications equipment, a controller(s), a timer(s), or other device(s) that monitors and/or controls an electrical load or a power production or storage source.

    (a) energy management system
    (b) power distribution system
    (c) energy storage system
    (d) interconnected power production system

51. An energy storage system (ESS) is defined as one or more devices installed as a system capable of storing energy and providing electrical energy into the _____ system or an electric power production and distribution network.

    (a) standby
    (b) emergency
    (c) premises wiring
    (d) UPS

52. "Exposed (as applied to _____)," is defined as on or attached to the surface, or behind access panels designed to allow access.

    (a) equipment
    (b) luminaires
    (c) wiring methods
    (d) motors

53. The largest amount of current capable of being delivered at a point on the system during a short-circuit condition is the definition of _____.

    (a) objectionable current
    (b) excessive current
    (c) induced current
    (d) available fault current

54. The *NEC* defines a "_____" as all circuit conductors between the service equipment, the source of a separately derived system, or other power supply source, and the final branch-circuit overcurrent device.

    (a) service
    (b) feeder
    (c) branch circuit
    (d) all of these

55. A(An) _____ that performs field evaluations of electrical or other equipment is known as a "Field Evaluation Body (FEB)."

    (a) home inspector
    (b) field installer
    (c) organization or part of an organization
    (d) insurance underwriter

56. Equipment or materials to which has been attached a(an) _____ of an FEB indicating the equipment or materials were evaluated and found to comply with requirements as described in an accompanying field evaluation report is known as "field labeled (as applied to evaluated products)."

    (a) symbol
    (b) label
    (c) other identifying mark
    (d) any of these

57. A _____ is a building or portion of a building in which one or more self-propelled vehicles can be kept for use, sale, storage, rental, repair, exhibition, or demonstration purposes.

    (a) garage
    (b) residential garage
    (c) service garage
    (d) commercial garage

58. A generator is a machine that converts mechanical energy into electrical energy by means of a _____ and alternator and/or inverter.

    (a) converter
    (b) rectifier
    (c) prime mover
    (d) turbine

59. Earth, as used in the *NEC* best describes the term _____.
    (a) bonded
    (b) ground
    (c) effective ground-fault current path
    (d) guarded

60. A(An) _____ is an unintentional, electrically conductive connection between an ungrounded conductor of an electrical circuit, and the normally noncurrent-carrying conductors, metal enclosures, metal raceways, metal equipment, or earth.
    (a) grounded conductor
    (b) ground fault
    (c) equipment ground
    (d) bonding jumper

61. Connected (connecting) to ground or to a conductive body that extends the ground connection is called "_____."
    (a) equipment grounding
    (b) bonded
    (c) grounded
    (d) all of these

62. A system or circuit conductor that is intentionally grounded is called a(an) "_____."
    (a) grounding conductor
    (b) unidentified conductor
    (c) grounded conductor
    (d) grounding electrode conductor

63. A(An) _____ grounded system is an electrical system that is grounded by intentionally connecting the system neutral point to ground through an impedance device.
    (a) impedance
    (b) solidly
    (c) isolated
    (d) separately

64. Connected to ground without the insertion of any resistor or impedance device is referred to as "_____."
    (a) grounded
    (b) solidly grounded
    (c) effectively grounded
    (d) a grounding conductor

65. A(An) "_____" is a device intended for the protection of personnel that functions to de-energize a circuit or portion thereof within an established period of time when a ground-fault current exceeds the values established for a Class A device.
    (a) dual-element fuse
    (b) inverse time breaker
    (c) ground-fault circuit interrupter
    (d) safety switch

66. A Class A GFCI trips when the ground-fault current is _____ or higher.
    (a) 4 mA
    (b) 5 mA
    (c) 6 mA
    (d) 7 mA

67. An effective ground-fault current path is an intentionally constructed, low-impedance electrically conductive path designed and intended to carry current during a ground-fault event from the point of a ground fault on a wiring system to _____.
    (a) ground
    (b) earth
    (c) the electrical supply source
    (d) the grounding electrode

68. A system intended to provide protection of equipment from damaging line-to-ground fault currents by causing a disconnecting means to open all ungrounded conductors of the faulted circuit at current levels less than the supply circuit overcurrent device defines "_____."
    (a) ground-fault protection of equipment
    (b) guarded
    (c) personal protection
    (d) automatic protection

69. A(An) _____ is a conductive path(s) that is part of an effective ground-fault current path and connects normally noncurrent-carrying metal parts of equipment together and to the system grounded conductor or to the grounding electrode conductor, or both.
    (a) grounding electrode conductor
    (b) main bonding jumper
    (c) system bonding jumper
    (d) equipment grounding conductor

Article 100 | Definitions

70. An impedance grounding conductor is a conductor that connects the system _____ to the impedance device in an impedance grounded system.

    (a) main bonding jumper
    (b) neutral point
    (c) supply-side bonding jumper
    (d) load-side bonding jumper

71. A conducting object through which a direct connection to earth is established is a "_____."

    (a) bonding conductor
    (b) grounding conductor
    (c) grounding electrode
    (d) grounded conductor

72. A conductor used to connect the system grounded conductor, or the equipment to a grounding electrode or to a point on the grounding electrode system, is called the "_____ conductor."

    (a) main grounding
    (b) common main
    (c) equipment grounding
    (d) grounding electrode

73. A _____ is an accommodation that combines living, sleeping, sanitary, and storage facilities within a compartment.

    (a) guest room
    (b) guest suite
    (c) dwelling unit
    (d) single-family dwelling

74. A _____ is an accommodation with two or more contiguous rooms comprising a compartment that provides living, sleeping, sanitary, and storage facilities.

    (a) guest room
    (b) guest suite
    (c) dwelling unit
    (d) single-family dwelling

75. A habitable room in a building is a room for _____, but excluding bathrooms, toilet rooms, closets, hallways, storage or utility spaces, and similar areas.

    (a) living
    (b) sleeping
    (c) eating or cooking
    (d) all of these

76. A handhole enclosure is an enclosure for use in underground systems, provided with an open or closed bottom, and sized to allow personnel to _____.

    (a) enter and exit freely
    (b) reach into but not enter
    (c) have full working space
    (d) visually examine the interior

77. Recognized as suitable for the specific purpose, function, use, environment, and application is the definition of "_____."

    (a) labeled
    (b) identified (as applied to equipment)
    (c) listed
    (d) approved

78. *In sight from* or "within sight from" is defined as equipment that is visible and not more than _____ distant from other equipment is in sight from that other equipment.

    (a) 10 feet
    (b) 20 feet
    (c) 25 feet
    (d) 50 feet

79. The highest current at rated voltage that a device is identified to interrupt under standard test conditions is the "_____."

    (a) interrupting rating
    (b) manufacturer's rating
    (c) interrupting capacity
    (d) withstand rating

80. A device that provides a means to connect intersystem bonding conductors for _____ systems to the grounding electrode system defines the term "intersystem bonding termination."

    (a) limited-energy
    (b) low-voltage
    (c) communications
    (d) power and lighting

81. A "kitchen" is defined as an area with a sink and _____ provisions for food preparation and cooking.

    (a) listed
    (b) labeled
    (c) temporary
    (d) permanent

82. Equipment or materials to which a label, symbol, or other identifying mark of a product evaluation organization that is acceptable to the authority having jurisdiction has been attached is known as "____."

    (a) listed
    (b) labeled
    (c) approved
    (d) identified

83. A laundry area is an area containing or designed to contain a ____.

    (a) laundry tray
    (b) clothes washer
    (c) clothes dryer
    (d) any of these

84. An outlet intended for the direct connection of a lampholder or a luminaire is a(an) "____."

    (a) outlet
    (b) receptacle outlet
    (c) lighting outlet
    (d) general-purpose outlet

85. A "limited care facility" is defined as a building or portion thereof used on a(an) ____ basis for the housing of four or more persons who are incapable of self-preservation because of age; physical limitation due to accident or illness; or limitations such as intellectual disability/developmental disability, mental illness, or chemical dependency.

    (a) occasional
    (b) 10-hour or less per day
    (c) 24-hour
    (d) temporary

86. Equipment, materials, or services included in a list published by an organization that is acceptable to the authority having jurisdiction defines the term "____."

    (a) booked
    (b) a digest
    (c) a manifest
    (d) listed

87. A location protected from weather and not subject to saturation with water or other liquids, but subject to moderate degrees of moisture defines a ____ location.

    (a) dry
    (b) damp
    (c) wet
    (d) moist

88. A location not normally subject to dampness or wetness but may be temporarily subject to dampness and wetness as in the case of a building under construction defines a ____ location.

    (a) dry
    (b) damp
    (c) moist
    (d) wet

89. A location unprotected and exposed to weather, subject to saturation, underground, or in concrete slabs in direct contact with the earth defines a ____ location.

    (a) dry
    (b) damp
    (c) wet
    (d) moist

90. A "luminaire" is a complete lighting unit consisting of a light source such as a lamp or lamps, together with the parts designed to position the ____ and connect it to the power supply.

    (a) lampholder
    (b) light source
    (c) fixture
    (d) bulb

91. A "neutral conductor" is the conductor connected to the ____ of a system, which is intended to carry current under normal conditions.

    (a) grounding electrode
    (b) neutral point
    (c) intersystem bonding termination
    (d) electrical grid

92. The ____ is the "neutral point."

    (a) common point on a wye-connection in a polyphase system
    (b) midpoint on a single-phase, 3-wire system
    (c) midpoint of a single-phase portion of a 3-phase delta system
    (d) any of these

Article 100 | Definitions

93. A(An) "_____" is a point on the wiring system at which current is taken to supply utilization equipment.

    (a) box
    (b) receptacle
    (c) outlet
    (d) device

94. Any current in excess of the rated current of equipment or the ampacity of a conductor is called "_____."

    (a) trip current
    (b) fault current
    (c) overcurrent
    (d) a short circuit

95. A(An) "_____" is intended to provide limited overcurrent protection for specific applications and utilization equipment such as luminaires and appliances. This limited protection is in addition to the protection provided by the required branch-circuit overcurrent protective device.

    (a) supplementary overcurrent protective device
    (b) surge protection device
    (c) arc-fault circuit interrupter
    (d) Class A GFCI

96. An 'overload' is defined as the operation of equipment in excess of normal, full load rating, or of a conductor in excess of its ampacity that, when it persists for a_____, would cause damage or dangerous overheating.

    (a) sufficient length of time
    (b) short time
    (c) long time
    (d) none of these

97. A panel, including buses and automatic overcurrent devices, designed to be placed in a cabinet, enclosure, or cutout box and accessible only from the front is known as a "_____."

    (a) switchboard
    (b) disconnect
    (c) panelboard
    (d) switchgear

98. An enclosed panelboard is an assembly of _____ or other equipment, installed in a cabinet, cutout box, or enclosure suitable for a panelboard application.

    (a) buses and connections
    (b) overcurrent devices
    (c) control apparatus with or without switches
    (d) any of these

99. A "power supply cord" is an assembly consisting of an attachment plug and a length of _____ cord connected to utilization equipment.

    (a) heavy duty
    (b) hard usage
    (c) flexible
    (d) light duty

100. A "_____" is the machine that supplies the mechanical horsepower to a generator.

    (a) prime mover
    (b) motor
    (c) capacitor
    (d) starter

101. The *NEC* defines a(an) "_____" as one who has skills and knowledge related to the construction and operation of the electrical equipment and installations and has received safety training to recognize and avoid the hazards involved.

    (a) inspector
    (b) master electrician
    (c) journeyman electrician
    (d) qualified person

102. NFPA 70E, *Standard for Electrical Safety in the Workplace*, provides information to help determine the electrical safety training requirements expected of a(an) "_____."

    (a) qualified person
    (b) electrical engineer
    (c) journeyman electrician
    (d) trained individual

Definitions | Article 100

103. A "raceway" is an enclosed channel designed expressly for holding _____, with additional functions as permitted in this *Code*.
    (a) wires
    (b) cables
    (c) busbars
    (d) any of these

104. A "surface metal raceway" is a metal raceway that is intended to be mounted to the surface of a structure, with associated couplings, connectors, boxes, and fittings for the _____ of electrical conductors.
    (a) installation
    (b) protection
    (c) routing
    (d) enclosure

105. A contact device installed at an outlet for the connection of an attachment plug is known as a(an) "_____."
    (a) attachment point
    (b) tap
    (c) receptacle
    (d) wall plug

106. A single "receptacle" is a single contact device with no other contact device on the same _____.
    (a) circuit
    (b) yoke or strap
    (c) run
    (d) equipment

107. An outlet where one or more receptacles are installed is called a(an) "_____."
    (a) device
    (b) equipment
    (c) receptacle
    (d) receptacle outlet

108. A duplex "receptacle" is an example of a multiple receptacle that has two receptacles on the same _____.
    (a) yoke or strap
    (b) strap
    (c) device
    (d) cover plate

109. Article 100 contains only those definitions essential to the application of this *Code*. An article number in parentheses following the definition indicates that the definition only applies to that article.
    (a) True
    (b) False

110. A "_____ system" is an electrical power supply output, other than a service, having no direct connection(s) to circuit conductors of any other electrical source other than those established by grounding and bonding connections.
    (a) separately derived
    (b) classified
    (c) direct
    (d) emergency

111. The conductors and equipment connecting the serving utility to the wiring system of the premises served is called a "_____."
    (a) branch circuit
    (b) feeder
    (c) service
    (d) service attachment

112. "Service conductors" are the conductors from the service point to the _____.
    (a) service disconnecting means
    (b) panelboard
    (c) switchgear
    (d) fire switch

113. "Overhead service conductors" are the conductors between the _____ and the first point of connection to the service-entrance conductors at the building or other structure.
    (a) service disconnect
    (b) service point
    (c) grounding electrode
    (d) equipment grounding conductor

114. "Underground service conductors" are the underground conductors between the service point and the first point of connection to the service-entrance conductors in a terminal box, meter, or other enclosure, _____ the building wall.
    (a) inside or outside
    (b) concealed within
    (c) above
    (d) below

Article 100 | Definitions

115. A "service drop" is defined as the overhead conductors between the serving utility and the _____.
    (a) service equipment
    (b) service point
    (c) grounding electrode conductor
    (d) equipment grounding conductor

116. The "_____" is the necessary equipment, consisting of a circuit breaker(s) or switch(es) and fuse(s) and their accessories, connected to the serving utility and intended to constitute the main control and disconnect of the serving utility.
    (a) service equipment
    (b) feeder equipment
    (c) feeder disconnect
    (d) none of these

117. The underground conductors between the utility electric supply system and the service point are known as the "_____."
    (a) utility service
    (b) service lateral
    (c) service drop
    (d) main service conductors

118. The "_____" is the point of connection between the facilities of the serving utility and the premises wiring.
    (a) service entrance
    (b) service point
    (c) overcurrent protection
    (d) beginning of the wiring system

119. "Service-entrance conductors" are the service conductors between the terminals of the _____ and the service drop, overhead service conductors, service lateral, or underground service conductors.
    (a) service equipment
    (b) service point
    (c) grounding electrode conductor
    (d) equipment grounding conductor

120. "_____" is the process of following a manufacturer's set of instructions or applicable industry standards to analyze, adjust, or perform prescribed actions upon equipment with the intention to preserve or restore the operational performance of the equipment.
    (a) Maintenance
    (b) Inspection
    (c) Servicing
    (d) Operating Procedure

121. A(An) _____ is an abnormal connection (including an arc) of relatively low impedance, whether made accidentally or intentionally, between two or more points of different potential.
    (a) ground fault
    (b) arc fault
    (c) system fault
    (d) short circuit

122. The prospective symmetrical fault current at a nominal voltage to which an apparatus or system is able to be connected without sustaining damage exceeding defined acceptance criteria is known as the "_____."
    (a) short-circuit current rating
    (b) arc-flash rating
    (c) overcurrent rating
    (d) available fault current

123. A "structure" is that which is _____, other than equipment.
    (a) built
    (b) constructed
    (c) built or constructed
    (d) none of these

124. A "surge-protective device" (SPD) is intended to limit _____ voltages by diverting or limiting surge current and preventing its continued flow while remaining capable of repeating these functions.
    (a) spike
    (b) transient
    (c) high
    (d) low

125. A switch constructed so that it can be installed in device boxes or on box covers, or otherwise used in conjunction with wiring systems recognized by this *Code* is called a "_____ switch."

(a) transfer
(b) motor-circuit
(c) general-use snap
(d) bypass isolation

126. A conductor, other than a service conductor, which has overcurrent protection ahead of its point of supply that exceeds the value permitted for similar conductors is known as a "_____."

(a) feeder conductor
(b) service conductor
(c) tap conductor
(d) conductor extension

127. "_____" is an unthreaded thinwall raceway of circular cross section designed for the physical protection and routing of conductors and cables and for use as an equipment grounding conductor when installed utilizing appropriate fittings.

(a) LFNC
(b) EMT
(c) NUCC
(d) RTRC

128. "_____" is a pliable corrugated raceway of circular cross section, with integral or associated couplings, connectors, and fittings that are listed for the installation of electrical conductors.

(a) PVC
(b) ENT
(c) RMC
(d) IMC

129. "Utilization equipment" is equipment that utilizes electric energy for _____ purposes.

(a) electromechanical
(b) heating
(c) lighting
(d) any of these

130. "_____" is, for grounded circuits, the voltage between the given conductor and that point or conductor of the circuit that is grounded; for ungrounded circuits, the greatest voltage between the given conductor and any other conductor of the circuit.

(a) Line-to-line voltage
(b) Voltage to ground
(c) Phase-to-phase voltage
(d) Neutral to ground voltage

131. A nominal value assigned to a circuit or system for the purpose of conveniently designating its voltage class, such as 120/240V, is called "_____ voltage."

(a) root-mean-square
(b) circuit
(c) nominal
(d) source

132. A(An) "_____" enclosure is constructed or protected so that exposure to the weather will not interfere with successful operation.

(a) weatherproof
(b) weathertight
(c) weather-resistant
(d) all weather

Notes

ARTICLE 110 — GENERAL REQUIREMENTS FOR ELECTRICAL INSTALLATIONS

Introduction to Article 110—General Requirements for Electrical Installations

Article 110 is the first article in the *NEC* that contains requirements as opposed to overall scope information or definitions. It contains the general rules that apply to all installations and, as such, is the foundation of the *Code*. Topics covered in our material for Article 110 include:

- How equipment is approved
- How to determine when or where equipment can be used
- How to arrange equipment so it is safe to operate and maintain for the end user
- How to identify the characteristics of the systems being installed so future alterations, service, or maintenance can be completed safely

This article is divided into five parts. The first two cover systems under 1000V, nominal and are the only parts of this article covered in this material. As you begin your journey to understanding the *NEC*, remember that many other *Code* rules were written with the understanding that you will come to Article 100 to determine the general requirements. Set yourself up for success by taking the time to read and understand each of these rules.

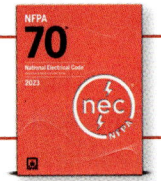

Please use the 2023 *Code* book to answer the following questions.

1. General requirements for the examination and approval, installation and use, access to and spaces about electrical conductors and equipment; enclosures intended for personnel entry; and tunnel installations are within the scope of _____.

   (a) Article 800
   (b) Article 300
   (c) Article 110
   (d) Annex J

2. The conductors and equipment required or permitted by this *Code* shall be acceptable only if _____.

   (a) labeled
   (b) listed
   (c) approved
   (d) identified

Article 110 | General Requirements for Electrical Installations

3. In judging equipment, considerations such as _____ shall be evaluated.
   (a) mechanical strength
   (b) wire-bending and connection space
   (c) arcing effects
   (d) all of these

4. In judging equipment, considerations such as cybersecurity for network-connected _____ to address its ability to withstand unauthorized updates and malicious attacks while continuing to perform its intended safety functionality shall be evaluated.
   (a) normal equipment
   (b) emergency equipment
   (c) standby power equipment
   (d) life safety equipment

5. Equipment that is _____ or identified for a use shall be installed and used in accordance with any instructions included in the listing, labeling, or identification.
   (a) listed, labeled, or both
   (b) listed
   (c) marked
   (d) suitable

6. The installation and use instructions for listed, labeled, or identified electrical equipment may be provided in the form of _____.
   (a) printed material
   (b) a quick response (QR) code
   (c) an internet address to download instructions
   (d) any of these

7. Product testing, evaluation, and listing (product certification) shall be performed by _____.
   (a) recognized qualified electrical testing laboratories
   (b) the manufacturer
   (c) a qualified person
   (d) an electrical engineer

8. If the conductor material is not specified, the sizes given in the Code shall apply to _____ conductors.
   (a) aluminum
   (b) copper-clad aluminum
   (c) copper
   (d) all of these

9. Conductor sizes are expressed in American Wire Gauge (AWG) or in _____.
   (a) inches
   (b) circular mils
   (c) square inches
   (d) cubic inches

10. Completed wiring installations shall be free from _____ other than as required or permitted elsewhere in this Code.
    (a) short circuits
    (b) ground faults
    (c) any connections to ground
    (d) all of these

11. Only wiring methods recognized as _____ are included in this Code.
    (a) expensive
    (b) efficient
    (c) suitable
    (d) cost effective

12. Equipment intended to interrupt current at _____ levels shall have an interrupting rating at nominal circuit voltage at least equal to the available fault current at the line terminals of the equipment.
    (a) fault
    (b) overcurrent
    (c) overload
    (d) incident energy

13. The _____, and other characteristics of the circuit to be protected shall be selected and coordinated to permit the circuit protective devices used to clear a fault to do so without extensive damage to the electrical equipment of the circuit.
    (a) overcurrent protective devices
    (b) total impedance
    (c) equipment short-circuit current ratings
    (d) all of these

14. Unless identified for use in the operating environment, no conductors or equipment shall be _____ having a deteriorating effect on the conductors or equipment.
    (a) located in damp or wet locations
    (b) exposed to fumes, vapors, liquids, or gases
    (c) exposed to excessive temperatures
    (d) all of these

15. Equipment not _____ for outdoor use and equipment identified only for indoor use such as "dry locations" or "indoor use only," shall be protected against damage from the weather during construction.

    (a) listed
    (b) identified
    (c) suitable
    (d) marked

16. Some _____ can cause severe deterioration of many plastic materials used for insulating and structural applications in equipment.

    (a) cleaning and lubricating compounds
    (b) protective coatings
    (c) paints and enamels
    (d) detergents

17. Electrical equipment shall be installed _____.

    (a) in a professional and skillful manner
    (b) under the supervision of a licensed person
    (c) completely before being inspected
    (d) all of these

18. Unused openings, other than those intended for the operation of equipment, those intended for mounting purposes, or permitted as part of the design for listed equipment shall be _____.

    (a) filled with cable clamps or connectors only
    (b) taped over with electrical tape
    (c) repaired only by welding or brazing in a metal slug
    (d) closed to afford protection substantially equivalent to the wall of the equipment

19. Internal parts of electrical equipment, including busbars, wiring terminals, insulators, and other surfaces, shall not be damaged or contaminated by foreign materials such as _____, or corrosive residues.

    (a) paint, plaster
    (b) cleaners
    (c) abrasives
    (d) any of these

20. Pressure terminal or pressure splicing connectors and soldering lugs shall be _____ for the material of the conductor and shall be properly installed and used.

    (a) listed
    (b) approved
    (c) identified
    (d) all of these

21. Connectors and terminals for conductors more finely stranded than Class B and Class C, as shown in Chapter 9, Table 10, shall be _____ for the specific conductor class or classes.

    (a) listed
    (b) approved
    (c) identified
    (d) all of these

22. Conductors of dissimilar metals shall not be intermixed in a terminal or splicing connector where physical contact occurs between dissimilar conductors unless the device is _____ for the purpose and conditions of use.

    (a) identified
    (b) listed
    (c) approved
    (d) designed

23. Connection of conductors to terminal parts shall ensure a mechanically secure electrical connection without damaging the conductors and shall be made by means of _____.

    (a) solder lugs
    (b) pressure connectors
    (c) splices to flexible leads
    (d) any of these

24. All _____ shall be covered with an insulation equivalent to that of the conductors or with an identified insulating device.

    (a) splices
    (b) joints
    (c) free ends of conductors
    (d) all of these

Article 110 | General Requirements for Electrical Installations

25. Separately installed pressure connectors shall be used with conductors at the _____ not exceeding the ampacity at the listed and identified temperature rating of the connector.

    (a) voltages
    (b) temperatures
    (c) listings
    (d) ampacities

26. Tightening torque values for terminal connections shall be as indicated on equipment or in installation instructions provided by the manufacturer. An approved means shall be used to achieve the _____ torque value.

    (a) indicated
    (b) identified
    (c) maximum
    (d) minimum

27. Examples of approved means of achieving the indicated _____ values include torque tools or devices such as shear bolts or breakaway-style devices with visual indicators that demonstrate that the proper torque has been applied.

    (a) pressure
    (b) torque
    (c) tightening
    (d) tension

28. On a 4-wire, delta-connected system where the midpoint of one phase winding is grounded, only the conductor or busbar having the higher phase voltage-to-ground shall be durably and permanently marked by an outer finish that is _____ in color.

    (a) black
    (b) red
    (c) blue
    (d) orange

29. Electrical equipment such as switchboards, switchgear, enclosed panelboards, industrial control panels, meter socket enclosures, and motor control centers, which are in other than dwelling units, and are likely to require _____ while energized, shall be field or factory marked to warn qualified persons of potential electric arc-flash hazards.

    (a) examination
    (b) adjustment
    (c) servicing or maintenance
    (d) any of these

30. In other than dwelling units, a permanent arc-flash label shall be field or factory applied to service equipment and feeder supplied equipment rated _____ or more.

    (a) 600A
    (b) 1000A
    (c) 1200A
    (d) 1600A

31. NFPA 70E, *Standard for Electrical Safety in the Workplace*, provides specific criteria for developing arc-flash labels for equipment that provides _____, and so forth.

    (a) nominal system voltage and incident energy levels
    (b) arc-flash boundaries
    (c) minimum required levels of personal protective equipment
    (d) all of these

32. Electrical equipment servicing and electrical preventive maintenance shall be performed by _____ trained in servicing and maintenance of equipment.

    (a) qualified persons
    (b) manufacturer's representatives
    (c) service specialists
    (d) licensed individuals

33. Equipment servicing and electrical preventive maintenance shall be performed in accordance with the original equipment manufacturer's instructions and _____.

    (a) information included in the listing information
    (b) applicable industry standards,
    (c) as approved by the authority having jurisdiction
    (d) any of these

34. Equipment that is reconditioned and required by the *Code* to be listed shall be listed or _____ as reconditioned using available instructions from the original equipment manufacturer.

    (a) identified
    (b) documented
    (c) field labeled
    (d) certified

35. Where caution, warning, or danger hazard markings such as labels or signs are required by this *Code*, the markings shall be of sufficient durability to withstand the environment involved and warn of these hazards using effective _____.

    (a) words
    (b) colors
    (c) symbols
    (d) any combination of words, colors, or symbols

36. Each disconnecting means shall be legibly marked to indicate its purpose unless located and arranged so _____.

    (a) that it can be locked out and tagged
    (b) it is not readily accessible
    (c) the purpose is evident
    (d) that it operates at less than 300 volts-to-ground

37. Equipment enclosures for circuit breakers or fuses applied in compliance with the series combination ratings marked on the equipment by the manufacturer in accordance with 240.86(B) shall be _____ to indicate the equipment has been applied with a series combination rating.

    (a) legibly marked in the field
    (b) inspected and tagged
    (c) installed
    (d) listed

38. _____ at other than dwelling units shall be legibly field marked with the available fault current, include the date the fault-current calculation was performed, and be of sufficient durability to withstand the environment involved.

    (a) Service equipment
    (b) Sub panels
    (c) Motor control centers
    (d) all of these

39. When service equipment is required to be field marked with the available fault current, the value of available fault current for use in determining appropriate minimum short-circuit current ratings of service equipment is available from _____ in published or other forms.

    (a) the architect
    (b) the engineer
    (c) electric utilities
    (d) all of these

40. When modifications to the electrical installation occur that affect the available fault current at the service, the available fault current shall be verified or _____ as necessary to ensure the service equipment ratings are sufficient for the available fault current at the line terminals of the equipment.

    (a) recalculated
    (b) increased
    (c) decreased
    (d) adjusted

41. If a disconnecting means is required to be lockable open elsewhere in the *NEC*, it shall be capable of being locked in the open position. The provisions for locking shall remain in place with or without _____.

    (a) the power off
    (b) the lock installed
    (c) supervision
    (d) a lock-out tag

42. _____, and access to and egress from working space, shall be provided and maintained about all electrical equipment to permit ready and safe operation and maintenance of such equipment.

    (a) Ventilation
    (b) Unrestricted movement
    (c) Circulation
    (d) Working space

43. Access to or egress from the required working space about electrical equipment is considered impeded if one or more simultaneously opened equipment doors restrict working space access to be less than _____ wide and 6½ ft high.

    (a) 24 in.
    (b) 28 in.
    (c) 30 in.
    (d) 36 in.

44. Working space is required for equipment operating at 1000V, nominal, or less to ground and likely to require _____ while energized.

    (a) examination
    (b) adjustment
    (c) servicing or maintenance
    (d) all of these

Article 110 | General Requirements for Electrical Installations

45. NFPA 70E, *Standard for Electrical Safety in the Workplace*, provides guidance, such as determining severity of potential exposure, planning safe work practices including establishing an electrically _____ work condition, arc-flash labeling, and selecting personal protective equipment.

    (a) safe
    (b) efficient
    (c) grounded
    (d) bonded

46. Working space distances for enclosed live parts shall be measured from the _____ of equipment if the live parts are enclosed.

    (a) enclosure or opening
    (b) front or back
    (c) mounting pad
    (d) footprint

47. Working space is not required at the back or sides of equipment where all _____ and all renewable, adjustable, or serviceable parts are accessible from the front.

    (a) screws
    (b) connections
    (c) bolts
    (d) doors

48. The minimum working space on a circuit for equipment operating at 120V to ground, with exposed live parts on one side and no live or grounded parts on the other side of the working space, is _____.

    (a) 1 ft
    (b) 3 ft
    (c) 4 ft
    (d) 6 ft

49. The required working space for access to live parts of equipment operating at 300V to ground, where there are exposed live parts on one side and grounded parts on the other side, is _____.

    (a) 3 ft
    (b) 3½ ft
    (c) 4 ft
    (d) 4½ ft

50. The required working space for access to live parts of equipment operating at 300V to ground, where there are exposed live parts on both sides of the workspace is _____.

    (a) 3 ft
    (b) 3½ ft
    (c) 4 ft
    (d) 4½ ft

51. The width of the working space shall be not be less than _____ wide, or the width of the equipment, whichever is greater.

    (a) 15 in.
    (b) 30 in.
    (c) 40 in.
    (d) 60 in.

52. The minimum height of working spaces shall be clear and extend from the grade, floor, or platform to a height of _____ ft or the height of the equipment, whichever is greater.

    (a) 3 ft
    (b) 6 ft
    (c) 6½ ft
    (d) 7 ft

53. The grade, floor, or platform in the required working space about electrical equipment shall be as level and flat as _____ for the entire required depth and width of the working space.

    (a) practical
    (b) possible
    (c) required
    (d) none of these

54. Working space required by Section 110.26 shall not be used for _____.

    (a) storage
    (b) raceways
    (c) lighting
    (d) accessibility

55. When normally enclosed live parts are exposed for inspection or servicing, the working space, if in a passageway or general open space, shall be suitably _____.

    (a) accessible
    (b) guarded
    (c) open
    (d) enclosed

56. For large equipment that contains overcurrent devices, switching devices, or control devices, there shall be one entrance to and egress from the required working space not less than 24 in. wide and _____ high at each end of the working space.

    (a) 5½ ft
    (b) 6 ft
    (c) 6½ ft
    (d) 7 ft

57. For equipment rated 800A or more that contains overcurrent devices, switching devices, or control devices; and where the entrance to the working space has a personnel door(s) less than 25 ft from the nearest edge of the working space, the door shall open at least 90° _____.

    (a) in or out with simple pressure and shall not have any lock
    (b) in the direction of egress and be equipped with listed panic or fire exit hardware
    (c) and be equipped with a locking means
    (d) and be equipped with an electronic opener

58. Illumination shall be provided for all working spaces about service equipment, switchboards, switchgear, enclosed panelboards, or motor control centers _____.

    (a) over 600V
    (b) installed indoors
    (c) rated 1200A or more
    (d) using automatic means of control

59. All service equipment, switchboards, panelboards, and motor control centers shall be _____.

    (a) located in dedicated spaces
    (b) protected from damage
    (c) in weatherproof enclosures
    (d) located in dedicated spaces and protected from damage

60. The minimum height of dedicated equipment space for motor control centers installed indoors is _____ above the enclosure, or to the structural ceiling, whichever is lower.

    (a) 3 ft
    (b) 5 ft
    (c) 6 ft
    (d) 6½ ft

61. A dropped, suspended, or similar ceiling that does not add strength to the building structure shall not be considered a _____ ceiling.

    (a) structural
    (b) False
    (c) real
    (d) drop

62. All switchboards, switchgear, panelboards, and motor control centers located outdoors shall be _____.

    (a) installed in identified enclosures
    (b) protected from accidental contact by unauthorized personnel or by vehicular traffic
    (c) protected from accidental spillage or leakage from piping systems
    (d) all of these

63. A NEMA Type 1 enclosure is approved for the environmental condition where _____ might be present.

    (a) falling dirt
    (b) falling liquids
    (c) circulating dust
    (d) settling airborne dust

64. Enclosures of switchboards, switchgear, or panelboards that may become ice covered where exposed to sleet may be installed in a _____ enclosure.

    (a) Type 3 or 3R
    (b) Type 3X or RX
    (c) Type 3S or SX
    (d) Type 4 or 4X

65. Enclosure Type 3X for switchboards, switchgear, or panelboards located outdoors are suitable in locations subject to _____.

    (a) rain
    (b) windblown dust
    (c) corrosive agents
    (d) any of these

66. A Type 4X enclosure for switchboards, switchgear, or panelboards located indoors is suitable in locations subject to the environmental condition of _____.

    (a) falling dirt
    (b) falling liquids
    (c) corrosive agents
    (d) any of these

Article 110 | General Requirements for Electrical Installations

67. The term "rainproof" is typically used in conjunction with enclosure type(s) _____.

    (a) NEMA 3
    (b) NEMA 3R and 3RX
    (c) NEMA 4
    (d) NEMA 4R and 4RX

CHAPTER 2
WIRING AND PROTECTION

Introduction to Chapter 2—Wiring and Protection

Chapter 2 of the *Code* is divided into eleven articles containing the general rules for wiring and sizing circuits, overcurrent protection of conductors, overvoltage protection of equipment, and bonding and grounding. The rules in this chapter apply to all electrical installations covered by the *NEC*—except as modified in Chapters 5, 6, 7, or specifically referenced in Chapter 8 [90.3].

This chapter can be thought of as the preconstruction phase of a job because it is primarily focused on layout, sizing, and the protection of circuits. Every article in this chapter deals with a different aspect of designing safe wiring for an electrical system. The Chapter 2 articles covered by this material are:

▸ **Article 200—Use and Identification of Neutral and Grounded-Phase Conductors.** This article has one part containing the requirements for the use and identification of the grounded conductor—which in most cases is the neutral conductor.

▸ **Article 210—Branch Circuits.** Article 210 is comprised of three parts which contain requirements for the installation, sizing, and protection of branch circuits. General rules are found in Part I and include topics such as conductor sizing, identification, and AFCI and GFCI protection. Parts II and III contain the requirements for branch circuits and required outlets.

▸ **Article 215—Feeders.** This article covers the requirements for the installation, sizing, and protection of feeders.

▸ **Article 220—Branch-Circuit, Feeder, and Service Calculations.** Article 220 is comprised seven parts. It provides the requirements for calculating branch-circuit, feeder, and service loads. This article also contains the rules for the number of required branch circuits and the number of receptacles on each.

▸ **Article 225—Outside Feeders.** This article covers the requirements for outside wiring methods (both overhead and underground). It includes feeders that run on or between buildings, poles, and other structures which may be present on the premises and used to feed equipment.

▸ **Article 230—Services.** Article 230 covers the installation requirements for service conductors and equipment. It is very important to know where the service begins and ends when applying this article.

▸ **Article 240—Overcurrent Protection.** This article provides the requirements for overcurrent protection and overcurrent protective devices.

▸ **Article 242—Overvoltage Protection.** Part I of Article 242 covers the general installation and connection requirements for surge-protective devices (SPDs) permanently installed on both the line side and load sides of service disconnects. Part II covers SPDs permanently installed on wiring systems 1000V and less.

...

Chapter 2 | Wiring and Protection

> ▶ **Article 250—Bonding and Grounding.** Article 250 covers the grounding requirements for providing a path to the Earth to reduce overvoltage from lightning, and the bonding requirements for the low-impedance fault current path necessary to facilitate the operation of overcurrent protective devices in the event of a ground fault.

ARTICLE 200 USE AND IDENTIFICATION OF GROUNDED CONDUCTORS

Introduction to Article 200—Use and Identification of Grounded Conductors

Article 200 contains the requirements for the use and identification of grounded conductors and their terminals. This article has eleven sections covering the requirements for neutral conductors and grounded-phase conductors. Take some time to review electrical theory before you try to attack this article, you must understand how current flow is essential for these rules to make sense. Some topics covered in this material for Article 200 include:

- Grounded System Connections
- Conductor Identification
- Equipment Terminal Identification

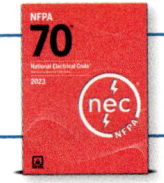

Please use the 2023 *Code* book to answer the following questions.

1. Article 200 provides the requirements for _____.
   (a) identification of terminals
   (b) grounded conductors in premises wiring systems
   (c) identification of grounded conductors
   (d) all of these

2. The continuity of a grounded conductor shall not depend on a connection to _____.
   (a) a metal enclosure
   (b) a raceway
   (c) cable armor
   (d) any of these

3. Where more than one neutral conductor is associated with different circuits in an enclosure, they shall be _____.
   (a) color coded
   (b) identified or grouped to correspond to the ungrounded circuit conductor(s)
   (c) tagged individually with individual stripes
   (d) together in one bundle

4. An insulated grounded conductor _____ or smaller shall be identified by a continuous white or gray outer finish, or by three continuous white or gray stripes along its entire length on other than green insulation.
   (a) 8 AWG
   (b) 6 AWG
   (c) 4 AWG
   (d) 3 AWG

5. At the time of installation, grounded conductors _____ or larger can be identified by a distinctive white or gray marking at their terminations.
    (a) 10 AWG
    (b) 8 AWG
    (c) 6 AWG
    (d) 4 AWG

6. Where grounded conductors of different nominal voltage systems are installed in the same raceway, cable, or enclosure, each grounded conductor shall be identified to distinguish the systems by _____.
    (a) a continuous white or gray outer finish
    (b) a grounded conductor with an outer covering of white or gray with a distinguishable colored stripe other than green
    (c) other identification allowed by 200.6(A) or (B) that distinguishes each nominal voltage system grounded conductor
    (d) any of these

7. The insulated grounded conductor(s) in a multiconductor cable _____ or larger, is permitted to be re-identified at the time of installation at its terminations in accordance with 200.6(B).
    (a) 8 AWG
    (b) 6 AWG
    (c) 4 AWG
    (d) 2 AWG

8. A _____ shall be used only for the grounded circuit conductor, unless otherwise permitted in 200.7(B) and (C).
    (a) conductor with continuous white or gray covering
    (b) conductor with three continuous white or gray stripes on other than green insulation
    (c) marking of white or gray color at the termination
    (d) any of these

9. The white conductor within a cable assembly can be used for a(an) _____ conductor where permanently reidentified to indicate its use as an ungrounded conductor at each location where the conductor is visible and accessible.
    (a) grounded
    (b) ungrounded
    (c) equipment grounding
    (d) grounding electrode

10. Receptacles shall have the terminal intended for connection to the grounded conductor identified by a metal or metal coating that is white or silver in color or by the word, "_____."
    (a) green
    (b) white
    (c) silver
    (d) neutral

11. For devices with screw shells, the terminal for the _____ shall be the one connected to the screw shell.
    (a) grounded conductor
    (b) ungrounded conductor
    (c) equipment grounding conductor
    (d) forming shell terminal

ARTICLE 210 BRANCH CIRCUITS

Introduction to Article 210—Branch Circuits

This article contains the general requirements for branch circuits which extend from the last point of overcurrent protection to the utilization equipment. Branch circuits account for most circuits run in any electrical installation, so you must be sure you are familiar with these rules. Some topics covered in this material for Article 210 include:

- Identification of Branch Circuits
- Multi-Wire Branch Circuits
- Voltage Limitations
- Required Branch Circuits
- GFCI and AFCI Requirements
- Branch-Circuit Ratings
- Permitted Loads
- Receptacle and Lighting Outlet Requirements

This article consists of three parts:

- Part I. General Provisions
- Part II. Branch-Circuit Ratings
- Part III. Required Outlets

Please use the 2023 *Code* book to answer the following questions.

1. Article 210 provides the general requirements for _____ not over 1000V ac, 1500V dc, nominal.

    (a) outside branch circuits
    (b) branch circuits
    (c) ungrounded conductors
    (d) feeder calculations

2. Each multiwire branch circuit shall be provided with a means that will simultaneously disconnect all _____ conductors at the point where the branch circuit originates.

    (a) circuit
    (b) grounded
    (c) grounding
    (d) ungrounded

Article 210 | Branch Circuits

3. Multiwire branch circuits shall supply only _____.

   (a) line-to-neutral loads
   (b) branch circuits in dwelling units
   (c) conductors originating from different panelboards
   (d) three-phase loads

4. Where the premises wiring system has branch circuits supplied from more than one nominal voltage system, each _____ conductor of a branch circuit shall be identified by phase or line and by nominal voltage system at all termination, connection, and splice points.

   (a) neutral
   (b) ungrounded
   (c) grounding
   (d) all of these

5. Where a different nominal voltage system is added to a(an) _____ installation, branch-circuit identification is only required for the new one.

   (a) new
   (b) existing
   (c) remodeled
   (d) repaired

6. In dwelling units and guest rooms or guest suites, voltage shall not exceed 120V for cord and plug equipment connected to loads rated _____.

   (a) 1440 VA
   (b) 1500 VA
   (c) 1800 VA
   (d) 2400 VA

7. If two or more branch circuits supply devices or equipment on the same yoke or mounting strap, a means to simultaneously disconnect the ungrounded supply conductors shall be provided _____.

   (a) at the point where the branch circuits originate
   (b) at the location of the device or equipment
   (c) at the point where the feeder originates
   (d) within sight of the device or equipment

8. A listed Class A GFCI shall provide protection in accordance with 210.8(A) through (F). The GFCI protective device shall be installed in a(an) _____ location.

   (a) circuit breaker type only
   (b) accessible
   (c) readily accessible
   (d) concealed

9. For the purposes of section 210.8, the distance from receptacles shall be measured as the shortest path the power supply cord connected to the receptacle would follow without piercing a _____ or fixed barrier.

   (a) floor
   (b) wall
   (c) ceiling
   (d) any of these

10. All 125V through 250V receptacles that are not readily accessible and supplied by single-phase branch circuits dedicated to electric _____ equipment shall be permitted to be installed in accordance with 426.28 or 427.22, as applicable.

    (a) snow-melting
    (b) deicing
    (c) pipeline and vessel heating
    (d) any of these

11. A receptacle supplying only a permanently installed premises _____ shall be permitted to omit ground-fault circuit-interrupter protection.

    (a) sump pump
    (b) refrigerator
    (c) security system
    (d) well pump

12. Factory-installed receptacles mounted internally to bathroom _____ assemblies shall not require GFCI protection unless required by the installation instructions or listing.

    (a) surface-mounted luminaire
    (b) exhaust fan
    (c) electric baseboard heat
    (d) all of these

13. All 125V through 250V receptacles installed in dwelling unit _____ and supplied by single-phase branch circuits rated 150V or less to ground shall have ground-fault circuit-interrupter protection for personnel.

    (a) hallways
    (b) bedrooms
    (c) closets
    (d) bathrooms

14. GFCI protection shall be provided for all 125V through 250V receptacles installed in dwelling unit _____.

    (a) attics
    (b) garages and accessory buildings
    (c) utility rooms
    (d) dens

15. All 125V through 250V receptacles installed in crawl spaces at or below grade level of dwelling units shall have _____ protection.

    (a) AFCI
    (b) GFCI
    (c) GFPE
    (d) none of these

16. GFCI protection shall be provided for all 125V through 250V _____ in dwelling unit basements.

    (a) receptacles
    (b) switches
    (c) outlets
    (d) disconnects

17. In dwelling unit kitchens, GFCI protection shall be provided for 125V through 250V receptacles _____.

    (a) installed to serve the countertop surfaces
    (b) within 6 ft from the top inside edge of the bowl of the sink
    (c) installed to serve above or below the countertop surfaces
    (d) serving the kitchen

18. In dwelling units, GFCI protection shall be provided for 125V through 250V receptacles installed in areas with sinks and permanent provisions for _____.

    (a) food preparation
    (b) beverage preparation
    (c) cooking
    (d) any of these

19. All 125V through 250V receptacles installed in dwelling unit boathouses shall have _____ protection.

    (a) GFCI
    (b) AFCI
    (c) GFPE
    (d) SPGFCI

20. In other than dwelling units, all 125V through 250V receptacles supplied by single-phase branch circuits rated 150 volts-to-ground or less, 50A or less, and three-phase branch circuits rated 100A or less, installed in(on) _____ shall have GFCI protection for personnel.

    (a) rooftops
    (b) kitchens
    (c) bathrooms
    (d) all of these

21. In other than dwelling units, GFCI protection is required for receptacles installed in _____.

    (a) kitchens
    (b) unfinished areas of basements
    (c) laundry areas
    (d) all of these

22. In other than dwelling units, GFCI protection shall be provided for receptacles installed in areas with sinks and permanent provisions for _____.

    (a) food preparation
    (b) beverage preparation
    (c) cooking
    (d) any of these

23. In other than dwelling units, GFCI protection shall be provided for receptacles installed within _____ serving areas with permanent provisions for food serving, beverage serving, or cooking.

    (a) picnic
    (b) banquet
    (c) recreational
    (d) buffet

Article 210 | Branch Circuits

24. In other than dwelling units, GFCI protection shall be provided for all outdoor receptacles supplied by branch circuits rated _____ or less to ground.

    (a) 125V
    (b) 150V
    (c) 208V
    (d) 277V

25. In other than dwelling units, GFCI protection shall be provided for receptacles and cord-and-plug connected appliances installed within _____ from the top inside edge of the bowl of a sink.

    (a) 3 ft
    (b) 4 ft
    (c) 5 ft
    (d) 6 ft

26. In other than dwelling units, all single-phase receptacles rated 150V to ground or less, 50A or less and three-phase receptacles rated 150V to ground or less, 100A or less installed in indoor _____ or wet locations shall be GFCI protected.

    (a) dry
    (b) damp
    (c) humid
    (d) rainy

27. In other than dwelling units, GFCI protection is required for all single-phase receptacles rated 150V to ground or less, 50A or less and three-phase receptacles rated 150V to ground or less, 100A or less in _____.

    (a) indoor damp and wet locations
    (b) locker rooms with associated showering facilities
    (c) garages, service bays, and similar areas other than vehicle exhibition halls and showrooms
    (d) all of these

28. All single-phase receptacles rated 150V to ground or less, 50A or less and three-phase receptacles rated 150V to ground or less, _____ or less installed in locker rooms with associated showering facilities shall be GFCI protected.

    (a) 60A
    (b) 75A
    (c) 100A
    (d) 125A

29. In other than dwelling units, GFCI protection is required for all single-phase receptacles rated 150V to ground or less, 50A or less and three-phase receptacles rated 150V to ground or less, 100A or less in _____ areas of the basement.

    (a) unfinished
    (b) finished
    (c) wet
    (d) dry

30. In other than dwelling units, GFCI protection is required where receptacles are installed within _____ from the top inside edge or rim or from the conductive support framing of aquariums, bait wells, and similar open aquatic vessels or containers.

    (a) 3 ft
    (b) 5 ft
    (c) 6 ft
    (d) 10 ft

31. In other than dwelling units, all 125-volt through 250-volt receptacles supplied by single-phase branch circuits rated 150 volts or less to ground, 50 amperes or less, and all receptacles supplied by three-phase branch circuits rated 150 volts or less to ground, 100 amperes or less, installed in _____, shall be provided with GFCI protection.

    (a) laundry areas
    (b) finished basements
    (c) attics
    (d) guest rooms and suites

32. In other than dwelling units, receptacles installed within _____ of the outside edge of a bathtub or shower stall shall have GFCI protection.

    (a) 2 ft
    (b) 3 ft
    (c) 4 ft
    (d) 6 ft

33. GFCI protection shall be provided for crawl space lighting outlets not exceeding _____.

    (a) 120V
    (b) 125V
    (c) 240V
    (d) 250V

34. According to Article 210, GFCI protection shall be provided for the branch circuit or outlet supplying _____ rated 150V or less to ground and 60A or less, single- or three-phase.

    (a) sump pumps
    (b) wall-mounted ovens
    (c) clothes dryers
    (d) all of these

35. For equipment requiring servicing, GFCI protection shall be provided for the receptacles within 25 ft of HVAC equipment required by _____.

    (a) 210.1
    (b) 210.25(B)
    (c) 210.62
    (d) 210.63(A)

36. For dwellings, all outdoor outlets, other than those covered in 210.8(A) Ex 1, and supplied by single-phase branch circuits rated 150V or less to ground, _____, shall be provided with GFCI protection.

    (a) 15A or more
    (b) 20A or less
    (c) 30A or less
    (d) 50A or less

37. For dwellings, all outdoor outlets, other than those covered in 210.8(A) Ex 1, including outlets installed in _____, rated 50A or less, shall be provided with GFCI protection

    (a) garages that have floors located at or below grade level
    (b) accessory buildings
    (c) boathouses
    (d) all of these

38. Two or more _____ small-appliance branch circuits shall be provided for all receptacle outlets specified by 210.52(B).

    (a) 15A
    (b) 20A
    (c) auxiliary
    (d) supplemental

39. There shall be a minimum of one additional _____ branch circuit for dwelling unit laundry receptacle outlet(s).

    (a) 15A
    (b) 20A
    (c) auxiliary
    (d) supplemental

40. At least _____ or more 120V, 20A branch circuit(s) shall be provided to supply dwelling unit bathroom(s) receptacle outlet(s).

    (a) one
    (b) two
    (c) three
    (d) four

41. At least one 120V, 20A branch circuit shall be installed to supply receptacle outlets, including those required by 210.52(G)(1) for _____ and in _____ with electric power.

    (a) attached decks, detached gazebos
    (b) attached garages, detached sheds
    (c) attached garages, unfinished accessory buildings
    (d) attached garages, detached garages

42. All 120V, single-phase, 10A, 15A, and 20A branch circuits supplying outlets or devices installed in dwelling unit _____ shall be AFCI protected.

    (a) kitchens
    (b) garages
    (c) bathrooms
    (d) outdoor areas

43. All 120V, single-phase, 10A, 15A, and 20A branch circuits supplying outlets or devices installed in dwelling unit _____ shall be AFCI protected by any of the means described in 210.12(A)(1) through (6).

    (a) kitchens
    (b) family rooms
    (c) dining rooms
    (d) all of these

44. All 120V, single-phase, 10A, 15A, or 20A branch circuits supplying outlets or devices installed in the _____ of dormitory units shall be AFCI protected.

    (a) bedrooms
    (b) living rooms
    (c) closets
    (d) all of these

Article 210 | Branch Circuits

45. All 120V, single-phase, 10A, 15A, or 20A branch circuits supplying outlets or devices installed in areas designed for use exclusively as _____ in fire stations, police stations, ambulance stations, rescue stations, ranger stations, and similar locations shall be AFCI protected.

    (a) sleeping quarters
    (b) recreational areas
    (c) offices
    (d) all of these

46. If branch-circuit wiring for any of the areas specified in 210.12(B), (C), or (D) is modified, replaced, or extended, the branch circuit shall be protected by a _____.

    (a) listed outlet branch-circuit type AFCI located at the first receptacle outlet of the existing branch circuit
    (b) listed combination GFPE circuit breaker only
    (c) GFCI circuit breaker
    (d) GFCI at first receptacle in the circuit

47. Guest rooms and guest suites in _____ that are provided with permanent provisions for cooking shall have branch circuits installed to meet the rules for dwelling units.

    (a) hotels
    (b) motels
    (c) assisted living facilities
    (d) all of these

48. Conductors for branch circuits [Article 210] are sized to prevent a voltage drop exceeding _____ at the farthest outlet of power, heating, and lighting loads, or combinations of such loads.

    (a) 2 percent
    (b) 3 percent
    (c) 4 percent
    (d) 6 percent

49. Where a branch circuit supplies continuous loads and/or noncontinuous loads, the rating of the overcurrent device shall not be less than the noncontinuous load plus _____ of the continuous load.

    (a) 80 percent
    (b) 115 percent
    (c) 120 percent
    (d) 125 percent

50. A single receptacle installed on an individual branch circuit shall have an ampere rating not less than the rating of the _____.

    (a) branch circuit
    (b) device listing
    (c) manufacturer's instructions
    (d) equipment current rating

51. The rating of any one cord-and plug-connected utilization equipment on a 15A, 120V branch circuit shall not exceed _____.

    (a) 12A
    (b) 15A
    (c) 16A
    (d) 20A

52. If a 20A branch circuit supplies multiple receptacles, the receptacles shall have an ampere rating of no less than _____.

    (a) 10A
    (b) 15A
    (c) 20A
    (d) 30A

53. A 15A or 20A branch circuit shall be permitted to supply lighting outlets, lighting units, or other utilization equipment, or any combination of them, if the rating of any one cord-and-plug-connected utilization equipment not fastened in place does not exceed _____ of the branch-circuit ampere rating.

    (a) 25 percent
    (b) 50 percent
    (c) 80 percent
    (d) 100 percent

54. The total rating of utilization equipment fastened in place shall not exceed _____ of the rating of a 20A multiple outlet branch circuit.

    (a) 25 percent
    (b) 50 percent
    (c) 80 percent
    (d) 100 percent

55. An appliance receptacle outlet installed for a specific appliance shall be installed within _____ of the intended location of the appliance.

    (a) sight
    (b) 3 ft
    (c) 6 ft
    (d) the length of the cord

56. The dwelling unit 15- and 20A receptacle outlets required by the *Code* are in addition to any receptacles that are _____.

    (a) part of a luminaire or appliance
    (b) located within cabinets or cupboards
    (c) located more than 5½ ft above the floor
    (d) any of these

57. A receptacle outlet shall be installed so no point along the floor line of any wall is more than _____, measured horizontally along the floor line, from a receptacle outlet.

    (a) 6 ft
    (b) 8 ft
    (c) 10 ft
    (d) 12 ft

58. In a dwelling unit, any wall space including space measured around corners and unbroken along the floor line by doorways, fireplaces, fixed cabinets, and similar openings shall be considered wall space when the wall space is at least _____ wide.

    (a) 2 ft
    (b) 3 ft
    (c) 4 ft
    (d) 6 ft

59. In dwelling units, when determining the spacing of receptacle outlets, _____ on exterior walls shall not be considered wall space.

    (a) fixed panels
    (b) fixed glass
    (c) sliding panels
    (d) all of these

60. Floor receptacle outlets shall not be counted as part of the required number of receptacle outlets for dwelling unit wall spaces, unless they are located within _____ of the wall.

    (a) 6 in.
    (b) 12 in.
    (c) 18 in.
    (d) 24 in.

61. Receptacles installed for _____ and similar work surfaces as specified in 210.52(C) shall not be considered as the receptacle outlets required by 210.52(A).

    (a) countertops
    (b) tables
    (c) peninsulas
    (d) none of these

62. The two or more small-appliance branch circuits specified in 210.52(B)(1) shall have _____.

    (a) no more than one outlet
    (b) no other outlets
    (c) unlimited outlets
    (d) supply only one appliance

63. Receptacles installed in a dwelling unit kitchen to serve countertop surfaces shall be supplied by not fewer than _____ small-appliance branch circuit(s).

    (a) one
    (b) two
    (c) three
    (d) four

64. Receptacle outlets are required for kitchen countertops and work surfaces that are _____ and wider.

    (a) 12 in.
    (b) 15 in.
    (c) 18 in.
    (d) 24 in.

65. Kitchen wall countertop and work surface space receptacle outlets shall be installed so that no point along the wall line is more than _____ measured horizontally from a receptacle outlet in that space.

    (a) 10 in.
    (b) 12 in.
    (c) 16 in.
    (d) 24 in.

Article 210 | Branch Circuits

66. If a receptacle outlet is not provided to serve an island or peninsular countertop or work surface, provisions shall be provided at the island or peninsula for the _____ addition of a receptacle outlet to serve the island or peninsular countertop or work surface.

    (a) future
    (b) permanent
    (c) possible
    (d) none of these

67. Kitchen and dining room countertop receptacle outlets in dwelling units shall be installed on or above the countertop or work surface, but not more than _____ above the countertop or work surface.

    (a) 12 in.
    (b) 18 in.
    (c) 20 in.
    (d) 24 in.

68. In dwelling units, the required bathroom receptacle outlet can be installed on the side or face of the sink cabinet if not more than _____ below the top of the sink or sink countertop.

    (a) 12 in.
    (b) 18 in.
    (c) 20 in.
    (d) 24 in.

69. In dwelling unit bathrooms, not less than one 15A or 20A, 125V receptacle outlet shall be installed within _____ of the outside edge of each bathroom basin.

    (a) 2 ft
    (b) 3 ft
    (c) 4 ft
    (d) 5 ft

70. There shall be at least _____ receptacle(s) installed outdoors at a one-family dwelling and each unit of a two-family dwelling unit that is at grade level.

    (a) one
    (b) two
    (c) three
    (d) four

71. At least one receptacle outlet not more than _____ above a balcony, deck, or porch shall be installed at each balcony, deck, or porch that is attached to and accessible from a dwelling unit.

    (a) 2 ft
    (b) 3 ft
    (c) 6½ ft
    (d) 8 ft

72. A laundry receptacle outlet shall not be required in each dwelling unit of a multifamily building if laundry facilities are provided on the _____ for all building occupants.

    (a) premises
    (b) outside
    (c) inside
    (d) roof

73. For one- and two-family dwellings, at least one receptacle outlet shall be installed in each _____.

    (a) separate unfinished portion of a basement
    (b) attached or detached garage with electric power
    (c) accessory building with electric power
    (d) all of these

74. For one- and two-family dwellings, and multifamily dwellings, at least one receptacle outlet shall be installed in each separate _____ of a basement.

    (a) unfinished portion
    (b) hallway
    (c) stairway
    (d) all of these

75. Hallways in dwelling units that are _____ or longer require a receptacle outlet.

    (a) 6 ft
    (b) 8 ft
    (c) 10 ft
    (d) 12 ft

76. Foyers with an area greater than _____ shall have a receptacle located in each wall space 3 ft or more in width unbroken by doorways, windows next to doors that extend to the floor, and similar openings.

    (a) 40 sq ft
    (b) 60 sq ft
    (c) 80 sq ft
    (d) 100 sq ft

77. Guest rooms or guest suites provided with permanent provisions for _____ shall have receptacle outlets installed in accordance with all of the applicable requirements for a dwelling unit in accordance with 210.52.

    (a) whirlpool tubs
    (b) bathing
    (c) cooking
    (d) Internet access

78. The number of receptacle outlets for guest rooms in hotels and motels shall not be less than that required for a dwelling unit. These receptacles shall be located to be convenient for permanent furniture layout, but at least _____ receptacle outlet(s) shall be readily accessible.

    (a) one
    (b) two
    (c) three
    (d) four

79. At least one 125-volt, single-phase, 15- or 20-ampere-rated receptacle outlet shall be installed within 18 in. of the top of each show window. No point along the top of the window shall be farther than _____ from a receptacle outlet.

    (a) 3 ft
    (b) 4 ft
    (c) 6 ft
    (d) 8 ft

80. A 125V, single-phase, 15A- or 20A-rated receptacle outlet shall be installed at an accessible location within _____ of equipment requiring servicing.

    (a) 8 ft
    (b) 10 ft
    (c) 25 ft
    (d) 50 ft

81. The required heating, air-conditioning, and refrigeration equipment receptacle outlet shall be located _____ the equipment.

    (a) 6 ft above
    (b) not over 8 ft from
    (c) on
    (d) on the same level as

82. The required heating, air-conditioning, and refrigeration equipment receptacle outlet can be connected to the _____ side of the equipment disconnecting means.

    (a) line
    (b) load
    (c) high
    (d) low

83. Where equipment, other than service equipment, requires dedicated equipment space as specified in 110.26(E), the required receptacle outlet shall be located within _____ the electrical equipment.

    (a) the same room or area as
    (b) or adjacent to
    (c) sight of
    (d) or below

84. Each meeting room of not more than _____ in other than dwelling units shall have outlets for nonlocking-type, 125V, 15A or 20A receptacles installed in accordance with 210.65(B).

    (a) 500 sq ft
    (b) 1000 sq ft
    (c) 1500 sq ft
    (d) 2000 sq ft

85. For the purposes of 210.65, meeting rooms are typically designed or intended for the gathering of seated occupants for such purposes as conferences, deliberations, or similar purposes, where _____ electronic equipment such as computers, projectors, or similar equipment is likely to be used.

    (a) approved
    (b) portable
    (c) listed
    (d) permanently installed

86. For the purposes of 210.65, examples of rooms that are not meeting rooms include _____.

    (a) auditoriums
    (b) schoolrooms
    (c) coffee shops
    (d) all of these

Article 210 | Branch Circuits

87. Receptacle outlets in meeting room fixed walls shall be installed in accordance with _____.

    (a) 210.52(A)(1)
    (b) 210.52(A)(1) and (A)(2)
    (c) 210.52(A)(1) through (A)(3)
    (d) 210.52(A)(1) through (A)(4)

88. A meeting room with any floor dimension that is _____ or greater in any direction and that has a floor area of at least 215 sq ft shall have at least one floor receptacle outlet.

    (a) 8 ft
    (b) 10 ft
    (c) 12 ft
    (d) 15 ft

89. A meeting room that is at least 12 ft wide and that has a floor area of at least 215 sq ft shall have at least one receptacle outlet located in the floor at a distance not less than _____ from any fixed wall for each 215 sq ft or fraction thereof.

    (a) 6 ft
    (b) 6 ft 6 in.
    (c) 7 ft
    (d) 7 ft 6 in.

90. Required lighting outlet switch or wall-mounted control devices shall not rely exclusively on a _____ unless a means is provided for automatically energizing the lighting outlets upon battery failure.

    (a) battery
    (b) solar cell
    (c) thermocouple
    (d) none of these

91. At least one lighting outlet controlled by a listed _____ shall be installed in every habitable room, kitchen, laundry area, and bathroom of a dwelling unit.

    (a) wall-mounted control device
    (b) switch
    (c) occupancy sensor
    (d) motion detector

92. In rooms other than kitchens, laundry areas, and bathrooms of dwelling units, one or more receptacles controlled by a listed wall-mounted control device shall be permitted in lieu of _____.

    (a) lighting outlets
    (b) luminaires
    (c) the receptacles required by 210.52(B) and (D)
    (d) all of these

93. At least one lighting outlet controlled by a listed wall-mounted control device shall be installed in dwelling unit hallways, stairways, and _____.

    (a) attached garages
    (b) detached garages with electric power
    (c) accessory buildings with electric power
    (d) all of these

94. For dwelling units, attached garages, detached garages with electric power, and accessory buildings with electric power, at least _____ exterior lighting outlet(s) controlled by a listed wall-mounted control device shall be installed to provide illumination on the exterior side of outdoor entrances or exits with grade-level access.

    (a) one
    (b) two
    (c) three
    (d) one or two

95. Where lighting outlets are installed for an interior stairway with _____ risers between floor levels, there shall be a listed wall-mounted control device at each floor level and at each landing level that includes a stairway entry to control the lighting outlets.

    (a) three or more
    (b) four or more
    (c) six or more
    (d) any number of

96. In a dwelling unit, dimmer control of lighting outlets for interior stairways installed in accordance with 210.70(A)(2)(3) shall not be permitted unless the listed control devices can provide dimming control _____ at each control location for the interior stairway illumination.

    (a) for illumination
    (b) for emergency lighting
    (c) to maximum brightness
    (d) for effective lighting

97. At least one lighting outlet _____ shall be located at the point of entry to the attic, underfloor space, utility room, or basement where these spaces are used for storage or contain equipment requiring servicing.

    (a) that is unswitched
    (b) containing or controlled by a switch or listed wall-mounted control device
    (c) that is GFCI protected
    (d) that is shielded from damage

Notes

ARTICLE 215 FEEDERS

Introduction to Article 215—Feeders

Article 215 contains the general requirements for feeder conductors which extend between a service disconnect, transformer, generator, PV system output circuit, or other power-supply source and the branch-circuit overcurrent protective device. Feeders have specific requirement permissions that differ from branch circuits making the proper identification of feeders critical. Some topics covered in this material for Article 215 include:

- Feeder Rating and Size
- Overcurrent Protection
- Feeder GFPE
- Identification
- Barrier Requirements
- Surge-Protective Requirements

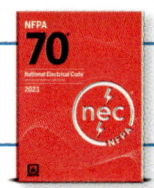

Please use the 2023 *Code* book to answer the following questions.

1. Each feeder disconnect rated 1000A or more and installed on solidly grounded wye electrical systems of more than 150V to ground, but not exceeding _____ phase-to-phase, shall be provided with ground-fault protection of equipment in accordance with 230.95.

    (a) 50V
    (b) 150V
    (c) 600V
    (d) 1000V

2. Where a feeder supplies continuous loads or any combination of continuous and noncontinuous loads, the conductor ampacity shall be no less than the noncontinuous load plus _____ of the continuous load.

    (a) 80 percent
    (b) 100 percent
    (c) 125 percent
    (d) 150 percent

Article 215 | Feeders

3. Where a portion of a feeder is connected at both its supply and load ends to separately installed pressure connections in accordance with 110.14(C)(2), it shall be permitted to have an allowable ampacity _____ the sum of the continuous load plus the noncontinuous load.

   (a) not less than
   (b) equal to
   (c) not greater than
   (d) of 80 percent of

4. Feeder grounded conductors not connected to an overcurrent device can be sized at _____ of the continuous and noncontinuous load.

   (a) 80 percent
   (b) 100 percent
   (c) 125 percent
   (d) 150 percent

5. Where a premises wiring system contains feeders supplied from more than one nominal voltage system, each ungrounded conductor of a feeder shall be identified by phase or line and system by _____, or other approved means.

   (a) color coding
   (b) marking tape
   (c) tagging
   (d) any of these

6. Barriers shall be placed such that no uninsulated, ungrounded busbar or terminal is exposed to inadvertent contact by persons or maintenance equipment while servicing load terminations in _____ supplied by feeder taps.

   (a) panelboards
   (b) switchboards and switchgear
   (c) motor control centers
   (d) any of these

7. Where a feeder supplies _____, a surge-protective device (SPD) shall be installed.

   (a) dwelling units
   (b) dormitory units
   (c) guest rooms and suites of hotels and motels
   (d) any of these

8. Surge-protective devices shall be installed in or adjacent to distribution equipment, connected to the _____ side of the feeder that contains branch circuit overcurrent protective device(s) that supply dwelling units, dormitory units, and guest rooms and suites.

   (a) line
   (b) load
   (c) supply
   (d) line or supply

9. Where a feeder supplies dwelling units, the required SPD shall be a _____.

   (a) Type 1
   (b) Type 1 or 2
   (c) Type 3
   (d) any of these

10. Where dwelling units are supplied by a feeder and the distribution equipment is _____, the required Type 1 or Type 2 SPD shall be installed.

    (a) replaced
    (b) repaired
    (c) due for maintenance
    (d) replaced or repaired

11. Where dwelling units are supplied by a feeder the required SPD shall have a nominal discharge current rating (In) of not less than _____.

    (a) 5 kA
    (b) 7.50 kA
    (c) 10 kA
    (d) the available fault current

ARTICLE 220 — BRANCH-CIRCUIT, FEEDER, AND SERVICE LOAD CALCULATIONS

Introduction to Article 220—Branch-Circuit, Feeder, and Service Load Calculations

This article contains the requirements necessary for calculating demand loads for branch circuits, feeders, and services. The *Code* recognizes that not all demand for power will occur at the same time. This load diversity allows us to apply the rules contained in this article to reduce the required size of circuits and equipment. Some topics covered in our material for Article 220 include:

- Branch-Circuit Load Calculations
- Existing Installation Load Calculations
- Service Load Calculations
- Special Application Load Calculations

This article consists of seven parts:

- Part I. General
- Part II. Branch-Circuit Load Calculations
- Part III. Feeder and Service Load Calculations
- Part IV. Optional Feeder and Service Load Calculations
- Part V. Farm Load Calculations
- Part VI. Health Care Facility Load Calculations
- Part VII. Marinas, Boatyards, Floating Buildings, and Docking Facility Calculations

As you work through Article 220, be sure to study the illustrations and review the examples in Annex D to help you fully understand this article's requirements.

Article 220 | Branch-Circuit, Feeder, and Service Load Calculations

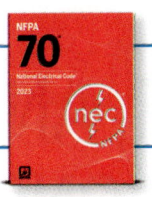

Please use the 2023 *Code* book to answer the following questions.

1. Article _____ provides requirements for calculating branch-circuit, feeder, and service loads.

   (a) 200
   (b) 210
   (c) 220
   (d) 230

2. Unless otherwise specified, for purposes of calculating branch-circuit and feeder loads, _____ system voltages of 120V, 120/240V, 208Y/120V, 240V, 347V, 480Y/277V, 480V, 600Y/347V, and 600V shall be used.

   (a) nominal
   (b) separately derived
   (c) utility
   (d) secondary

3. When calculations in Article 220 result in a fraction of an ampere that is less than _____, such fractions can be dropped.

   (a) 0.49
   (b) 0.5
   (c) 0.51
   (d) 0.8

4. For dwelling units, the calculated floor area for the general lighting load shall not include _____.

   (a) finished basements
   (b) finished attics
   (c) open porches
   (d) utility rooms

5. Outlets supplying luminaires shall be calculated based on the maximum _____ rating of the equipment.

   (a) power
   (b) true power
   (c) voltage
   (d) volt-ampere

6. Sign and outline lighting outlets are to be calculated at a minimum of _____ for each required branch circuit specified in 600.5(A).

   (a) 1000 VA
   (b) 1200 VA
   (c) 1500 VA
   (d) 2000 VA

7. Show window loads shall be calculated at _____ per linear ft of show window.

   (a) 90 VA
   (b) 120 VA
   (c) 200 VA
   (d) 240 VA

8. Nondwelling unit motors rated less than _____ and connected to a lighting circuit shall be considered general lighting load.

   (a) 1/16 hp
   (b) 1/8 hp
   (c) 1/4 hp
   (d) 1/3 hp

9. The lighting load unit values of Table 220.42(A) are based on minimum load conditions and _____ power factor and might not provide sufficient capacity for the installation contemplated.

   (a) 80 percent
   (b) 85 percent
   (c) 90 percent
   (d) 92 percent

10. The general lighting load for a school is _____.

    (a) 1.50 VA
    (b) 2.50 VA
    (c) 3 VA
    (d) 3.50 VA

11. The 125 percent multiplier for a continuous load as specified in 210.20(A) _____ included when using the unit loads in table 220.12 for calculating the minimum lighting load for a specified occupancy.

    (a) is
    (b) is not
    (c) is permitted to be
    (d) shall not be

12. Where the building is designed to comply with an energy code, the lighting load shall be calculated using the unit values specified in the _____.

    (a) *NEC*
    (b) building code
    (c) energy code
    (d) any of these

13. For other than dwelling units or guest rooms of hotels or motels, the feeder and service calculation for track lighting shall be calculated at 150 VA for every _____ of lighting track or fraction thereof.

    (a) 1 ft
    (b) 2 ft
    (c) 3 ft
    (d) 4 ft

14. Feeder and service loads for fixed electric space-heating loads shall be calculated at _____ of the total connected load.

    (a) 80 percent
    (b) 100 percent
    (c) 125 percent
    (d) 200 percent

15. For dwelling unit load calculations in accordance Article 220, a load of not less than _____ for each 2-wire small-appliance branch circuit shall be applied.

    (a) 1000 VA
    (b) 1200 VA
    (c) 1500 VA
    (d) 2000 VA

16. For dwelling unit load calculations in accordance Article 220, a load of not less than _____ for the laundry branch circuit shall be applied.

    (a) 1000 VA
    (b) 1200 VA
    (c) 1500 VA
    (d) 2000 VA

17. When sizing a service or feeder for fixed appliances in dwelling units, a demand factor of 75 percent of the total nameplate ratings can be applied if there are _____ or more appliances fastened in place.

    (a) two
    (b) three
    (c) four
    (d) five

18. Applying a demand factor of 75 percent to the nameplate rating load of four or more appliances rated ¼ hp or greater, or 500 watts or greater, that are fastened in place, and that are served by the same feeder or service in a one-family, two-family, or multifamily dwelling shall be permitted. This demand factor shall not apply to _____.

    (a) electric vehicle supply equipment
    (b) dishwashers
    (c) waste disposals
    (d) microwave/hoods

19. The load for electric clothes dryers in a dwelling unit shall be _____ or the nameplate rating, whichever is larger, for each dryer served.

    (a) 1500W
    (b) 4500W
    (c) 5000W
    (d) 8000W

20. For dwelling unit load calculations in accordance Article 220, the branch-circuit load for one 10-kW range is _____.

    (a) 8 kW
    (b) 10 kW
    (c) 12 kW
    (d) 14 kW

Article 220 | Branch-Circuit, Feeder, and Service Load Calculations

21. For dwelling unit load calculations in accordance Article 220, the branch-circuit load for one wall-mounted oven and one counter-mounted cooking unit shall be the _____ rating of the appliance.

    (a) nameplate
    (b) ampere
    (c) wattage
    (d) voltage

22. Using the standard load calculation method, the feeder demand factor for a duplex containing two 12 kW ranges is _____.

    (a) 11 kW
    (b) 14 kW
    (c) 16 kW
    (d) 24 kW

23. Table 220.56 may be applied to determine the load for thermostatically controlled or intermittently used _____ and other kitchen equipment in a commercial kitchen.

    (a) commercial electric cooking equipment
    (b) dishwasher booster heaters
    (c) water heaters
    (d) all of these

24. The demand factors in Table 220.56 shall apply to _____ equipment.

    (a) space-heating
    (b) ventilating
    (c) air-conditioning
    (d) none of these

25. When applying the demand factors of Table 220.56, the feeder or service demand load shall not be less than the sum of the _____.

    (a) total number of receptacles at 180 VA per receptacle outlet
    (b) VA ratings of all of the small-appliance branch circuits combined
    (c) largest two kitchen equipment loads
    (d) kitchen heating and air-conditioning loads

26. The electrical vehicle supply equipment (EVSE) load shall be calculated at the larger of _____ or the nameplate rating of the equipment.

    (a) 5000W
    (b) 7200W
    (c) 10,000W
    (d) 12,500W

27. If a motor or air-conditioning load is part of the noncoincident load and is not the largest of the noncoincident loads, 125 percent of either the motor load or air-conditioning load, whichever is _____, shall be used in the calculation.

    (a) less
    (b) smaller
    (c) larger
    (d) less or smaller

28. There shall be no reduction in the size of the neutral or grounded conductor on _____ loads supplied from a 4-wire, wye-connected, three-phase system.

    (a) dwelling unit
    (b) hospital
    (c) nonlinear
    (d) motel

29. If an energy management system (EMS) is used to limit the current to a feeder or service, the set point value of the EMS shall be considered _____.

    (a) at 80 percent
    (b) at 90 percent
    (c) at 100 percent
    (d) a continuous load

30. Under the optional method for calculating a single-family dwelling unit service, general loads beyond the initial 10 kVA are assessed at a _____ demand factor.

    (a) 40 percent
    (b) 50 percent
    (c) 60 percent
    (d) 75 percent

31. A demand factor of _____ applies to a multifamily dwelling with ten units if the optional calculation method is used.

    (a) 43 percent
    (b) 50 percent
    (c) 60 percent
    (d) 75 percent

32. Where two dwelling units are supplied by a single feeder or service and the calculated load under Part III of this article exceeds that for _____ identical units calculated under 220.84, the lesser of the two loads is permitted to be used.

    (a) two
    (b) three
    (c) four
    (d) five

33. When calculating a feeder or service load for existing installations, if the maximum demand data for a 1-year period is not available, the calculated load shall be permitted to be based on the maximum demand (the _____ kilowatts) reached and maintained for a 15-minute interval continuously recorded over a minimum 30-day period.

    (a) lowest recorded
    (b) highest recorded
    (c) lowest average
    (d) highest average

34. Where shore power accommodations provide two receptacles specifically for an individual boat slip, and these receptacles have different voltages, only the receptacle with the _____ shall be required to be calculated.

    (a) smaller kW demand
    (b) larger kW demand
    (c) higher voltage
    (d) nominal voltage

Notes

ARTICLE 225 — OUTSIDE BRANCH CIRCUITS AND FEEDERS

Introduction to Article 225—Outside Branch Circuits and Feeders

Article 225 contains the installation requirements for outside branch circuits and feeders not over 1000V ac or 1500V dc, installed on or between buildings, structures, or poles. Conductors installed outdoors can serve many purposes such as area lighting, power for outdoor equipment, or to provide power to separate buildings or structures. Some topics covered in our material for this article include:

- Conductor Support and Attachment
- Clearance for Overhead Conductors and Cables
- Raceways on Exterior Surfaces of Buildings or Other Structures
- Raceway Seals
- Grouping and Identification of Disconnects
- Emergency Disconnects
- Surge Protection

Article 225 consists of two parts:

- Part I—General Requirements
- Part II—Buildings or Other Structures Supplied by a Feeder(s) or Branch Circuit(s)

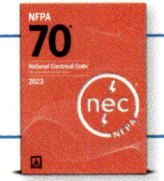

Please use the 2023 *Code* book to answer the following questions.

1. Article _____ covers requirements for outside branch circuits and feeders not over 1000V ac or 1500V dc, nominal, run on or between buildings, structures, or poles on the premises.

    (a) 200
    (b) 210
    (c) 220
    (d) 225

2. In accordance with Article 225—Outside Branch Circuits and Feeders, open individual conductors shall not be smaller than _____ copper for spans up to 50 ft in length and _____ copper for a longer span, unless supported by a messenger wire.

    (a) 10 AWG, 8 AWG
    (b) 8 AWG, 8 AWG
    (c) 6 AWG, 8 AWG
    (d) 6 AWG, 6 AWG

Article 225 | Outside Branch Circuits and Feeders

3. The point of attachment of overhead premises wiring to a building shall in no case be less than _____ above finished grade.

   (a) 8 ft
   (b) 10 ft
   (c) 12 ft
   (d) 15 ft

4. Where a mast is used for overhead branch-circuit or feeder conductor support, it shall have adequate _____ or be supported by braces or guy wires to safely withstand the strain imposed by the conductors.

   (a) strength
   (b) mobility
   (c) length
   (d) size

5. Overhead feeder and/or branch-circuit conductors shall not be attached to a mast where the connection is _____ a weatherhead or the end of the conduit and a coupling where the coupling is located above the last point of securement to the building or other structure, or where the coupling is located above the building or other structure.

   (a) above
   (b) below
   (c) between
   (d) even with

6. Overhead feeder conductors shall have a minimum vertical clearance of _____ over residential property and driveways, as well as those commercial areas not subject to truck traffic, where the voltage does not exceed 300V to ground.

   (a) 10 ft
   (b) 12 ft
   (c) 15 ft
   (d) 18 ft

7. The minimum clearance for overhead feeder conductors not exceeding 1000V that pass over public streets, alleys, roads, and parking areas subject to truck traffic is _____.

   (a) 10 ft
   (b) 12 ft
   (c) 15 ft
   (d) 18 ft

8. Overhead feeder conductors installed over roofs shall have a vertical clearance of not less than _____ above the roof surface, unless otherwise permitted by an exception.

   (a) 3 ft
   (b) 8 ft 6 in.
   (c) 12 ft
   (d) 15 ft 6 in.

9. If a set of 120/240V overhead feeder conductors terminates at a through-the-roof raceway or approved support, with not more than 6 ft of these conductors, 4 ft horizontally, passing over the roof overhang, the minimum clearance above the roof for these conductors shall not be less than _____.

   (a) 12 in.
   (b) 18 in.
   (c) 2 ft
   (d) 5 ft

10. The requirement for maintaining a 3-ft vertical clearance from the edge of the roof shall not apply to the final feeder conductor span where the conductors are attached to _____.

    (a) a building pole
    (b) the side of a building
    (c) an antenna
    (d) the base of a building

11. Overhead feeder and branch-circuit clearances from chimneys, radio and television antennas, tanks, and other nonbuilding or nonbridge structures, shall not be less than _____.

    (a) 3 ft
    (b) 6 ft
    (c) 8 ft
    (d) 10 ft

12. The vertical clearance of final spans of overhead conductors above or within _____ measured horizontally of platforms, projections, or surfaces that will permit personal contact shall be maintained in accordance with 225.18.

    (a) 3 ft
    (b) 6 ft
    (c) 8 ft
    (d) 10 ft

13. Overhead branch-circuit and feeder conductors shall not be installed beneath openings through which materials may be moved, such as openings in farm and commercial buildings, and shall not be installed where they obstruct _____ these openings.

    (a) entrance to
    (b) egress from
    (c) access to
    (d) a safe descent from

14. In accordance with Article 225—Outside Branch Circuits and Feeders, raceways on exteriors of buildings or other structures shall be arranged to drain and shall be _____ for use in wet locations.

    (a) labeled
    (b) listed
    (c) approved
    (d) listed or approved

15. In accordance with Article 225—Outside Branch Circuits and Feeders, vegetation such as trees shall not be used for support of _____.

    (a) overhead conductor spans
    (b) surface wiring methods
    (c) luminaires
    (d) electric equipment

16. Where a raceway enters a(an) _____ from outside, it shall be sealed in accordance with 300.5(G) and 300.7(A).

    (a) building or structure
    (b) crawlspace
    (c) highway right-of-way
    (d) easement

17. In accordance with Article 225—Outside Branch Circuits and Feeders, a building or structure shall be supplied by a maximum of _____ feeder(s) or branch circuit(s), unless specifically permitted otherwise.

    (a) one
    (b) two
    (c) three
    (d) four

18. Where multiple outside feeder conductors to a building originate in the same panelboard, switchboard, or other distribution equipment, and each feeder terminates in a single disconnecting means, not more than _____ feeders are permitted to be run to the building.

    (a) two
    (b) four
    (c) six
    (d) eight

19. Where more than one outside feeder is installed in accordance with 225.30(B), all feeder disconnects in the building shall be _____ in the same location.

    (a) grouped
    (b) identified
    (c) labeled
    (d) grouped and labeled

20. In accordance with Article 225—Outside Branch Circuits and Feeders, the disconnecting means for a building supplied by a feeder shall be installed at a(an) _____ location.

    (a) accessible
    (b) readily accessible
    (c) outdoor
    (d) indoor

21. In accordance with Article 225—Outside Branch Circuits and Feeders, there shall be no more than _____ switches or circuit breakers to serve as the disconnecting means for a building supplied by a feeder.

    (a) two
    (b) four
    (c) six
    (d) eight

22. In accordance with Article 225—Outside Branch Circuits and Feeders, the two to six disconnects for a disconnecting means for a building supplied by a feeder shall be _____.

    (a) the same size
    (b) grouped
    (c) in the same enclosure
    (d) of the same manufacturer

Article 225 | Outside Branch Circuits and Feeders

23. Where a building has multiple outside feeders, a permanent _____ shall be installed at each outside feeder disconnect location denoting all other services and feeders and the area served by each.

    (a) plaque or directory
    (b) map
    (c) label
    (d) guide

24. In accordance with Article 225—Outside Branch Circuits and Feeders, a building disconnecting means that supplies only limited loads of a single branch circuit shall have a rating of not less than _____.

    (a) 15A
    (b) 20A
    (c) 25A
    (d) 30A

25. In accordance with Article 225—Outside Branch Circuits and Feeders, for installations consisting of not more than two 2-wire branch circuits, the building disconnecting means shall have a rating of not less than _____.

    (a) 15A
    (b) 20A
    (c) 25A
    (d) 30A

26. In accordance with Article 225—Outside Branch Circuits and Feeders, for a one-family dwelling, the feeder disconnecting means shall have a rating of not less than _____, 3-wire.

    (a) 60A
    (b) 100A
    (c) 150A
    (d) 200A

27. For all other installations supplied by a feeder(s) or branch circuit(s) and not specifically identified in 225.39(A) through (C), the feeder or branch-circuit disconnecting means shall have a rating of not less than _____.

    (a) 20A
    (b) 30A
    (c) 40A
    (d) 60A

28. For one-and two-family dwelling units supplied by an outside feeder, an emergency disconnecting means _____ be installed.

    (a) shall not
    (b) shall
    (c) shall be permitted to
    (d) none these

29. The emergency disconnecting means for one-and two-family dwelling units supplied by an outside feeder shall be installed in a readily accessible outdoor location on or _____.

    (a) within sight of the dwelling unit
    (b) at the source of power
    (c) in the panelboard
    (d) closest to the entrance of the feeder cable assembly

30. The emergency disconnecting means for one- and two-family dwelling units supplied by an outside feeder shall have a short-circuit current rating equal to or greater than _____.

    (a) 5 kAIC
    (b) 10 kAIC
    (c) 22 kAIC
    (d) the available fault current

31. Where the is more than one emergency disconnecting means for one- and two-family dwelling units supplied by an outside feeder provide, they shall be _____.

    (a) separated
    (b) adjacent to each other
    (c) grouped
    (d) away from each other

32. Where equipment for isolation of other energy source systems is not located adjacent to the emergency disconnect required for one- and two-family dwellings supplied by an outside feeder, a plaque or directory identifying the location of all equipment for isolation of other energy sources shall be located _____ the disconnecting means.

    (a) inside
    (b) on
    (c) adjacent to
    (d) within sight of

33. The emergency disconnecting means for one- and two-family dwellings supplied by an outside feeder shall be marked as "EMERGENCY DISCONNECT" and the marking or labels shall _____.

    (a) be located on the outside front of the disconnect enclosure
    (b) have a red background with white text
    (c) have lettering at least ½ in. high
    (d) all of these

34. Where a feeder supplies _____, a surge-protective device (SPD) shall be installed.

    (a) dwelling and dormitory units
    (b) hotel and motel guest rooms and suites
    (c) patient sleeping rooms of nursing homes and limited care facilities
    (d) all of these

35. SPD's required by 225.42(A), shall be installed _____ the distribution equipment that is connected to the load side of the feeder and contains branch circuit overcurrent protective device(s).

    (a) in or adjacent to
    (b) within 3 ft of
    (c) within 10 ft of
    (d) within sight of

Notes

ARTICLE 230 SERVICES

Introduction to Article 230—Services

Article 230 covers the installation requirements for service conductors and service disconnects. It is crucial to understand what a service is, where it starts, and where it ends to properly apply many of these rules. Some topics covered by our material in this article include:

- Number of Services
- Raceway Sealing
- Clearances on Buildings
- Support and Attachment
- Conductor Size and Ampacity
- Service Equipment Marking and Protection
- Emergency Disconnects

This article consists of seven parts:

- Part I. General
- Part II. Overhead Service Conductors
- Part III. Underground Service Conductors
- Part IV. Service-Entrance Conductors
- Part V. Service Equipment—General
- Part VI. Disconnecting Means
- Part VII. Overcurrent Protection

Article 230 | Services

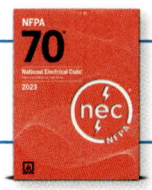

Please use the 2023 Code book to answer the following questions.

1. Service conductors and equipment for control and protection of services not over 1000V ac or 1500V dc nominal, and their installation requirements are covered in Article _____.
   (a) 210
   (b) 220
   (c) 230
   (d) 240

2. A building or structure shall be supplied by a maximum of _____ service(s), unless specifically permitted otherwise.
   (a) one
   (b) two
   (c) three
   (d) four

3. Under special conditions additional services are permitted for a(an) _____.
   (a) fire pump
   (b) emergency system
   (c) optional standby system
   (d) any of these

4. If necessary to meet capacity requirements, additional services are permitted for a single building or other structure by _____.
   (a) the registered design professional
   (b) special permission
   (c) the engineer of record
   (d) master electricians

5. Additional services are permitted for different voltages, frequencies, or phases, or for different uses, such as for _____.
   (a) gymnasiums
   (b) different rate schedules
   (c) flea markets
   (d) special entertainment events

6. Where a building or structure is supplied by more than _____, a permanent plaque or directory shall be installed at each service disconnect location denoting all other services supplying that building or structure and the area served by each.
   (a) one service
   (b) two services
   (c) three services
   (d) six services

7. Service conductors supplying a building or other structure shall not _____ another building or other structure.
   (a) be installed on the exterior walls of
   (b) pass through the interior of
   (c) be installed underneath
   (d) span the roof of

8. Service conductors shall be considered outside of a building or other structure where installed under not less than _____ of concrete beneath a building or other structure.
   (a) 2 in.
   (b) 4 in.
   (c) 5 in.
   (d) 6 in.

9. Circuit conductors other than service conductors, shall not be installed in the same _____ as the service conductors.
   (a) raceway or cable
   (b) handhole enclosure
   (c) underground box
   (d) all of these

10. Where a service _____ enters a building or structure, it shall be sealed in accordance with 300.5(G) and 300.7(A).
    (a) raceway
    (b) cable assembly
    (c) cable tray
    (d) any of these

11. Service conductors installed as unjacketed multiconductor cable shall have a minimum clearance of _____ from windows that are designed to be opened, doors, porches, balconies, ladders, stairs, fire escapes, or similar locations.

    (a) 3 ft
    (b) 4 ft
    (c) 6 ft
    (d) 10 ft

12. The vertical clearance of final spans of overhead service conductors above, or within _____ measured horizontally of platforms, projections, or surfaces that will permit personal contact shall be maintained.

    (a) 3 ft
    (b) 4 ft
    (c) 5 ft
    (d) 6 ft

13. Overhead service conductors shall not be installed beneath openings through which materials may be moved, such as openings in farm and commercial buildings, and shall not be installed where they obstruct _____ these building openings.

    (a) entrance to
    (b) egress from
    (c) access to
    (d) a safe descent from

14. Vegetation such as _____ shall not be used for support of overhead service conductors or service equipment.

    (a) shrubs
    (b) trees
    (c) potted plants
    (d) all of these

15. Service-drop conductors shall have _____.

    (a) sufficient ampacity to carry the load
    (b) adequate mechanical strength
    (c) sufficient ampacity to carry the load or adequate mechanical strength
    (d) sufficient ampacity to carry the load and adequate mechanical strength

16. The minimum size service-drop conductor permitted is _____ copper or _____ aluminum or copper-clad aluminum.

    (a) 8 AWG, 8 AWG
    (b) 8 AWG, 6 AWG
    (c) 6 AWG, 8 AWG
    (d) 6 AWG, 6 AWG

17. Overhead service conductors installed over roofs shall have a vertical clearance of not less than _____ above the roof surface.

    (a) 3 ft
    (b) 4 ft
    (c) 5 ft
    (d) 8 ft 6 in.

18. Where the voltage between conductors does not exceed 300 and the roof has a slope of 4 in. in 12 in. or greater, a reduction in clearance to _____ over the roof is permitted.

    (a) 3 ft
    (b) 4 ft
    (c) 5 ft
    (d) 8 ft

19. Where the voltage between conductors does not exceed 300, a reduction in clearance above only the overhanging portion of the roof to not less than _____ shall be permitted if not more than 6 ft of overhead service conductors, pass above the roof overhang 4 ft horizontally.

    (a) 12 in.
    (b) 18 in.
    (c) 2 ft
    (d) 5 ft

20. The requirement to maintain a 3-foot vertical clearance from the edge of a roof does not apply to the final conductor span where the service drop is attached to _____.

    (a) a service pole
    (b) the side of a building
    (c) an antenna
    (d) the base of a building

21. Where the voltage between overhead service conductors does not exceed 300V and the roof area is guarded or isolated, a reduction in clearance to _____ is permitted.

    (a) 1 ft
    (b) 2 ft
    (c) 3 ft
    (d) 6 ft

22. Overhead service conductors shall have a minimum clearance from final grade of _____ above areas or sidewalks accessible only to pedestrians, measured from final grade or other accessible surface where the voltage does not exceed 150V to ground.

    (a) 8 ft
    (b) 10 ft
    (c) 12 ft
    (d) 15 ft

23. Overhead service conductors shall have a minimum vertical clearance of _____ from final grade over residential property and driveways, as well as over commercial areas not subject to truck traffic where the voltage does not exceed 300V to ground.

    (a) 10 ft
    (b) 12 ft
    (c) 15 ft
    (d) 18 ft

24. The minimum clearance for overhead service conductors that pass over public streets, alleys, roads, parking areas subject to truck traffic is _____.

    (a) 10 ft
    (b) 12 ft
    (c) 15 ft
    (d) 18 ft

25. Overhead service conductors shall have a horizontal clearance of not less than _____ from a pool.

    (a) 8 ft
    (b) 10 ft
    (c) 12 ft
    (d) 14 ft

26. The minimum point of attachment of overhead service conductors to a building shall not be less than _____ above finished grade.

    (a) 8 ft
    (b) 10 ft
    (c) 12 ft
    (d) 15 ft

27. Where conduits are used as service masts, hubs shall be _____ for use with service-entrance equipment.

    (a) identified
    (b) approved
    (c) of a heavy-duty type
    (d) listed

28. Underground service conductors shall have _____.

    (a) adequate mechanical strength
    (b) no splices
    (c) 90°C conductors
    (d) sufficient ampacity for the loads calculated

29. Underground copper service conductors shall not be smaller than _____.

    (a) 3 AWG
    (b) 4 AWG
    (c) 6 AWG
    (d) 8 AWG

30. Underground service conductors that supply power to limited loads of a single branch circuit shall not be smaller than _____.

    (a) 14 AWG copper
    (b) 14 AWG aluminum
    (c) 12 AWG copper
    (d) 12 AWG aluminum

31. Underground service conductors shall be protected from damage in accordance with _____ including minimum cover requirements.

    (a) 240.6(A)
    (b) 300.5
    (c) 310.16
    (d) 430.52

32. The general requirement for each service drop, set of overhead service conductors, set of underground service conductors, or service lateral is that it shall supply _____ set(s) of service-entrance conductors.

    (a) only one
    (b) only two
    (c) up to six
    (d) an unlimited number of

33. One set of service-entrance conductors connected to the _____ side of the normal service disconnecting means shall be permitted to supply each or several systems covered by 230.82(5) or 230.82(6).

    (a) supply
    (b) load
    (c) high
    (d) low

34. The minimum service-entrance conductor size shall have an ampacity not less than the maximum load to be served after the application of any _____ factors.

    (a) adjustment
    (b) correction
    (c) demand
    (d) adjustment or correction

35. Wiring methods permitted for service-entrance conductors include _____.

    (a) Type IGS cable
    (b) Type NM cable
    (c) Type UF cable
    (d) all of these

36. Wiring methods permitted for service-entrance conductors include _____.

    (a) rigid metal conduit
    (b) electrical metallic tubing
    (c) PVC conduit
    (d) all of these

37. Power distribution blocks installed on service conductors shall be _____ "suitable for use on the line side of the service equipment" or equivalent.

    (a) approved as
    (b) identified as
    (c) labeled
    (d) marked

38. Underground service-entrance conductors shall be protected against _____ damage.

    (a) physical
    (b) extensive
    (c) severe
    (d) impact

39. Service-entrance cables which are not installed underground, where subject to physical damage, shall be protected by _____.

    (a) rigid metal conduit
    (b) IMC
    (c) Schedule 80 PVC conduit
    (d) any of these

40. Service-entrance cables mounted in contact with a building shall be supported at intervals not exceeding _____.

    (a) 24 in.
    (b) 30 in.
    (c) 3 ft
    (d) 4 ft

41. Where exposed to the weather, raceways enclosing service-entrance conductors shall be _____ for use in wet locations and arranged to drain.

    (a) approved or listed
    (b) listed and identified
    (c) suitable
    (d) listed and labeled

42. Overhead service-entrance cables shall be equipped with a _____.

    (a) raceway
    (b) service head
    (c) cover
    (d) all of these

Article 230 | Services

43. Service heads on raceways or service-entrance cables and goosenecks in service-entrance cables shall be located _____ the point of attachment, unless impracticable.

    (a) above
    (b) below
    (c) even with
    (d) any of these

44. To prevent the entrance of _____, service-entrance conductors shall be connected to the service drop or overhead service conductors either below the level of the service head or below the level of the termination of the service-entrance cable sheath.

    (a) rain
    (b) snow
    (c) ice crystals
    (d) moisture

45. Service-entrance and overhead service conductors shall be arranged so that _____ will not enter the service raceway or equipment.

    (a) dust
    (b) vapor
    (c) water
    (d) lightning

46. On a three-phase, 4-wire, delta-connected service where the midpoint of one phase winding is grounded, the service conductor having the higher phase voltage-to-ground shall be durably and permanently marked by an outer finish that is _____ in color, or by other effective means, at each termination or junction point.

    (a) orange
    (b) red
    (c) blue
    (d) any of these

47. Barriers shall be placed in service equipment such that no uninsulated, ungrounded service busbar or service _____ is exposed to inadvertent contact by persons or maintenance equipment while servicing load terminations with the service disconnect in the open position.

    (a) phase conductor
    (b) neutral conductor
    (c) terminal
    (d) disconnect

48. The service disconnecting means shall be marked to identify it as being suitable for use as service equipment and shall be _____.

    (a) weatherproof
    (b) listed or field evaluated
    (c) approved
    (d) moisture resistant

49. Individual meter socket enclosures shall not be considered service equipment but shall be _____ for the voltage and ampacity of the service.

    (a) listed and rated
    (b) labeled and approved
    (c) inspected and rated
    (d) suitable

50. Meter sockets supplied by and under the exclusive control of an electric utility shall not be required to be _____.

    (a) approved
    (b) rated
    (c) listed
    (d) all of these

51. All services supplying _____ shall be provided with a surge-protective device (SPD).

    (a) dwelling units and dormitory units
    (b) guest rooms and suites of hotels and motels
    (c) patient sleeping rooms in nursing homes and limited care facilities
    (d) all of these

52. Where the service equipment for areas of nursing homes and limited care facilities used exclusively as _____ is replaced, a surge-protective device (SPD) shall be installed.

    (a) patient sleeping rooms
    (b) critical care areas
    (c) public areas
    (d) emergency egress

53. SPD's required by 230.67(A) shall be an integral part of the service equipment or shall be located _____.

    (a) immediately adjacent thereto
    (b) within 3 ft of the service equipment
    (c) within 10 ft of the service equipment
    (d) within sight of the service equipment

54. The surge-protective device (SPD) required for a dwelling unit shall be an integral part of the service equipment or be located immediately adjacent thereto.

    (a) True
    (b) False

55. The surge-protective device (SPD) required for a dwelling unit shall be _____.

    (a) Type 1 or 2
    (b) Type 2 or 3
    (c) Type 3
    (d) Type 4

56. A service disconnecting means shall be installed at a(an) _____ location.

    (a) dry
    (b) readily accessible
    (c) outdoor
    (d) indoor

57. A service disconnecting means shall not be installed in _____.

    (a) bathrooms
    (b) hallways
    (c) outside
    (d) electrical rooms

58. Each service disconnecting means shall be permanently _____ to identify it as a service disconnect.

    (a) identified
    (b) positioned
    (c) marked
    (d) arranged

59. There shall be no more than _____ service disconnects installed for each service or for each set of service-entrance conductors as permitted in 230.2 and 230.40.

    (a) two
    (b) four
    (c) six
    (d) eight

60. Existing service equipment, installed in compliance _____ that permitted multiple service disconnecting means in a single enclosure, section, or compartment, shall be permitted to contain a maximum of six service disconnecting means.

    (a) with OSHA standards
    (b) with the manufacturer's instructions
    (c) with previous editions of this *Code*
    (d) with local codes

61. When the service contains two to six service disconnecting means, they shall be _____ and marked to indicate the load served.

    (a) the same size
    (b) grouped
    (c) in the same enclosure
    (d) from the same manufacturer

62. The additional service disconnecting means for fire pumps, emergency systems, legally required standby, or optional standby services shall be installed remote from the one to six service disconnecting means for normal service to minimize the possibility of _____ interruption of supply.

    (a) intentional
    (b) accidental
    (c) simultaneous
    (d) prolonged

63. For installations that supply only limited loads of a single branch circuit, the service disconnecting means shall have a rating of not less than _____.

    (a) 15A
    (b) 20A
    (c) 25A
    (d) 30A

64. For installations consisting of not more than two 2-wire branch circuits, the service disconnecting means shall have a rating of not less than _____.

    (a) 15A
    (b) 20A
    (c) 25A
    (d) 30A

65. For a one-family dwelling, the service disconnecting means shall have a rating of not less than _____, 3-wire.

    (a) 90A
    (b) 100A
    (c) 125A
    (d) 200A

66. _____ are permitted to be connected to the supply side of the service disconnecting means.

    (a) Cable limiters
    (b) Meter sockets
    (c) Solar PV systems
    (d) all of these

67. A meter-mounted transfer switch shall be listed and be capable of transferring _____.

    (a) the load served
    (b) 125 percent of the continuous load served
    (c) the maximum short-circuit current
    (d) all of these

68. For one- and two-family dwelling unit service conductors, an emergency disconnecting means shall be installed in a readily accessible _____ location.

    (a) indoor
    (b) outdoor
    (c) indoor or outdoor
    (d) enclosed

69. One- and two-family dwelling emergency disconnecting means are permitted to be a listed disconnect switch or circuit breaker that is marked _____ for use as service equipment, but not marked as suitable only for use as service equipment, installed on the supply side of each service disconnect.

    (a) suitable
    (b) appropriate
    (c) ready
    (d) none of these

70. Where equipment for isolation of other energy source systems is not located adjacent to the emergency disconnect required for one- and two-family dwelling services, a plaque or directory identifying the location of all equipment for isolation of other energy sources shall be located _____ the disconnecting means.

    (a) inside
    (b) on
    (c) adjacent to
    (d) within sight of

71. The markings for the required emergency disconnecting means for one- and two-family dwelling services shall _____.

    (a) be permanently affixed and be sufficiently durable to withstand the environment involved
    (b) be located on the outside front of the disconnect enclosure with red background and white text
    (c) have lettering at least ½ in. high
    (d) all of these

72. Each _____ service conductor shall have overload protection.

    (a) overhead
    (b) underground
    (c) ungrounded
    (d) individual

73. Where _____ are used as the service overcurrent device, the disconnecting means shall be located ahead of the supply side of the fuses in accordance with 230.91.

    (a) fuses
    (b) circuit breakers
    (c) GFCIs
    (d) AFCIs

74. Ground-fault protection of equipment shall be provided for solidly grounded wye electrical services of more than 150V to ground, but not exceeding 1000V phase-to-phase for each service disconnecting means rated _____ or more.

    (a) 1000A
    (b) 1500A
    (c) 2000A
    (d) 2500A

ARTICLE 240 — OVERCURRENT PROTECTION

Introduction to Article 240—Overcurrent Protection

Article 240 covers the general requirements for overcurrent protection and the installation requirements of overcurrent protective devices—typically circuit breakers or fuses. Overcurrent protection is installed to protect the circuit if the current reaches a value that will cause damage to conductors, conductor insulation, or equipment. Some topics covered in our material for Article 240 include:

- Protection of Conductors and Cords
- Standard Ampere Ratings
- Supplementary Overcurrent Protection
- Location iln the Circuit
- Location in the Premises
- Enclosure Requirements
- Fuse Requirements
- Breaker Requirements

This article consists of eight parts:

- Part I. General
- Part II. Location
- Part III. Enclosures
- Part IV. Disconnecting and Guarding
- Part V. Plug Fuses
- Part VI. Cartridge Fuses
- Part VII. Circuit Breakers
- Part VIII. Supervised Industrial Installations

Article 240 | Overcurrent Protection

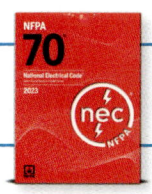

Please use the 2023 *Code* book to answer the following questions.

1. Each _____ service conductor shall have overload protection.
   (a) overhead
   (b) underground
   (c) ungrounded
   (d) individual

2. The general requirements for overcurrent protection and overcurrent protective devices not more than 1000V, nominal are provided in Article _____.
   (a) 230
   (b) 240
   (c) 242
   (d) 250

3. Overcurrent protection for conductors and equipment is provided to _____ the circuit if the current reaches a value that will cause an excessive or dangerous temperature in conductors or conductor insulation.
   (a) open
   (b) close
   (c) monitor
   (d) record

4. Conductor overload protection shall not be required where the interruption of the _____ would create a hazard, such as in a material-handling magnet circuit or fire pump circuit. However, short-circuit protection is required.
   (a) circuit
   (b) line
   (c) phase
   (d) system

5. If an _____ or less overcurrent protective device is an adjustable trip device installed in accordance with 240.4(B)(1), (B)(2), and (B)(3), it shall be permitted to be set to a value that does not exceed the next higher standard value above the ampacity of the conductors being protected as shown in Table 240.6(A) where restricted access in accordance with 240.6(C) is provided.
   (a) 600A
   (b) 800A
   (c) 1000A
   (d) 1200A

6. The next higher standard rating overcurrent device above the ampacity of the ungrounded conductors being protected is permitted to be used, provided the _____.
   (a) conductors being protected are not part of a branch circuit supplying more than one receptacle for cord-and-plug-connected portable loads
   (b) ampacity of the conductors does not correspond with the standard ampere rating of a fuse or circuit breaker
   (c) next higher standard rating selected does not exceed 800A
   (d) all of these

7. If the circuit's overcurrent device exceeds _____, the conductor ampacity shall have a rating not less than the rating of the overcurrent device.
   (a) 800A
   (b) 1000A
   (c) 1200A
   (d) 2000A

8. Overcurrent protection shall not exceed _____.
   (a) 15A for 14 AWG copper
   (b) 20A for 12 AWG copper
   (c) 30A for 10 AWG copper
   (d) all of these

9. Fixture wire is permitted to be tapped to the branch-circuit conductor in accordance with which of the following?
   (a) 15A or 20A circuits—18 AWG, up to 50 ft of run length
   (b) 15A or 20A circuits—16 AWG, up to 100 ft of run length
   (c) 20A circuits—14 AWG and larger
   (d) all of these

10. The standard ampere rating(s) for fuses is(are) _____.
    (a) 1A
    (b) 6A
    (c) 601A
    (d) all of these

11. Standard ampere ratings for circuit breakers and fuses do not include _____.
    (a) 10A
    (b) 35A
    (c) 75A
    (d) 225A

12. For adjustable trip circuit breakers, restricted access is defined as _____.
    (a) located behind bolted equipment enclosure doors
    (b) located behind locked doors accessible only to qualified personnel
    (c) password protected, with password accessible only to qualified personnel
    (d) any of these

13. _____ is a specialized field requiring constant, vigilant attention to security vulnerabilities that could arise due to software defects, system configuration changes, or user interactions.
    (a) Special security
    (b) Cybersecurity
    (c) Physical security
    (d) none of these

14. Remote access for an adjustable trip circuit breaker is permitted to be achieved by being connected directly through a _____.
    (a) secure network
    (b) local non-networked interface
    (c) hardwired ethernet cable
    (d) secure VPN

15. Remote access for an adjustable trip circuit breaker is permitted to be achieved by being connected through a networked interface where the circuit breaker and associated software for adjusting the settings are identified as being evaluated for _____.
    (a) cybersecurity
    (b) tamper resistance
    (c) observable consequence of the adjustment
    (d) overload prevention

16. Documentation of the cybersecurity assessment for remote access for an adjustable trip circuit breaker connected through a networked interface shall be made available to those authorized to _____ the system.
    (a) inspect
    (b) operate
    (c) maintain
    (d) all of these

17. Supplementary overcurrent protective devices are not permitted to be used _____.
    (a) to provide additional overcurrent protection for luminaires
    (b) to provide additional overcurrent protection for appliances
    (c) as the required branch-circuit overcurrent protective device
    (d) none of these

18. Ground-fault protection of equipment shall be provided for solidly grounded wye electrical systems of more than 150 volts-to-ground, but not exceeding 1000V phase-to-phase for each individual device used as a building or structure main disconnecting means rated _____ or more, unless specifically exempted.
    (a) 1000A
    (b) 1500A
    (c) 2000A
    (d) 2500A

19. Circuit breakers shall _____ all ungrounded conductors of the circuit both manually and automatically unless specifically permitted otherwise.
    (a) open
    (b) close
    (c) isolate
    (d) inhibit

Article 240 | Overcurrent Protection

20. For multiwire branch circuits, single-pole breakers with identified handle ties can be used to protect each _____ conductor for line-to-neutral connected loads.

    (a) ungrounded
    (b) grounded
    (c) grounding
    (d) neutral

21. Overcurrent protection shall be provided in each ungrounded circuit conductor and shall be located at the point where the conductors receive their _____ except as specified in 240.21(A) through (H).

    (a) power
    (b) supply
    (c) source
    (d) energy

22. Feeder taps are permitted to be located at any point on the _____ side of the feeder overcurrent protective device.

    (a) load
    (b) line
    (c) supply
    (d) end

23. When feeder taps not over 10 ft long leave the enclosure in which the tap is made, the ampacity of the tap conductors cannot be less than _____ of the rating of the device protecting the feeder.

    (a) one-tenth
    (b) one-fifth
    (c) one-half
    (d) two-thirds

24. Tap conductors not over 25 ft in length are permitted, providing the _____.

    (a) ampacity of the tap conductors is not less than one-third the rating of the overcurrent device protecting the feeder conductors being tapped
    (b) tap conductors terminate in a single circuit breaker or set of fuses that limits the load to the ampacity of the tap conductors
    (c) tap conductors are suitably protected from physical damage
    (d) all of these

25. Outside feeder tap conductors can be of unlimited length without overcurrent protection at the point they receive their supply if the tap conductors _____.

    (a) are protected from physical damage
    (b) terminate at a single circuit breaker or a single set of fuses that limits the load to the ampacity of the tap conductors
    (c) the overcurrent device is an integral part of a disconnecting means
    (d) all of these

26. The next size up rule in 240.4(B) is not permitted for _____ secondary conductors.

    (a) transformer
    (b) generator
    (c) motor
    (d) relay

27. Secondary conductors not over 10 ft long shall be enclosed in a(an) _____.

    (a) cable
    (b) enclosure
    (c) raceway
    (d) all of these

28. Outside secondary conductors can be of unlimited length without overcurrent protection at the point they receive their supply if the _____.

    (a) conductors are protected from physical damage
    (b) conductors terminate at a single overcurrent device equal to or less than their ampacity
    (c) overcurrent device is part of the building disconnect
    (d) all of these

29. Circuit breakers and switches containing fuses shall be readily accessible and installed so the center of the grip of the operating handle of the switch or circuit breaker, when in its highest position, is not more than _____ above the floor or working platform.

    (a) 6 ft 4 in.
    (b) 6 ft 5 in.
    (c) 6 ft 6 in.
    (d) 6 ft 7 in.

30. Overcurrent protective devices shall not be located _____.
    (a) where exposed to physical damage
    (b) near easily ignitible materials, such as in clothes closets
    (c) in bathrooms, showering facilities, or locker rooms with showering facilities
    (d) all of these

31. _____ shall not be located over the steps of a stairway.
    (a) Disconnect switches
    (b) Overcurrent protective devices
    (c) Knife switches
    (d) Transformers

32. Circuit breaker enclosures shall be permitted to be installed _____ where the circuit breaker is installed in accordance with 240.81
    (a) vertically
    (b) horizontally
    (c) face up
    (d) face down

33. Plug fuses of the Edison-base type shall have a maximum rating of _____.
    (a) 20A at 125V
    (b) 30A at 125V
    (c) 40A at 125V
    (d) 50A at 125V

34. Plug fuses of the Edison-base type shall be used only _____.
    (a) where over fusing is necessary
    (b) for replacement in existing installations
    (c) as a replacement for Type S fuses
    (d) if rated 50A and above

35. Where the circuit breaker handles are operated vertically, the "up" position of the handle shall be the "_____" position.
    (a) on
    (b) off
    (c) tripped
    (d) any of these

36. Circuit breakers used to switch high-intensity discharge lighting circuits shall be listed and marked as _____.
    (a) SWD
    (b) HID
    (c) SWD or HID
    (d) SWD and HID

37. A circuit breaker with a _____ voltage rating, such as 240V or 480V, can be used where the nominal voltage between any two conductors does not exceed the circuit-breaker voltage rating.
    (a) straight
    (b) slash
    (c) high
    (d) low

38. A circuit breaker with a _____ rating, such as 120/240V or 277/480V can be used on a solidly grounded circuit where the nominal voltage of any conductor to ground does not exceed the lower of the two values, and the nominal voltage between any two conductors does not exceed the higher value.
    (a) straight
    (b) slash
    (c) high
    (d) low

39. A circuit breaker with a slash rating, such as 120/240V or 480Y/277V, shall be permitted to be applied in a solidly grounded circuit where the nominal voltage of any conductor to ground _____ the lower of the two values of the circuit breakers voltage rating and the nominal voltage between any two conductors does not exceed the higher value of the circuit breaker's voltage rating.
    (a) is equal to
    (b) is equal to or greater than
    (c) does not exceed
    (d) is equal to 125 percent of

Notes

ARTICLE 242 — OVERVOLTAGE PROTECTION

Introduction to Article 242—Overvoltage Protection

This article provides the general, installation, and connection requirements for overvoltage protection and overvoltage protective devices (surge-protective devices or SPDs). Surge-protective devices are installed to reduce transient voltages present on the premises electrical system to protect electronic safety equipment such as smoke detectors, AFCIs, GFCIs, and electronic breakers from damage. Some topics covered in this material for Article 242 include:

- Short-Circuit Current Rating
- SPD Types
- Location
- Conductor Routing and Sizing

Please use the 2023 *Code* book to answer the following questions.

1. Article _____ provides the general requirements, installation requirements, and connection requirements for overvoltage protection and overvoltage protective devices.
   - (a) 242
   - (b) 285
   - (c) 286
   - (d) 287

2. Surge-protective devices shall be _____.
   - (a) listed
   - (b) identified
   - (c) marked
   - (d) labeled

3. An SPD shall provide _____ that it is functioning properly.
   - (a) indication
   - (b) notification
   - (c) a sign
   - (d) a label

4. A surge-protective device shall not be installed in circuits over _____.
   - (a) 480V
   - (b) 600V
   - (c) 1000V
   - (d) 4160V

Article 242 | Overvoltage Protection

5. Type 1 SPDs shall be permitted to be connected on the supply side of the _____ disconnect.

    (a) service
    (b) feeder
    (c) branch-circuit
    (d) outside feeder

6. A _____ surge-protective device is permitted to be connected on either the line or load side of a service disconnect overcurrent device.

    (a) Type 1
    (b) Type 2
    (c) Type 3
    (d) Type 4

7. Type 2 SPDs shall be connected at the building or structure anywhere on the load side of the _____.

    (a) first overcurrent device
    (b) service attachment point
    (c) meter socket
    (d) transformer

8. Type 2 surge-protective device(s) shall be connected on the load side of the _____ in a separately derived system.

    (a) first overcurrent device
    (b) metering device
    (c) service disconnect
    (d) service entrance

9. The conductors used to connect the surge-protective device to the line or bus and to ground shall not be any longer than _____ and shall avoid unnecessary bends.

    (a) 6 in.
    (b) 12 in.
    (c) 18 in.
    (d) necessary

ARTICLE 250 — GROUNDING AND BONDING

Introduction to Article 250—Grounding and Bonding

Article 250 covers the general requirements for bonding and grounding electrical installations. The terminology used in this article has been a source of much confusion over the years so pay careful attention to the definitions pertaining to Article 250. Understanding the difference between bonding and grounding will help you correctly apply the provisions of this article. Because of the massive size and scope of Article 250, Figure 250.1 in the *NEC* is provided as a reference for the locations of the different types of rules. Of the ten parts contained in this article only parts one through seven are covered in this material. Some topics covered in this material include:

- General Requirements for Grounding and Bonding
- Objectionable Current
- Protection of Clamps and Fittings
- System Grounding Requirements
- Bonding Jumpers
- Generator Bonding
- Grounding Electrode System
- Service Equipment Bonding
- Piping System and Structural Steel Bonding
- Equipment Grounding Conductors (EGCs)

This article consists of ten parts:

- Part I. General
- Part II. System Grounding
- Part III. Grounding Electrode System and Grounding Electrode Conductor (GEC)
- Part IV. Enclosure, Raceway, and Service Cable Connections
- Part V. Bonding
- Part VI. Equipment Grounding Conductors (EGC)
- Part VII. Methods of EGC Connections
- Part VIII. Direct-Current Systems
- Part IX. Instruments, Meters, and Relays
- Part X. Grounding of Systems and Circuits of over 1000 Volts

Article 250 | Grounding and Bonding

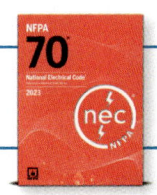

Please use the 2023 *Code* book to answer the following questions.

1. General requirements for grounding and bonding of electrical installations and the location of grounding connections are within the scope of _____.

    (a) Article 110
    (b) Article 200
    (c) Article 250
    (d) Article 680

2. Grounded electrical systems shall be connected to earth in a manner that will _____.

    (a) limit voltages due to lightning, line surges, or unintentional contact with higher-voltage lines
    (b) stabilize the voltage to earth during normal operation
    (c) facilitate overcurrent device operation in case of ground faults
    (d) limit voltages due to lightning, line surges, or unintentional contact with higher-voltage lines and stabilize the voltage to earth during normal operation

3. An important consideration for limiting imposed voltage on electrical systems is to remember that bonding and grounding electrode conductors should not be any longer than _____ and unnecessary bends and loops should be avoided.

    (a) necessary
    (b) 10 ft
    (c) 25 ft
    (d) 50 ft

4. For grounded systems, normally noncurrent-carrying conductive materials enclosing electrical conductors or equipment shall be connected to earth so as to limit _____ on these materials.

    (a) the voltage to ground
    (b) current
    (c) arcing
    (d) resistance

5. For grounded systems, normally noncurrent-carrying conductive materials enclosing electrical conductors shall be connected together and to the _____ to establish an effective ground-fault current path.

    (a) ground
    (b) earth
    (c) electrical supply source
    (d) enclosure

6. In grounded systems, normally noncurrent-carrying electrically conductive materials that are likely to become energized shall be connected _____ in a manner that establishes an effective ground-fault current path.

    (a) together
    (b) to the electrical supply source
    (c) to the closest grounded conductor
    (d) together and to the electrical supply source

7. For grounded systems, electrical equipment, and other electrically conductive material likely to become energized shall be installed in a manner that creates a _____ from any point on the wiring system where a ground fault occurs to the electrical supply source.

    (a) circuit facilitating the operation of the overcurrent device
    (b) low-impedance circuit
    (c) circuit capable of safely carrying the ground-fault current likely to be imposed on it
    (d) all of these

8. For grounded systems, the earth _____ considered an effective ground-fault current path.

    (a) shall be
    (b) shall not be
    (c) is
    (d) is not

9. The grounding and bonding of electrical systems, circuit conductors, surge arresters, surge-protective devices, and conductive normally noncurrent-carrying metal parts of equipment shall be installed and arranged in a manner that will prevent _____.

    (a) objectionable current
    (b) voltage transients
    (c) neutral to earth voltage
    (d) an arc flash

10. Equipment grounding conductors, grounding electrode conductors, and bonding jumpers shall be connected by _____.

    (a) listed pressure connectors
    (b) terminal bars
    (c) exothermic welding
    (d) any of these

11. Ground clamps and fittings that are exposed to physical damage shall be enclosed in _____ or equivalent protective covering.

    (a) metal or wood
    (b) wood or rubber
    (c) concrete
    (d) metal or plastic

12. _____ on equipment to be grounded shall be removed from contact surfaces to ensure electrical continuity.

    (a) Paint
    (b) Lacquer
    (c) Enamel
    (d) any of these

13. Alternating-current circuits of less than 50V shall be grounded if supplied by a transformer whose supply system exceeds _____.

    (a) 150V to ground
    (b) 300V to ground
    (c) 600V to ground
    (d) 1000V to ground

14. _____ alternating-current systems operating at 480V shall have ground detectors installed on the system.

    (a) Grounded
    (b) Solidly grounded
    (c) Effectively grounded
    (d) Ungrounded

15. Ungrounded alternating-current systems from 50V to 1000V or less that are not required to be grounded in accordance with 250.21(B) shall have _____.

    (a) ground detectors installed for ac systems operating at not less than 100V and at 1000V or less
    (b) the ground detection sensing equipment connected as far as practicable to where the system receives its supply
    (c) ground detectors installed for ac systems operating at not less than 120V and at 1000V or less, and have the ground detection sensing equipment connected as close as practicable to where the system receives its supply
    (d) ground-fault protection for equipment

16. Ungrounded alternating-current systems from 50V to less than 1000V shall be legibly marked "CAUTION: UNGROUNDED SYSTEM—OPERATING _____ VOLTS BETWEEN CONDUCTORS" at the _____ of the system, with sufficient durability to withstand the environment involved.

    (a) source
    (b) first disconnecting means
    (c) every junction box
    (d) the source or the first disconnecting means

17. The grounding electrode conductor connection shall be made at any accessible point from the load end of the overhead service conductors, _____ to the terminal or bus to which the grounded service conductor is connected at the service disconnecting means.

    (a) service drop
    (b) underground service conductors
    (c) service lateral
    (d) any of these

18. If the main bonding jumper is a wire or busbar and is installed from the grounded conductor terminal bar to the equipment grounding terminal bar in the service equipment, the _____ is permitted to be connected to the equipment grounding terminal bar to which the main bonding jumper is connected.

    (a) equipment grounding conductor
    (b) grounded service conductor
    (c) grounding electrode conductor
    (d) system bonding jumper

Article 250 | Grounding and Bonding

19. A grounded conductor shall not be connected to normally noncurrent-carrying metal parts of equipment, to equipment grounding conductor(s), or be reconnected to ground on the load side of the _____ except as otherwise permitted.

    (a) service disconnecting means
    (b) distribution panel
    (c) switchgear
    (d) switchboard

20. For a grounded system, an unspliced _____ shall be used to connect the equipment grounding conductor(s) and the service disconnect enclosure to the grounded conductor of the system within the enclosure for each service disconnect.

    (a) grounding electrode
    (b) main bonding jumper
    (c) busbar
    (d) insulated copper conductor

21. If an ac system operating at 1000V or less is grounded at any point, the _____ shall be routed with the ungrounded conductors to each service disconnecting means and shall be connected to each disconnecting means grounded conductor(s) terminal or bus.

    (a) system bonding jumper
    (b) supply-side bonding jumper
    (c) grounded conductor
    (d) equipment grounding conductor

22. The grounded conductor brought to service equipment shall be routed with the phase conductors and shall not be smaller than specified in Table _____ when the service-entrance conductors are 1100 kcmil copper and smaller.

    (a) 250.102(C)(1)
    (b) 250.122
    (c) 310.16
    (d) 430.52

23. If ungrounded service-entrance conductors are connected in parallel, the size of the grounded conductors in each raceway shall be based on the total circular mil area of the parallel ungrounded service-entrance conductors in the raceway, sized in accordance with 250.24(D)(1), but not smaller than _____.

    (a) 1/0 AWG
    (b) 2/0 AWG
    (c) 3/0 AWG
    (d) 4/0 AWG

24. A grounding electrode conductor, sized in accordance with _____, shall be used to connect the equipment grounding conductors, the service-equipment enclosures, and, if the system is grounded, the grounded service conductor to the grounding electrode(s).

    (a) 250.66
    (b) 250.102(C)(1)
    (c) 250.122
    (d) 310.16

25. A main bonding jumper shall be a _____ or similar suitable conductor.

    (a) wire
    (b) bus
    (c) screw
    (d) any of these

26. If a main bonding jumper is a screw only, the screw shall be identified with a(an) _____ that shall be visible with the screw installed.

    (a) silver or white finish
    (b) etched ground symbol
    (c) hexagonal head
    (d) green finish

27. Main bonding jumpers and system bonding jumpers shall not be smaller than specified in _____.

    (a) Table 250.102(C)(1)
    (b) Table 250.122
    (c) Table 310.16
    (d) Chapter 9, Table 8

28. Where the supply conductors are larger than 1100 kcmil copper or 1750 kcmil aluminum, the main bonding jumper shall have an area that is _____ the area of the largest phase conductor when of the same material.

    (a) at least equal to
    (b) at least 50 percent of
    (c) not less than 12½ percent of
    (d) not more than 12½ percent of

29. A grounded conductor shall not be connected to normally noncurrent-carrying metal parts of equipment on the _____ side of the system bonding jumper of a separately derived system except as otherwise permitted.

    (a) supply
    (b) grounded
    (c) high-voltage
    (d) load

30. The connection of the system bonding jumper for a separately derived system shall be made _____ on the separately derived system from the source to the first system disconnecting means or overcurrent device.

    (a) in at least two locations
    (b) in every location that the grounded conductor is present
    (c) at any single point
    (d) effectively

31. If a building or structure is supplied by a feeder from an outdoor separately derived system, a system bonding jumper at both the source and the first disconnecting means shall be permitted if doing so does not establish a(an) _____ path for the grounded conductor.

    (a) series
    (b) parallel
    (c) conductive
    (d) effective

32. A separately derived ac system supply-side bonding jumper shall be installed to the first disconnecting means enclosure, and it is not required to be larger than the _____.

    (a) neutral conductor
    (b) derived ungrounded conductors
    (c) equipment grounding conductor
    (d) main service grounding electrode conductor

33. If the source of a separately derived system and the first disconnecting means are located in separate enclosures, a supply-side bonding jumper of the wire type shall comply with 250.102(C), based on _____.

    (a) the size of the primary conductors
    (b) the size of the secondary overcurrent protection
    (c) the size of the derived ungrounded conductors
    (d) one-third the size of the primary grounded conductor

34. The building or structure grounding electrode system shall be used as the _____ electrode for the separately derived system.

    (a) grounding
    (b) bonding
    (c) grounded
    (d) bonded

35. For a single separately derived system, the grounding electrode conductor connects the grounded conductor of the derived system to the grounding electrode at the same point on the separately derived system where the _____ is connected.

    (a) metering equipment
    (b) transfer switch
    (c) system bonding jumper
    (d) largest circuit breaker

36. Grounding electrode conductor taps from a separately derived system to a common grounding electrode conductor are permitted when a building or structure has multiple separately derived systems, provided that the taps terminate at the same point as the _____.

    (a) system bonding jumper
    (b) main bonding jumper
    (c) supply-side bonding jumper
    (d) neutral conductor

37. The common grounding electrode conductor installed for multiple separately derived systems shall not be smaller than _____ copper when using a wire-type conductor.

    (a) 1/0 AWG
    (b) 2/0 AWG
    (c) 3/0 AWG
    (d) 4/0 AWG

38. The common grounding electrode conductor installed for multiple separately derived systems shall be permitted to be a _____ pipe in accordance with 250.68(C)(1).

    (a) metal gas
    (b) metal water
    (c) PVC water
    (d) any of these

Article 250 | Grounding and Bonding

39. The common grounding electrode conductor installed for multiple separately derived systems shall be permitted to be the metal structural frame of the building or structure in accordance with 250.68(C)(2) or connected to the grounding electrode system by a conductor not smaller than _____.

    (a) 6 AWG copper
    (b) 1/0 AWG copper
    (c) 3/0 AWG copper or 250 kcmil aluminum
    (d) 4/0 AWG aluminum

40. Each tap conductor to a common grounding electrode conductor for multiple separately derived systems shall be sized in accordance with _____, based on the derived ungrounded conductors of the separately derived system it serves.

    (a) 250.66
    (b) 250.118
    (c) 250.122
    (d) 310.15

41. Tap connections to a common grounding electrode conductor for multiple separately derived systems may be made to a copper or aluminum busbar that is _____ and of sufficient length to accommodate the number of terminations necessary for the installation.

    (a) smaller than ¼ in. thick × 4 in. wide
    (b) not smaller than ¼ in. thick × 2 in. wide
    (c) not smaller than ½ in. thick × 2 in. wide
    (d) not smaller than ¼ in. thick × 2½ in. wide

42. Tap connections to a common grounding electrode conductor for multiple separately derived systems shall be made at an accessible location by _____.

    (a) a connector listed as grounding and bonding equipment
    (b) listed connections to aluminum or copper busbars
    (c) the exothermic welding process
    (d) any of these

43. A grounding electrode system and grounding electrode conductor at a building or structure shall not be required if only a _____ supplies the building or structure.

    (a) 4-wire service
    (b) single or multiwire branch circuit
    (c) 3-wire service
    (d) any of these

44. An equipment grounding conductor shall be run with the supply conductors and be connected to the building or structure _____ and to the grounding electrode.

    (a) rebar
    (b) disconnecting means
    (c) structural steel
    (d) ground rod

45. The size of the grounding electrode conductor for a building or structure supplied by a feeder shall not be smaller than that identified in _____, based on the largest ungrounded supply conductor.

    (a) 250.66
    (b) 250.102
    (c) 250.122
    (d) Table 310.16

46. Impedance grounded systems in which a grounding impedance device, typically a resistor, limits the ground-fault current for a 480V up to 1000V three-phase system are permitted where _____.

    (a) the conditions of maintenance and supervision ensure that only qualified persons service the installation
    (b) ground detectors are installed on the system
    (c) line-to-neutral loads are not served
    (d) all of these

47. Concrete-encased electrodes _____ shall not be required to be part of the grounding electrode system if the rebar is not accessible for use without disturbing the concrete.

    (a) in hazardous (classified) locations
    (b) in health care facilities
    (c) of existing buildings or structures
    (d) in agricultural buildings with equipotential planes

48. In order for a metal underground water pipe to be used as a grounding electrode, it shall be in direct contact with the earth for _____.

    (a) 5 ft
    (b) 10 ft or more
    (c) less than 10 ft
    (d) 20 ft or more

49. One or more metal in-ground support structure(s) in direct contact with the earth vertically for _____ or more, with or without concrete encasement, is permitted to be a grounding electrode in accordance with 250.52.
    (a) 4 ft
    (b) 6 ft
    (c) 8 ft
    (d) 10 ft

50. The minimum length of a 4 AWG concrete-encased electrode is at least _____.
    (a) 10 ft
    (b) 20 ft
    (c) 25 ft
    (d) 50 ft

51. Rebar in multiple pieces used as a concrete-encased electrode shall be connected together by _____ tie wires or other effective means.
    (a) steel
    (b) plastic
    (c) aluminum
    (d) fiber glass

52. An electrode encased by at least 2 in. of concrete, located horizontally near the bottom or vertically and within that portion of a concrete foundation or footing that is in direct contact with the earth, is permitted as a grounding electrode when it consists of a bare copper conductor not smaller than _____.
    (a) 8 AWG
    (b) 6 AWG
    (c) 4 AWG
    (d) 1/0 AWG

53. If multiple concrete-encased electrodes are present at a building or structure, it shall be permissible to bond only _____ into the grounding electrode system.
    (a) one
    (b) two
    (c) three
    (d) four

54. Concrete-encased grounding electrodes that are installed where the concrete is installed with _____ is not considered to be in direct contact with the earth.
    (a) insulation
    (b) vapor barriers
    (c) films
    (d) any of these

55. A ground ring encircling the building or structure can be used as a grounding electrode when the _____.
    (a) ring is in direct contact with the earth
    (b) ring consists of at least 20 ft of bare copper conductor
    (c) bare copper conductor is not smaller than 2 AWG
    (d) all of these

56. Rod and pipe grounding electrodes shall not be less than _____ in length.
    (a) 6 ft
    (b) 8 ft
    (c) 10 ft
    (d) 20 ft

57. Grounding electrodes of the rod type less than _____ in diameter shall be listed.
    (a) ½ in.
    (b) ⅝ in.
    (c) ¾ in.
    (d) 1 in.

58. A buried iron or steel plate used as a grounding electrode shall expose not less than _____ of surface area to exterior soil.
    (a) 2 sq ft
    (b) 4 sq ft
    (c) 9 sq ft
    (d) 10 sq ft

59. Grounding electrodes of bare or electrically conductive coated iron or steel plates shall be at least _____ thick.
    (a) ⅛ in.
    (b) ¼ in.
    (c) ½ in.
    (d) ¾ in.

Article 250 | Grounding and Bonding

60. Metal underground systems or structures such as piping systems, underground tanks, and underground metal well casings that are not bonded to a metal _____ are permitted as grounding electrodes.

    (a) gas pipe
    (b) fire-sprinkler pipe
    (c) water pipe
    (d) none of these

61. _____ shall not be used as a grounding electrode(s).

    (a) Metal underground gas piping systems
    (b) Aluminum
    (c) Swimming pool structures and structural rebar
    (d) all of these

62. _____ electrodes shall be free from nonconductive coatings such as paint or enamel.

    (a) Rod
    (b) Pipe
    (c) Plate
    (d) all of these

63. If practicable, rod, pipe, and plate electrodes shall be embedded _____.

    (a) directly below the electrical meter
    (b) on the north side of the building
    (c) below permanent moisture level
    (d) all of these

64. The grounding electrode conductor to a ground rod that serves as a supplemental electrode for the metal water pipe electrode is not required to be larger than _____ copper wire.

    (a) 8 AWG
    (b) 6 AWG
    (c) 4 AWG
    (d) 3 AWG

65. Where the resistance-to-ground of 25 ohms or less is not achieved for a single rod electrode, _____.

    (a) other means besides electrodes shall be used in order to provide grounding
    (b) the single rod electrode shall be supplemented by one additional electrode
    (c) additional electrodes shall be added until 25 ohms is achieved
    (d) any of these

66. If multiple rod, pipe, or plate electrodes are installed to supplement the water pipe electrode, they shall not be less than _____ apart.

    (a) 3 ft
    (b) 4 ft
    (c) 5 ft
    (d) 6 ft

67. A rod or pipe electrode shall be installed such that at least _____ of length is in contact with the soil.

    (a) 30 in.
    (b) 6 ft
    (c) 8 ft
    (d) 10 ft

68. Where rock bottom is encountered, a rod or pipe electrode shall be driven at an angle not to exceed _____ from the vertical.

    (a) 15 degrees
    (b) 30 degrees
    (c) 45 degrees
    (d) 60 degrees

69. The upper end of the rod electrode shall be _____ ground level unless the aboveground end and the grounding electrode conductor attachment are protected against physical damage as specified in 250.10.

    (a) no more than 1 in. above
    (b) no more than 2 in. above
    (c) no more than 3 in. above
    (d) flush with or below ground level

70. Plate electrodes shall be installed not less than _____ below the surface of the earth.

    (a) 30 in.
    (b) 4 ft
    (c) 5 ft
    (d) 6 ft

71. Where bonding jumper(s) are used to connect the grounding electrodes together to form the grounding electrode system, _____ is not permitted to be used as a conductor to interconnect the electrodes.

    (a) rebar
    (b) structural steel
    (c) a grounding plate
    (d) none of these

72. Where a metal underground water pipe is used as a grounding electrode, the continuity of the grounding path or the bonding connection to interior piping shall not rely on _____ and similar equipment.

    (a) bonding jumpers
    (b) water meters or filtering devices
    (c) grounding clamps
    (d) all of these

73. If the supplemental electrode is a rod, pipe, or plate electrode, that portion of the bonding jumper that is the sole connection to the supplemental grounding electrode is not required to be larger than _____ copper.

    (a) 8 AWG
    (b) 6 AWG
    (c) 4 AWG
    (d) 1 AWG

74. When a ground ring is used as a grounding electrode, it shall be installed at a depth below the earth's surface of not less than _____.

    (a) 18 in.
    (b) 24 in.
    (c) 30 in.
    (d) 8 ft

75. When installing _____ electrodes, the earth shall not be used as an effective ground-fault current path.

    (a) auxiliary
    (b) supplemental
    (c) oversized
    (d) aluminum

76. Grounding electrode conductors of the wire type shall be _____.

    (a) solid
    (b) stranded
    (c) insulated or bare
    (d) any of these

77. Bare or covered aluminum or copper-clad aluminum grounding electrode conductors without an extruded polymeric covering shall not be installed where subject to corrosive conditions or be installed in direct contact with _____.

    (a) concrete
    (b) bare copper conductors
    (c) wooden framing members
    (d) all of these

78. Aluminum or copper-clad aluminum grounding electrode conductors external to buildings or equipment enclosures shall not terminate within _____ of the earth.

    (a) 12 in.
    (b) 18 in.
    (c) 20 in.
    (d) 24 in.

79. If _____, a grounding electrode conductor or its enclosure shall be securely fastened to the surface on which it is carried.

    (a) concealed
    (b) exposed
    (c) accessible
    (d) none of these

80. Grounding electrode conductors _____ and larger that are not exposed to physical damage can be run along the surface of the building construction without metal covering or protection.

    (a) 10 AWG
    (b) 8 AWG
    (c) 6 AWG
    (d) 4 AWG

81. A(An) _____ or larger grounding electrode conductor exposed to physical damage shall be protected in rigid metal conduit, IMC, Schedule 80 PVC conduit, reinforced thermosetting resin conduit Type XW (RTRC-XW), EMT, or cable armor.

    (a) 10 AWG
    (b) 8 AWG
    (c) 6 AWG
    (d) 4 AWG

Article 250 | Grounding and Bonding

82. Grounding electrode conductors smaller than _____ shall be protected in rigid metal conduit, IMC, PVC conduit, electrical metallic tubing, or cable armor.

    (a) 10 AWG
    (b) 8 AWG
    (c) 6 AWG
    (d) 4 AWG

83. Grounding electrode conductors in contact with _____ shall not be required to comply with 300.5 but shall be protected if subject to physical damage.

    (a) water
    (b) the earth
    (c) metal
    (d) all of these

84. Grounding electrode conductors shall be installed in one continuous length without a splice or joint, unless spliced by _____.

    (a) connecting together sections of a busbar
    (b) irreversible compression-type connectors listed as grounding and bonding equipment
    (c) the exothermic welding process
    (d) any of these

85. The common grounding electrode conductor shall be sized in accordance with 250.66, based on the sum of the circular mil area of the _____ ungrounded conductor(s) of each set of conductors that supplies the disconnecting means.

    (a) smallest
    (b) largest
    (c) color of the
    (d) material of the

86. Ferrous metal raceways for grounding electrode conductors shall be _____ continuous from the point of attachment to cabinets or equipment to the grounding electrode.

    (a) electrically
    (b) physically
    (c) mechanically
    (d) integrally

87. Ferrous metal raceways for grounding electrode conductors shall be bonded at each end of the raceway or enclosure to the grounding electrode or grounding electrode conductor to create a(an) _____ parallel path.

    (a) mechanically
    (b) electrically
    (c) physically
    (d) effective

88. The grounding electrode conductor is permitted to be run to any _____ available in the grounding electrode system.

    (a) panelboards
    (b) bonding jumper
    (c) switchgear
    (d) convenient grounding electrode

89. Bonding jumpers from grounding electrodes are permitted to be connected to a busbar not less than _____.

    (a) ⅛ in. thick × 1 in. wide
    (b) ⅛ in. thick × 2 in. wide
    (c) ¼ in. thick × 1 in. wide
    (d) ¼ in. thick × 2 in. wide

90. Grounding electrode conductors shall not be installed through a ventilation opening of a(an) _____.

    (a) enclosure
    (b) cabinet
    (c) motor control center
    (d) environmental air system

91. A metal water pipe grounding electrode conductor sized at _____ is required for a 400A service supplied with 500 kcmil conductors.

    (a) 1 AWG
    (b) 1/0 AWG
    (c) 2/0 AWG
    (d) 3/0 AWG

92. The minimum grounding electrode conductor to a rod, pipe, or plate electrode for a 30A service with 10 AWG conductors is _____.

    (a) 8 AWG
    (b) 6 AWG
    (c) 1/0 AWG
    (d) 4/0 AWG

93. A metal water pipe grounding electrode conductor sized at _____ is required for a service supplied with 350 kcmil conductors.

    (a) 6 AWG
    (b) 3 AWG
    (c) 2 AWG
    (d) 1/0 AWG

94. A(An) _____ is the smallest size grounding electrode conductor permitted for a solidly grounded ac system.

    (a) 8 AWG
    (b) 6 AWG
    (c) 1/0 AWG
    (d) 4/0 AWG

95. A service consisting of 12 AWG service-entrance conductors requires a grounding electrode conductor sized no less than _____.

    (a) 10 AWG
    (b) 8 AWG
    (c) 6 AWG
    (d) 4 AWG

96. The largest size copper grounding electrode conductor required based on Table 250.66 is _____.

    (a) 6 AWG
    (b) 1/0 AWG
    (c) 3/0 AWG
    (d) 250 kcmil

97. A grounding electrode conductor sized at _____ is required for a service supplied with 400 kcmil parallel conductors in three raceways.

    (a) 1 AWG
    (b) 1/0 AWG
    (c) 2/0 AWG
    (d) 3/0 AWG

98. A grounding electrode conductor sized at _____ is required for a service supplied with 250 kcmil conductors paralleled in two raceways.

    (a) 1 AWG
    (b) 1/0 AWG
    (c) 2/0 AWG
    (d) 3/0 AWG

99. The largest sized grounding electrode conductor to a rod, pipe, or plate electrode required for a 400A service with 500 kcmil conductors is _____.

    (a) 8 AWG
    (b) 6 AWG
    (c) 1/0 AWG
    (d) 4/0 AWG aluminum

100. If the grounding electrode conductor to a ground rod does not extend on to other types of electrodes, the grounding electrode conductor shall not be required to be larger than _____ copper wire.

    (a) 10 AWG
    (b) 8 AWG
    (c) 6 AWG
    (d) 4 AWG

101. If the grounding electrode conductor to a concrete-encased electrode does not extend on to other types of electrodes, the grounding electrode conductor shall not be required to be larger than _____ copper wire.

    (a) 10 AWG
    (b) 8 AWG
    (c) 6 AWG
    (d) 4 AWG

102. All mechanical elements used to terminate a grounding electrode conductor or bonding jumper to a grounding electrode shall be _____.

    (a) accessible
    (b) concealed
    (c) exposed
    (d) protected

103. An encased or buried grounding electrode conductor or bonding jumper connection to a concrete-encased, driven, or buried grounding electrode shall not be required to be _____.

    (a) readily accessible
    (b) accessible
    (c) available
    (d) any of these

104. When an underground metal _____ piping system is used as a grounding electrode, bonding shall be provided around insulated joints and around any equipment that is likely to be disconnected for repairs or replacement.

    (a) water
    (b) gas
    (c) fire-sprinkled
    (d) none of these

105. Interior metal water piping that is electrically continuous with a metal underground water pipe electrode and is located not more than _____ from the point of entrance to the building, as measured along the water piping, is permitted to extend the connection to an electrode(s).

    (a) 2 ft
    (b) 3 ft
    (c) 4 ft
    (d) 5 ft

106. The metal structural frame of a building is permitted to be used as a conductor to _____ electrodes that are part of the grounding electrode system, or as a grounding electrode conductor.

    (a) interconnect
    (b) identify
    (c) separate
    (d) none of these

107. A rebar-type concrete-encased electrode with an additional rebar section extended from its location within the concrete foundation or footing to an accessible location that is not subject to _____ is permitted for connection of grounding electrode conductors.

    (a) physical damage
    (b) moisture
    (c) corrosion
    (d) any of these

108. Not more than _____ grounding or bonding conductor shall be connected to the grounding electrode by a single clamp or fitting unless the clamp or fitting is listed for multiple conductors.

    (a) one
    (b) two
    (c) three
    (d) four

109. The grounding conductor connection to the grounding electrode shall be made by _____.

    (a) listed lugs
    (b) exothermic welding
    (c) listed pressure connectors
    (d) any of these

110. Listed ground clamps that are identified for _____ are also suitable for concrete encasement.

    (a) wet locations
    (b) outdoor use
    (c) direct burial
    (d) corrosive environments

111. Metal enclosures and raceways containing _____ conductors shall be connected to the grounded system conductor if the electrical system is grounded.

    (a) service
    (b) feeder
    (c) branch-circuit
    (d) outside feeder or branch-circuit

112. Metal components that are installed in a run of an underground nonmetallic raceway(s) and are isolated from possible contact by a minimum cover of _____ to all parts of the metal components shall not be required to be connected to the grounded conductor, supply-side bonding jumper, or grounding electrode conductor.

    (a) 12 in.
    (b) 18 in.
    (c) 24 in.
    (d) 30 in.

113. Metal enclosures and raceways for other than service conductors shall be connected to the _____ conductor.

    (a) neutral
    (b) equipment grounding
    (c) ungrounded
    (d) grounded

114. Short sections of metal enclosures or raceways used to provide support or protection of _____ from physical damage shall not be required to be connected to the equipment grounding conductor.

    (a) conduit
    (b) feeders under 600V
    (c) cable assemblies
    (d) grounding electrode conductors

115. The normally noncurrent-carrying metal parts of service equipment, such as service _____, shall be bonded together.

    (a) raceways or service cable armor
    (b) equipment enclosures containing service conductors, including meter fittings, boxes, or the like, interposed in the service raceway or armor
    (c) cable trays
    (d) all of these

116. Bonding jumpers for service raceways shall be used around impaired connections such as _____.

    (a) oversized concentric knockouts
    (b) oversized eccentric knockouts
    (c) reducing washers
    (d) any of these

117. Electrical continuity at service equipment, service raceways, and service conductor enclosures shall be ensured by _____.

    (a) bonding equipment to the grounded service conductor
    (b) connections made up wrenchtight utilizing threaded couplings
    (c) other listed bonding devices, such as bonding-type locknuts, bushings, or bushings with bonding jumpers
    (d) any of these

118. Connections of wrenchtight threaded couplings, threaded entries, or listed threaded hubs are considered to be effectively _____ to the service metal enclosure.

    (a) attached
    (b) bonded
    (c) grounded
    (d) secured

119. Service metal raceways and metal-clad cables are considered effectively bonded when using threadless couplings and connectors that are _____.

    (a) nonmetallic
    (b) made up tight
    (c) sealed
    (d) classified

120. A means external to enclosures for connecting intersystem _____ conductors shall be provided at the service equipment or metering equipment enclosure and disconnecting means of buildings or structures supplied by a feeder or branch circuit.

    (a) bonding
    (b) ungrounded
    (c) secondary
    (d) bonding and ungrounded

121. In accordance with 250.94(A), the intersystem bonding termination device shall _____.

    (a) be accessible for connection and inspection
    (b) consist of a set of terminals with the capacity for connection of not less than three intersystem bonding conductors
    (c) not interfere with opening the enclosure for a service, building/structure disconnecting means, or metering equipment
    (d) all of these

122. In accordance with 250.94(A), the intersystem bonding termination device shall _____.

    (a) be securely mounted and electrically connected to service equipment, the meter enclosure, or exposed nonflexible metallic service raceway, or be mounted at one of these enclosures and be connected to the enclosure or grounding electrode conductor with a minimum 6 AWG copper conductor
    (b) be securely mounted to the building/structure disconnecting means, or be mounted at the disconnecting means and be connected to the metallic enclosure or grounding electrode conductor with a minimum 6 AWG copper conductor
    (c) have terminals that are listed as grounding and bonding equipment
    (d) all of these

Article 250 | Grounding and Bonding

123. At existing buildings or structures, an intersystem bonding termination is not required if other acceptable means of bonding exists. An external accessible means for bonding communications systems together can be by the use of a(an) _____.

    (a) nonflexible metal raceway
    (b) exposed grounding electrode conductor
    (c) connection to a grounded raceway or equipment approved by the authority having jurisdiction
    (d) any of these

124. When bonding enclosures, metal raceways, frames, and fittings any nonconductive paint, enamel, or similar coating shall be removed at _____.

    (a) contact surfaces
    (b) threads
    (c) contact points
    (d) all of these

125. Expansion, expansion-deflection, or deflection fittings and telescoping sections of metal raceways shall be made _____ continuous by equipment bonding jumpers or other means.

    (a) physically
    (b) mechanically
    (c) electrically
    (d) directly

126. The minimum size supply-side bonding jumper for a service raceway containing 4/0 AWG aluminum conductors is _____.

    (a) 6 AWG aluminum
    (b) 4 AWG aluminum
    (c) 4 AWG copper
    (d) 3 AWG copper

127. Where ungrounded supply conductors are paralleled in two or more raceways, the bonding jumper for each raceway shall be based on the size of the _____ in each raceway.

    (a) overcurrent protection for conductors
    (b) grounded conductors
    (c) largest ungrounded supply conductors
    (d) sum of all conductors

128. If service conductors are connected in parallel in three separate metal raceways, with 600 kcmil conductors per phase, the supply-side bonding jumper size for each service raceway is _____.

    (a) 1/0 AWG
    (b) 3/0 AWG
    (c) 250 kcmil
    (d) 500 kcmil

129. The minimum size copper equipment bonding jumper for a 40A-rated circuit is _____.

    (a) 14 AWG
    (b) 12 AWG
    (c) 10 AWG
    (d) 8 AWG

130. An equipment bonding jumper can be installed on the outside of a raceway, provided the length of the equipment bonding jumper is not more than _____ long and the equipment bonding jumper is routed with the raceway.

    (a) 3 ft
    (b) 4 ft
    (c) 5 ft
    (d) 6 ft

131. Metal water piping systems shall be bonded to the _____, or to one or more grounding electrodes used if the grounding electrode conductor or bonding jumper to the grounding electrode is of sufficient size.

    (a) grounded conductor at the service
    (b) service equipment enclosure
    (c) grounding electrode conductor if of sufficient size
    (d) any of these

132. Bonding jumper(s) for the metal water piping systems shall not be required to be larger than _____ copper.

    (a) 1/0 AWG
    (b) 2/0 AWG
    (c) 3/0 AWG
    (d) 4/0 AWG

133. The metal water piping system(s) installed in or attached to a building or structure [250.104(A)(3)] shall be bonded to _____.
    (a) the building or structure disconnecting means enclosure where located at the building or structure
    (b) the equipment grounding conductor run with the supply conductors
    (c) one or more grounding electrodes
    (d) any of these

134. The bonding jumper(s) required for the metal water piping system(s) installed in or attached to a building or structure supplied by a feeder(s) or branch circuit(s) shall be sized in accordance with _____.
    (a) 250.66
    (b) 250.102(D)
    (c) 250.122
    (d) 310.16

135. If installed _____ a building or structure, a metal piping system that is likely to become energized shall be bonded.
    (a) in
    (b) on
    (c) under
    (d) in or on

136. The building structural steel bonding jumper size for a 400A service supplied with 500 kcmil conductors is _____.
    (a) 6 AWG
    (b) 3 AWG
    (c) 2 AWG
    (d) 1/0 AWG

137. Exposed structural metal that is interconnected to form a metal building frame, not intentionally grounded or bonded, and is likely to become energized shall be bonded to the _____.
    (a) service equipment enclosure
    (b) grounded conductor at the service
    (c) disconnecting means for buildings or structures supplied by a feeder or branch circuit
    (d) any of these

138. A transformer supplies power to a 100A panelboard with 2 AWG THWN-2 conductors. The size of the bonding jumper in copper required to bond the building steel to the secondary grounded conductor is _____.
    (a) 8 AWG
    (b) 6 AWG
    (c) 4 AWG
    (d) 2 AWG

139. A transformer supplies power to a 200A panelboard with 2 AWG THWN-2 conductors. The size of the bonding jumper in copper required to bond the building steel to the secondary grounded conductor is _____.
    (a) 8 AWG
    (b) 6 AWG
    (c) 4 AWG
    (d) 2 AWG

140. A separate bonding jumper to the building structural metal shall not be required if the metal in-ground support structure is used as a grounding electrode or the metal frame of a building or structure is used as the _____ for the separately derived system.
    (a) bonding jumper
    (b) ground-fault current path
    (c) grounding electrode or grounding electrode conductor
    (d) lightning protection

141. Lightning protection system ground terminals _____ bonded to the building or structure grounding electrode system.
    (a) shall be
    (b) shall not be
    (c) shall be permitted to be
    (d) shall be effectively

142. Metal enclosures shall be permitted to be used to connect bonding jumpers or _____ conductors, or both, together to become a part of an effective ground-fault current path.
    (a) grounded
    (b) neutral
    (c) equipment grounding
    (d) grounded phase

Article 250 | Grounding and Bonding

143. Exposed, normally noncurrent-carrying metal parts of cord-and-plug-connected equipment shall be connected to the equipment grounding conductor if operated at over _____ to ground.

    (a) 24V
    (b) 50V
    (c) 120V
    (d) 150V

144. An equipment grounding conductor of the wire type is required in _____.

    (a) rigid metal conduit
    (b) intermediate metal conduit
    (c) electrical metallic tubing
    (d) none of these

145. Flexible metal conduit used as an EGC where flexibility for movement of equipment is required after installation shall _____.

    (a) be provided with a wire type equipment grounding conductor or bonding jumper
    (b) not require a wire-type EGC if less than 6 ft
    (c) not require a wire-type EGC if protected by 20A or less
    (d) none of these

146. FMC can be used as the equipment grounding conductor if the length in any ground return path does not exceed 6 ft and the circuit conductors contained in the conduit are protected by overcurrent devices rated at _____ or less.

    (a) 15A
    (b) 20A
    (c) 30A
    (d) 60A

147. LFMC is acceptable as an equipment grounding conductor when it terminates in _____ and is protected by an overcurrent device rated 20A or less for trade sizes ⅜ through ½.

    (a) labeled fittings
    (b) identified fittings
    (c) approved fittings
    (d) listed fittings

148. The _____ of Type AC cable is recognized as an equipment grounding conductor.

    (a) armor
    (b) cover
    (c) sheath
    (d) any of these

149. Type MC cable is recognized as an equipment grounding conductor when _____.

    (a) it contains an insulated or uninsulated equipment grounding conductor in compliance with 250.118(1)
    (b) the cable assembly contains a bare copper conductor
    (c) it is only hospital grade Type MC cable
    (d) it is terminated with bonding bushings

150. A wire-type equipment grounding conductor can be identified by _____.

    (a) a continuous outer finish that is green
    (b) being bare
    (c) a continuous outer finish that is green with one or more yellow stripes
    (d) any of these

151. An insulated or covered conductor _____ and larger is permitted, at the time of installation, to be permanently identified as an equipment grounding conductor at each end and at every point where the conductor is accessible.

    (a) 8 AWG
    (b) 6 AWG
    (c) 4 AWG
    (d) 1/0 AWG

152. One or more insulated conductors in a multiconductor cable, at the time of installation, shall be permitted to be permanently identified as equipment grounding conductors at each end and at every point where the conductors are accessible by coloring the insulation _____.

    (a) green
    (b) grey
    (c) green with a yellow stripe
    (d) white or silver

153. Unless part of an applicable cable wiring method, bare or covered conductors shall not be installed if subject to _____ conditions or be installed in direct contact with concrete, masonry, or the earth.

    (a) corrosive
    (b) wet
    (c) damp
    (d) dry

154. Equipment grounding conductors are not required to be _____ than the circuit conductors.

    (a) larger
    (b) smaller
    (c) less
    (d) none of these

155. If the ungrounded conductors are increased in size for any reason other than as required in 310.15(B) or 310.15(C), wire-type equipment grounding conductors shall be increased in size proportionately to the increase in _____ of the ungrounded conductors.

    (a) ampacity
    (b) circular mil area
    (c) diameter
    (d) temperature rating

156. When a single equipment grounding conductor is used for multiple circuits in the same raceway, cable, or cable tray, the single equipment grounding conductor shall be sized according to the _____.

    (a) combined rating of all the overcurrent devices
    (b) largest overcurrent device protecting the circuit conductors
    (c) combined rating of all the loads
    (d) any of these

157. Equipment grounding conductors for motor branch circuits shall be sized in accordance with Table 250.122(A), based on the rating of the _____ device.

    (a) motor overload
    (b) motor over-temperature
    (c) branch-circuit short-circuit and ground-fault protective
    (d) feeder overcurrent protection

158. If circuit conductors are connected in parallel in the same raceway, a single wire-type conductor shall be permitted as the equipment grounding conductor and shall be sized in accordance with 250.122 based on the _____ for the feeder or branch circuit.

    (a) fuse
    (b) circuit breaker
    (c) overcurrent protective device
    (d) any of these

159. If conductors are installed in multiple raceways and are connected in _____, a wire-type equipment grounding conductor, if used, shall be installed in each raceway and shall be connected in parallel. The equipment grounding conductor installed in each raceway shall be sized in accordance with 250.122 based on the rating of the overcurrent protective device for the feeder or branch circuit.

    (a) parallel
    (b) series
    (c) combination
    (d) none of these

160. Except as provided in 250.122(F)(2)(C) for raceway or cable tray installations, the equipment grounding conductor in each multiconductor cable shall be sized in accordance with 250.122 based on the _____.

    (a) largest circuit conductor
    (b) overcurrent protective device for the feeder or branch circuit
    (c) smallest branch-circuit conductor
    (d) overcurrent protective device for the service

161. Equipment grounding conductors for feeder taps are not required to be _____ than the tap conductors.

    (a) larger
    (b) smaller
    (c) less
    (d) none of these

162. In accordance with 250.134, non-current-carrying metal parts of fastened in place equipment, raceways, and other enclosures, shall be connected to an _____.

    (a) grounded conductor
    (b) equipment grounding conductor
    (c) ungrounded conductor
    (d) none of these

163. Metal parts of cord-and-plug-connected equipment, shall be connected to an _____ run with the power supply conductors in a cable assembly or flexible cord properly terminated in a grounding-type attachment plug with one fixed grounding contact.

    (a) grounded conductor
    (b) equipment grounding conductor
    (c) ungrounded conductor
    (d) none of these

Article 250 | Grounding and Bonding

164. Frames of electric ranges, wall-mounted ovens, counter-mounted cooking units, _____, and outlet or junction boxes that are part of the circuit shall be connected to the equipment grounding conductor in accordance with 250.140(A) or the grounded conductor in accordance with 250.140(B).

    (a) washing machines
    (b) dishwashers
    (c) microwaves
    (d) clothes dryers

165. The circuit supplying _____ shall include an equipment grounding conductor. The frame of the appliance shall be connected to the equipment grounding conductor in the manner specified by 250.134 or 250.138.

    (a) electric ranges or clothes dryers
    (b) electric wall mounted ovens
    (c) electric counter-mounted cooking units
    (d) any of these

166. A(An) _____ shall be used to connect the grounding terminal of a grounding-type receptacle to a metal box that is connected to an equipment grounding conductor.

    (a) equipment bonding jumper
    (b) grounded conductor jumper
    (c) equipment bonding jumper or grounded conductor jumper
    (d) equipment bonding jumper and grounded conductor jumper

167. Where the metal box for a receptacle is surface mounted, direct metal-to-metal contact between the device yoke and the box shall be permitted to ground the receptacle to the box if at least _____ of the insulating washers of the receptacle is (are) removed.

    (a) one
    (b) two
    (c) three
    (d) four

168. A listed exposed work cover can be the grounding and bonding means for a surface-mounted metal box when the device is attached to the cover with at least _____ permanent fastener(s) and the exposed work cover mounting holes are located on a non-raised portion of the cover.

    (a) one
    (b) two
    (c) three
    (d) four

169. Receptacle yokes or contact devices designed and _____ as self-grounding can, in conjunction with the supporting screws, establish the equipment bonding between the device yoke and a flush-type box.

    (a) approved
    (b) advertised
    (c) listed
    (d) installed

170. The receptacle grounding terminal of an isolated ground receptacle shall be connected to a(an) _____ equipment grounding conductor run with the circuit conductors.

    (a) insulated
    (b) covered
    (c) bare
    (d) solid

171. All _____ that are spliced or terminated within the box shall be connected together. Connections and splices shall be made in accordance with 110.14(B) and 250.8 except that insulation shall not be required.

    (a) neutral conductors
    (b) equipment grounding conductors
    (c) phase conductors
    (d) switch-legs

172. The arrangement of grounding connections shall ensure that the disconnection or the removal of a luminaire, receptacle, or other device fed from the box does not interrupt the electrical continuity of the _____ conductor(s) providing an effective ground-fault current path.

    (a) grounded
    (b) ungrounded
    (c) equipment grounding
    (d) all of these

173. For the continuity of equipment grounding conductors and attachment in boxes, a connection used for _____ shall be made between the metal box and the equipment grounding conductor(s).

    (a) bonding
    (b) connections and splices
    (c) extending the length of the circuit
    (d) no other purpose

174. A connection used for no other purpose shall be made between the metal box and the equipment grounding conductor(s). The equipment bonding jumper or equipment grounding conductor shall be sized from Table 250.122 based on the largest _____ conductors in the box.

(a) overcurrent device protecting circuit
(b) ungrounded
(c) grounded
(d) neutral

175. One or more equipment grounding conductors brought into a nonmetallic outlet box shall be arranged to provide a connection to _____ in that box requiring connection to an equipment grounding conductor.

(a) any fitting or device
(b) a ground clip
(c) a clamp(s)
(d) the grounded conductor

Notes

CHAPTER 3

WIRING METHODS AND MATERIALS

Introduction to Chapter 3—Wiring Methods and Materials

Chapter 3 of the *Code* is divided into fifty-one articles containing the general rules for wiring and sizing circuits, overcurrent protection of conductors, overvoltage protection of equipment, and bonding and grounding. The rules in this chapter apply to all electrical installations covered by the *NEC*—except as modified in Chapters 5, 6, 7, or specifically referenced in Chapter 8 [90.3].

This chapter can be thought of as the rough in phase of a job because it is primarily focused on the wiring methods and materials used to rough out an installation. Every article in this chapter deals with a different method or material used to get wiring from point "A" to point "B" in a system. The Chapter 3 articles covered by this material are:

Wiring Method Articles

- **Article 300—General Requirements for Wiring Methods and Materials.** Article 300 contains the general requirements for all wiring methods included in the *Code*, except for Class 2 power-limited, fire alarm and coaxial cables, which are covered in Chapters 7 and 8.

- **Article 310—Conductors for General Wiring.** This article contains the general requirements for conductors such as insulation markings, ampacity ratings, and conductor use. There is also a section that addresses single-family dwelling service and feeder conductors exclusively. Article 310 does not apply to conductors that are part of flexible cords, fixture wires, or conductors that are an integral part of equipment [90.7 and 310.1].

- **Article 312—Cabinets, Cutout Boxes, and Meter Socket Enclosures.** Article 312 covers the installation and construction specifications for cabinets and meter socket enclosures.

- **Article 314—Outlet, Device, Pull, and Junction Boxes; Conduit Bodies; Fittings; and Handhole Enclosures.** Installation requirements for outlet boxes, pull and junction boxes, as well as conduit bodies and handhole enclosures are contained in this article.

Cable Articles

Articles 320 through 340 address specific types of cables. If you take the time to become familiar with the various types of cables, you will be able to:

- Understand what is available for doing the work.
- Recognize cable types having special *NEC* requirements.
- Avoid buying cable you cannot install due to *Code* requirements you cannot meet with that wiring method.

...

Chapter 3 | Wiring Methods and Materials

Here is a brief overview of the cable articles covered in this material:

- **Article 320—Armored Cable (Type AC).** Armored cable is an assembly of insulated conductors, 14 AWG through 1 AWG, individually wrapped with waxed paper. The conductors are contained within a flexible metal (steel or aluminum) spiral sheath that interlocks at the edges. Armored cable looks like flexible metal conduit. Many electricians call this metal cable "BX®."

- **Article 330—Metal-Clad Cable (Type MC).** Metal-clad cable encloses insulated conductors in a metal sheath of corrugated, smooth copper or aluminum tubing, or spiral interlocked steel or aluminum. The physical characteristics of Type MC cable make it a versatile wiring method permitted in almost any location and for almost any application. The most used Type MC cable is the interlocking kind, which looks like armored cable or flexible metal conduit.

- **Article 334—Nonmetallic-Sheathed Cable (Type NM).** Nonmetallic-sheathed cable is commonly referred to by its trade name "Romex®." It encloses two, three, or four insulated conductors, 14 AWG through 2 AWG, within a nonmetallic outer jacket. Because this cable is manufactured in this manner, it contains a separate (usually bare) equipment grounding conductor. Nonmetallic-sheathed cable is commonly used for residential wiring applications but may sometimes be permitted for use in commercial occupancies.

- **Article 336—Power and Control Tray Cable (Type TC).** Power and control tray cable is flexible, inexpensive, and easily installed. It provides very limited physical protection for the conductors, so the installation restrictions are rigorous. Its low cost and relative ease of installation make it a common wiring method for industrial applications.

- **Article 338—Service-Entrance Cable (Types SE and USE).** Service-entrance and underground service-entrance cables can be a single conductor or a multiconductor assembly within an overall nonmetallic outer jacket or covering. These cables are most often used for services not over 1000V but are also permitted for feeders and branch circuits. When used as a service conductor(s) or a service-entrance conductor(s), pre-manufactured Type "SE" cable assemblies will typically contain two insulated phase conductors and a bare neutral conductor. When permitted for use as a feeder or branch circuit, Type SE cable is usually designated as Type "SER" and will contain the same three conductors as Type SE but a fourth conductor (which is insulated) will be added to serve as the neutral conductor.

- **Article 340—Underground Feeder and Branch-Circuit Cable (Type UF).** Underground feeder cable is a moisture-, fungus-, and corrosion-resistant cable suitable for direct burial in the Earth and is available in sizes 14 AWG through 4/0 AWG [340.104]. Multiconductor UF cable is covered in molded plastic that surrounds the insulated conductors.

Raceway Articles

Articles 342 through 390 address specific types of raceways. Refer to Article 100 for the definition of a raceway. If you take the time to become familiar with the various types of raceways, you will be able to:

- Understand what is available for doing the work.
- Recognize raceway types having special *Code* requirements.
- Avoid buying a raceway you cannot install due to *NEC* requirements you cannot meet with that wiring method.

Here is a brief overview of the raceway articles included in this material:

- **Article 342—Intermediate Metal Conduit (IMC).** Intermediate metal conduit is a circular metal raceway with the same outside diameter as rigid metal conduit. The wall thickness of this type of conduit is less than that of rigid metal conduit, so it has a larger interior cross-sectional area for holding conductors. Intermediate metal conduit is lighter and less expensive than rigid metal conduit and is approved by the *Code* for use in the same applications as rigid metal conduit. This type of conduit also uses a different steel alloy, which makes it stronger than rigid metal conduit, even though the walls are thinner.

Wiring Methods and Materials | **Chapter 3**

▸ **Article 344—Rigid Metal Conduit (RMC).** Rigid metal conduit is like intermediate metal conduit, except the wall thickness is larger, so it has a smaller interior cross-sectional area. This type of conduit is heavier than intermediate metal conduit and is permitted for use in the same applications as intermediate metal conduit (IMC).

▸ **Article 348—Flexible Metal Conduit (FMC).** Flexible metal conduit is a raceway of circular cross section made of a helically wound, interlocked metal strip of either steel or aluminum. It is commonly called "Greenfield" (after its inventor) or "Flex."

▸ **Article 350—Liquidtight Flexible Metal Conduit (LFMC).** Liquidtight flexible metal conduit is a raceway of circular cross section with an outer liquidtight, nonmetallic, sunlight-resistant jacket over an inner flexible metal core, with associated couplings, connectors, and fittings. It is listed for the installation of electrical conductors. This type of conduit is commonly called "Sealtite®" or simply "liquidtight." Liquidtight flexible metal conduit is similar in construction to flexible metal conduit, but it has an outer thermoplastic covering.

▸ **Article 352—Rigid Polyvinyl Chloride Conduit (PVC).** Rigid polyvinyl chloride conduit is a nonmetallic raceway of circular cross section with integral or associated couplings, connectors, and fittings. It is listed for the installation of electrical conductors.

▸ **Article 356—Liquidtight Flexible Nonmetallic Conduit (LFNC).** Liquidtight flexible nonmetallic conduit (commonly referred to as "Carflex®") is a raceway of circular cross section with an outer liquidtight, nonmetallic, sunlight-resistant jacket over an inner flexible core, with associated couplings, connectors, and fittings.

▸ **Article 358—Electrical Metallic Tubing (EMT).** Electrical metallic tubing is a nonthreaded thinwall raceway of circular cross section designed for the physical protection and routing of conductors and cables. Compared to rigid metal conduit and intermediate metal conduit, electrical metallic tubing is relatively easy to bend, cut, and ream. EMT is not threaded, so all connectors and couplings are of the threadless type. It is available in a range of colors, such as red and blue.

▸ **Article 362—Electrical Nonmetallic Tubing (ENT).** Electrical nonmetallic tubing is a pliable, corrugated, circular raceway made of PVC. It is often referred to as "Smurf Pipe" or "Smurf Tube," because it was only available in blue when it was first available. The nickname is a reference to the children's cartoon characters "The Smurfs." It is now available in many other colors.

▸ **Article 376—Metal Wireways.** A metal wireway is a sheet metal trough with hinged or removable covers making the electrical conductors and cables housed and protected inside accessible. Metal wireways must be installed as complete and contiguous systems.

▸ **Article 380—Multioutlet Assemblies.** A multioutlet assembly is a surface, flush, or freestanding raceway designed to hold conductors and receptacles. It is assembled in the field or at the factory.

▸ **Article 386—Surface Metal Raceways.** A surface metal raceway is a metal raceway intended to be mounted to a surface with associated accessories, in which conductors are placed after the raceway has been installed as a complete system.

Cable Trays

▸ **Article 392—Cable Trays.** A cable tray system is a unit or assembly of units or sections with associated fittings forming a structural system used to securely fasten or support cables and raceways. A cable tray is not a raceway. It is a support system for raceways, cables, and enclosures.

Notice as you read through the various wiring methods that the *NEC* attempts to use similar section numbering for similar topics from one article to the next. It uses the same digits after the decimal point in the section numbers for the same topic. This makes it easier to locate the specific requirements of a particular article. For example, the rules for securing and supporting can be found in the section ending with ".30" of each article.

Notes

ARTICLE 300

GENERAL REQUIREMENTS FOR WIRING METHODS AND MATERIALS

Introduction to Article 300—General Requirements for Wiring Methods and Materials

Article 300 contains the general requirements for all installed wiring methods included in the *NEC*. Because the Code is an installation standard this article does not apply where these wiring methods are integral parts of electrical equipment.

Because Article 300 contains the general requirements for wiring methods and materials, you must have a solid understanding of these rules to correctly and safely install the wiring methods included in Chapter 3. Some topics covered in this material include:

- Conductors
- Terminations
- Burial Depth
- Electrical and Mechanical Continuity of Raceways and Cables
- Securing and Supporting
- Length of Free Conductors
- Induced Currents in Steel Enclosures
- Spread of Fire

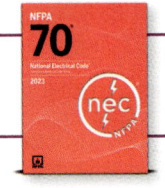

Please use the 2023 *Code* book to answer the following questions.

1. The requirements of Article 300 are not intended to apply to the conductors that form an _____ part of equipment or listed utilization equipment.

    (a) exterior
    (b) integral
    (c) interior
    (d) none of these

2. All conductors of the same circuit, including the grounded and equipment grounding conductors and bonding conductors shall be contained within the same _____, unless otherwise permitted elsewhere in the *Code*.

    (a) raceway
    (b) conduit body
    (c) trench
    (d) all of these

Article 300 | General Requirements for Wiring Methods and Materials

3. The requirement to run all paralleled circuit conductors within the same _____ applies separately to each portion of the paralleled installation.

   (a) raceway or auxiliary gutter
   (b) cable tray or trench
   (c) cable or cord
   (d) all of these

4. Conductors installed in nonmetallic raceways run underground shall be permitted to be arranged as isolated _____ installations. The raceways shall be installed in close proximity, and the conductors shall comply with 300.20(B).

   (a) neutral
   (b) grounded conductor
   (c) phase
   (d) all of these

5. Conductors for ac and dc circuits under 1000V ac and 1500V dc, can occupy the same _____ provided that all conductors have an insulation rating equal to the maximum voltage applied to any conductor.

   (a) equipment wiring enclosure
   (b) cable
   (c) raceway
   (d) any of these

6. Where a cable or raceway-type wiring method is installed through bored holes in joists, rafters, or wood members, the holes shall be bored so that the edge of the hole is _____ the edges of the wood member.

   (a) not less than 1¼ in. from
   (b) immediately adjacent to
   (c) not less than 1/16 in. from
   (d) 90° away from

7. Cables laid in wood notches require protection against nails or screws by using a steel plate at least _____ thick, installed before the building finish is applied.

   (a) 1/16 in.
   (b) 1/8 in.
   (c) ¼ in.
   (d) ½ in.

8. A 1/16-in. steel plate for _____ is not required for protection when installed in wood notches.

   (a) Type UF cable
   (b) Type NM cable
   (c) Type MC cable
   (d) intermediate metal conduit

9. Where Type NM cables pass through cut or drilled slots or holes in metal members, the cable shall be protected by _____ which are installed in the opening prior to the installation of the cable and which securely cover all metal edges.

   (a) anti-short devices
   (b) sleeves
   (c) plates
   (d) listed bushings or grommets

10. Where nails or screws are likely to penetrate nonmetallic-sheathed cable or ENT installed through metal framing members, a steel sleeve, steel plate, or steel clip not less than _____ in thickness shall be used to protect the cable or tubing.

    (a) 1/16 in.
    (b) 1/8 in.
    (c) ½ in.
    (d) ¾ in.

11. Where cables and nonmetallic raceways are installed parallel to framing members, the nearest outside surface of the cable or raceway shall be _____ the nearest edge of the framing member where nails or screws are likely to penetrate.

    (a) not less than 1¼ in. from
    (b) immediately adjacent to
    (c) not less than 1/16 in. from
    (d) 90 degrees away from

12. A cable, raceway, or box installed under metal-corrugated sheet roof decking shall be supported so the top of the cable, raceway, or box is not less than _____ from the lowest surface of the roof decking to the top of the cable, raceway, or box.

    (a) ½ in.
    (b) 1 in.
    (c) 1½ in.
    (d) 2 in.

13. When installed under metal-corrugated sheet roof decking, _____ and intermediate metal conduit, with listed steel or malleable iron fittings and boxes, shall not be required to comply with 300.4(E).

    (a) rigid metal conduit
    (b) electrical metallic tubing
    (c) Schedule 80 PVC
    (d) all of these

14. Where electrical equipment is installed under metal-corrugated sheet roof decking, the 1½-in. spacing is not required where metal-corrugated sheet roof decking is covered with a concrete slab with a minimum thickness of _____, measured from the top of the corrugated roofing.

    (a) ½ in.
    (b) 1 in.
    (c) 1½ in.
    (d) 2 in.

15. Conduit bushings installed to protect insulated conductors _____ or larger contained within raceways that are constructed wholly of insulating material, shall not be used to secure a fitting or raceway.

    (a) 4 AWG
    (b) 6 AWG
    (c) 8 AWG
    (d) 10 AWG

16. Where raceways contain 4 AWG or larger insulated circuit conductors and these conductors enter a cabinet, a box, an enclosure, or a raceway the conductors shall be protected from abrasion during and after installation by an identified fitting providing a smoothly rounded _____ surface.

    (a) fiberglass
    (b) plastic
    (c) insulating
    (d) gray

17. Where raceways contain 4 AWG or larger insulated circuit conductors and these conductors enter a cabinet, a box, an enclosure, or a raceway the conductors shall be protected from abrasion during and after installation by _____.

    (a) an identified fitting that provides a smooth rounded insulating surface
    (b) a listed metal fitting that has smooth rounded edges
    (c) threaded hubs that provide a smooth rounded or flared entry
    (d) any of these

18. A listed expansion/deflection fitting or other approved means shall be used where a raceway crosses a _____ intended for expansion, contraction, or deflection used in buildings, bridges, parking garages, or other structures.

    (a) junction box
    (b) structural joint
    (c) cable tray
    (d) Unistrut® hanger

19. The minimum cover requirement for Type UF cable that supplies a 120V, 30A circuit is _____.

    (a) 6 in.
    (b) 12 in.
    (c) 18 in.
    (d) 24 in.

20. Electrical metallic tubing that is directly buried under a two-family dwelling driveway shall have at least _____ of cover.

    (a) 6 in.
    (b) 12 in.
    (c) 18 in.
    (d) 24 in.

21. Rigid metal conduit that is directly buried outdoors shall have at least _____ of cover.

    (a) 6 in.
    (b) 12 in.
    (c) 18 in.
    (d) 24 in.

22. When installing PVC underground without concrete cover, there shall be a minimum of _____ of cover.

    (a) 6 in.
    (b) 12 in.
    (c) 18 in.
    (d) 22 in.

Article 300 | General Requirements for Wiring Methods and Materials

23. A PVC raceway covered in 2 in. of concrete is required to have a minimal buried depth of _____.

    (a) 6 in.
    (b) 18 in.
    (c) 12 in.
    (d) 24 in.

24. The minimum cover requirement for Type UF cable that supplies a 120V, 15A GFCI-protected circuit under a driveway of a one-family dwelling is _____.

    (a) 6 in.
    (b) 12 in.
    (c) 16 in.
    (d) 24 in.

25. For a dwelling location, direct buried cables that are GFCI protected at no more than 20A shall have a cover of _____.

    (a) 6 in.
    (b) 12 in.
    (c) 18 in.
    (d) 24 in.

26. Type UF cable used with a 24V landscape lighting system can have a minimum cover of _____.

    (a) 6 in.
    (b) 12 in.
    (c) 18 in.
    (d) 24 in.

27. "_____" shall be defined as the shortest distance measured between a point on the top surface of direct-buried cable and the top surface of finished grade.

    (a) Notched
    (b) Cover
    (c) Gap
    (d) Spacing

28. The interior of underground raceways shall be considered a _____ location.

    (a) wet
    (b) dry
    (c) damp
    (d) corrosive

29. Underground cable and conductors installed under a building shall be _____.

    (a) in the same trench
    (b) in a raceway
    (c) encased in concrete
    (d) under at least 2 in. of concrete

30. Type MC Cable _____ for direct burial or concrete encasement shall be permitted under a building without installation in a raceway in accordance with 330.10(A)(5).

    (a) listed
    (b) identified
    (c) tagged
    (d) labeled

31. Where direct-buried conductors and cables emerge from grade, they shall be protected by enclosures or raceways to a point at least _____ above finished grade.

    (a) 3 ft
    (b) 6 ft
    (c) 8 ft
    (d) 10 ft

32. Direct-buried service conductors that are not encased in concrete and that are buried 18 in. or more below grade shall have their location identified by a warning ribbon placed in the trench at least _____ above the underground installation.

    (a) 6 in.
    (b) 10 in.
    (c) 12 in.
    (d) 18 in.

33. _____ conductors or cables can be spliced or tapped without the use of splice boxes when the splice or tap is made in accordance with 110.14(B).

    (a) Direct-buried
    (b) Wet location
    (c) Ungrounded
    (d) Grounded

34. Backfill used for underground wiring shall not damage _____ or prevent adequate compaction of fill or contribute to corrosion.

    (a) raceways
    (b) cables
    (c) conductors
    (d) any of these

General Requirements for Wiring Methods and Materials | Article 300

35. Conduits or raceways through which moisture might contact live parts shall be _____ at either or both ends.
    (a) crimped
    (b) taped
    (c) bushed
    (d) sealed or plugged

36. A(An) _____, with an integral bushed opening shall be used at the end of a conduit or other raceway that terminates underground where the conductors or cables emerge as a direct burial wiring method.
    (a) splice kit
    (b) connector
    (c) adapter
    (d) bushing or terminal fitting

37. All conductors of the same circuit shall be _____, unless otherwise specifically permitted in the *Code*.
    (a) bonded
    (b) grounded
    (c) the same size
    (d) in the same raceway or cable or be in close proximity in the same trench

38. Direct-buried conductors, cables, or raceways which are subject to movement by settlement or frost shall be arranged to prevent damage to the _____ or to equipment connected to the raceways.
    (a) cable
    (b) raceway
    (c) enclosed conductors
    (d) expansion fitting

39. Raceways, cable trays, cablebus, auxiliary gutters, cable armor, boxes, cable sheathing, cabinets, enclosures (other than surrounding fences and walls), elbows, couplings, fittings, supports, and support hardware shall be of materials suitable for _____.
    (a) corrosive locations
    (b) wet locations
    (c) the environment in which they are to be installed
    (d) damp locations

40. Where corrosion protection is necessary and the conduit is threaded anywhere other than at the factory where the product is listed, the threads shall be coated with a(an) _____ electrically conductive, corrosion-resistant compound.
    (a) marked
    (b) listed
    (c) labeled
    (d) approved

41. Where portions of cable raceways or sleeves are required to be sealed due to different temperatures, sealants shall be identified for use with _____, a bare conductor, a shield, or other components.
    (a) low temperature conditions
    (b) high temperature conditions
    (c) a stranded conductor
    (d) cable insulation or conductor insulation

42. Raceways shall be provided with expansion, expansion-deflection, or deflection fittings where necessary to compensate for thermal expansion, deflection, and _____.
    (a) contraction
    (b) warping
    (c) bending
    (d) cracking

43. Where raceways are installed in wet locations above grade, the interior of these raceways shall be considered a _____ location.
    (a) wet
    (b) dry
    (c) damp
    (d) corrosive

44. Metal raceways, cable armor, and other metal enclosures shall be _____ joined together into a continuous electric conductor so as to provide effective electrical continuity.
    (a) electrically
    (b) permanently
    (c) metallically
    (d) physically

Article 300 | General Requirements for Wiring Methods and Materials

45. Raceways, cable assemblies, boxes, cabinets, and fittings shall be _____ fastened in place.

    (a) securely
    (b) supported and
    (c) approved as
    (d) none of these

46. Where independent support wires of a suspended ceiling assembly are used to support raceways, cable assemblies, or boxes above a ceiling, they shall be secured at _____ end(s).

    (a) one
    (b) both
    (c) the line and load
    (d) at the attachment to the structural member

47. Wiring located within the cavity of a fire-rated floor-ceiling or roof-ceiling assembly shall not be secured to, or supported by, the ceiling assembly, including the ceiling support _____.

    (a) wires
    (b) hangers
    (c) rods
    (d) none of these

48. Raceways may be used as a means of support where the raceway contains power-supply conductors for electrically controlled equipment and is used to _____ Class 2 or Class 3 circuit conductors or cables that are solely for the purpose of connection to the equipment control circuits.

    (a) support
    (b) secure
    (c) strap
    (d) none of these

49. Cable wiring methods shall not be used as a means of support for _____.

    (a) other cables
    (b) raceways
    (c) nonelectrical equipment
    (d) any of these

50. Raceways, cable armors, and cable sheaths shall be _____ between cabinets, boxes, conduit bodies, fittings, or other enclosures or outlets.

    (a) continuous
    (b) protected
    (c) buried
    (d) encased in concrete

51. Mechanical continuity of raceways, cable armors, and cable sheaths as required by 300.12 does not apply to _____.

    (a) Type MI Cable
    (b) Type MC Cable
    (c) short sections of raceways used for support or protection of cable assemblies
    (d) any of these

52. Conductors in raceways shall be _____ between outlets, boxes, devices, and so forth.

    (a) continuous
    (b) installed
    (c) copper
    (d) in conduit

53. In multiwire branch circuits, the continuity of a(an) _____ shall not depend on device connections such as lampholders, receptacles, and so forth.

    (a) ungrounded conductor
    (b) grounded conductor
    (c) grounding electrode
    (d) raceway

54. Where the opening to an outlet, junction, or switch point is less than 8 in. in any dimension, the length of free conductor of each conductor, spliced or unspliced, shall extend at least _____ outside the opening of the enclosure.

    (a) 1 in.
    (b) 3 in.
    (c) 6 in.
    (d) 12 in.

55. Fittings and connectors shall be used only with the specific wiring methods for which they are _____ and listed.

    (a) designed
    (b) identified
    (c) marked
    (d) labeled

56. A box or conduit body shall not be required for splices and taps in _____ conductors and cables as long as the splice is made with a splicing device that is identified for the purpose.

    (a) direct-buried
    (b) exposed
    (c) concealed
    (d) none of these

57. The number and size of conductors and cables in any raceway shall not be more than will _____.

    (a) permit dissipation of heat
    (b) prevent damage to insulation during installation
    (c) prevent damage to insulation during removal of conductors
    (d) all of these

58. Raceways shall be _____ between outlet, junction, or splicing points prior to the installation of conductors.

    (a) installed complete
    (b) tested for ground faults
    (c) a minimum of 80 percent complete
    (d) torqued

59. Short sections of raceways used for _____ shall not be required to be installed complete between outlet, junction, or splicing points.

    (a) meter to service enclosure connection(s)
    (b) protection of cables from physical damage
    (c) nipples
    (d) separately derived systems

60. A vertical run of 4/0 AWG shall be supported at intervals not exceeding _____.

    (a) 40 ft
    (b) 80 ft
    (c) 100 ft
    (d) 120 ft

61. Size 3/0 AWG conductors installed in vertical raceways shall be supported at least every _____.

    (a) 60 ft
    (b) 80 ft
    (c) 100 ft
    (d) 180 ft

62. Conductors carrying alternating current installed in ferrous metal raceways or enclosures shall be arranged so as to avoid heating the surrounding ferrous metal by induction. To accomplish this, the _____ conductor(s) shall be grouped together.

    (a) phase
    (b) grounded
    (c) equipment grounding
    (d) all of these

63. _____ is(are) a nonferrous, nonmagnetic metal that has no heating due to hysteresis heating.

    (a) Steel
    (b) Iron
    (c) Aluminum
    (d) all of these

64. Electrical installations in hollow spaces, vertical shafts, and ventilation or air-handling ducts shall be made so that the possible spread of fire or products of combustion will not be _____.

    (a) substantially increased
    (b) allowed
    (c) inherent
    (d) possible

65. Electrical installations in hollow spaces shall be made so as to not increase the spread of fire, such as boxes installed in a wall cavity on opposite sides of a fire-rated wall where a minimum horizontal separation of _____ usually applies between boxes.

    (a) 6 in.
    (b) 12 in.
    (c) 18 in.
    (d) 24 in.

66. No wiring of any type shall be installed in ducts used to transport _____.

    (a) dust
    (b) flammable vapors
    (c) loose stock
    (d) all of these

Article 300 | General Requirements for Wiring Methods and Materials

67. Equipment and devices shall only be permitted within ducts to transport environmental air if necessary for their direct action upon, or sensing of, the _____.

    (a) contained air
    (b) air quality
    (c) air temperature
    (d) humidity

68. The space above a hung ceiling used for environmental air-handling purposes is an example of _____.

    (a) a specifically fabricated duct used for environmental air [300.22(B)]
    (b) other space used for environmental air (plenum) [300.22(C)]
    (c) a supply duct used for environmental air [300.22(B)]
    (d) a supplemental return duct used for environmental air [300.22(C)]

69. Wiring methods permitted in ceiling areas used for environmental air include _____.

    (a) electrical metallic tubing
    (b) flexible metallic conduit
    (c) RMC without an overall nonmetallic covering
    (d) all of these

70. _____ is(are) permitted to support the wiring methods and equipment in other spaces used for environmental air.

    (a) Metal cable tray systems
    (b) Nonmetallic wireways
    (c) PVC conduit
    (d) Surface nonmetallic raceways

71. Electrical equipment with a metal enclosure, or electrical equipment with a nonmetallic enclosure listed for use within an air-handling space and having low _____ release properties are permitted to be installed in other spaces used for environmental air.

    (a) resistance
    (b) impedance
    (c) and high temperature
    (d) smoke and heat

72. Cables, raceways, and _____ installed behind suspended-ceiling panels shall be arranged and secured to allow access to the electrical equipment.

    (a) equipment
    (b) appliances
    (c) cords
    (d) conductors

73. Where an exit enclosure (stair tower) is required to have a fire-resistance rating, only electrical wiring methods serving equipment permitted by the _____ in the exit enclosure shall be installed within the exit enclosure.

    (a) fire code official
    (b) building code official
    (c) authority having jurisdiction
    (d) electrical engineer

74. Where an exit enclosure (stair tower) is required to have _____ lighting on outside exterior doorways from the exit enclosure, luminaires shall be permitted to be supplied from the inside of the exit enclosure.

    (a) normal
    (b) emergency
    (c) egress
    (d) standby

ARTICLE 310 — CONDUCTORS FOR GENERAL WIRING

Introduction to Article 310—Conductors for General Wiring

This article contains the general requirements for conductors such as their insulation markings, ampacity ratings, and conditions of use. It does not apply to conductors that are part of flexible cords, fixture wires, or to those that are an integral part of equipment [90.7 and 300.1(B)]. Some topics covered in this material include:

- Conductor Size and Material
- Insulation Types
- Conductor Identification and Marking
- Conductor Ampacity

Article 310 consists of three parts:

- Part I. General
- Part II. Construction Specifications
- Part III. Installation

Please use the 2023 *Code* book to answer the following questions.

1. The minimum size copper conductor permitted for voltage ratings up to 2000V is _____.

    (a) 14 AWG
    (b) 12 AWG
    (c) 10 AWG
    (d) 8 AWG

2. Solid aluminum conductors of 8 AWG, 10 AWG, and 12 AWG shall be made of an AA-_____ series electrical grade aluminum alloy conductor material.

    (a) 1350
    (b) 2000
    (c) 6000
    (d) 8000

Article 310 | Conductors for General Wiring

3. Stranded aluminum conductors 8 AWG through 1000 kcmil marked as _____ shall be made of an AA-8000 series electrical grade aluminum alloy conductor material.
   (a) Type UF
   (b) Type NM
   (c) Type NMC
   (d) Type SE

4. The _____ core of a copper-clad aluminum conductor shall be made of an AA-8000 series electrical grade aluminum alloy conductor material.
   (a) aluminum
   (b) copper
   (c) steel
   (d) iron

5. Conductors in Article 300 shall be of copper, aluminum, or copper-clad aluminum, unless otherwise specified. Copper-clad aluminum conductor material shall be _____.
   (a) identified for the use
   (b) listed
   (c) indicated as suitable
   (d) approved

6. Where installed in raceways, conductors _____ and larger shall be stranded, unless specifically permitted or required elsewhere in the *NEC*.
   (a) 10 AWG
   (b) 8 AWG
   (c) 6 AWG
   (d) 4 AWG

7. Conductors for general wiring not specifically permitted elsewhere in this *Code* to be covered or bare shall _____.
   (a) not be permitted
   (b) be insulated
   (c) be rated
   (d) be listed

8. Insulated conductors with the letters "HH" in their designation have a _____ insulation rating in a dry location.
   (a) 60°C
   (b) 75°C
   (c) 90°C
   (d) 110°C

9. Insulated conductors with letter designation of _____, are permitted in a wet location with a maximum operating temperature of 90°C.
   (a) USE
   (b) RHW
   (c) XHWN
   (d) THWN-2

10. Conductors with Type TW insulation have a temperature rating of _____.
    (a) 60°C
    (b) 75°C
    (c) 90°C
    (d) 110°C

11. The insulation of USE-2 cable is _____ resistant.
    (a) heat
    (b) moisture
    (c) sunlight
    (d) heat and moisture

12. Conductors that are intended for use as ungrounded conductors, whether used as a single conductor or in multiconductor cables, shall be finished to be clearly distinguishable from _____ conductors.
    (a) grounded
    (b) ungrounded
    (c) equipment grounding
    (d) grounded and equipment grounding

13. The conductors described in 310.4 shall be permitted for use in any of the _____ covered in Chapter 3 and as specified in their respective tables or as permitted elsewhere in this *Code*.
    (a) wiring methods
    (b) cables
    (c) conduits
    (d) tubing

14. Insulated conductors and cables used in _____ shall be any of the types identified in this *Code*.
    (a) dry and damp locations
    (b) dry locations
    (c) damp locations
    (d) wet and damp locations

15. Insulated conductors and cables used in _____ shall be Types FEP, FEPB, MTW, PFA, RHH, RHW, RHW-2, SA, THHN, THW, THW-2, THHW, THWN, THWN-2, TW, XHH, XHHW, XHHW-2, XHHN, XHWN, XHWN-2, Z, or ZW.

    (a) dry and damp locations
    (b) dry locations
    (c) damp locations
    (d) wet and damp locations

16. Insulated conductors and cables used in wet locations shall be _____.

    (a) moisture-impervious metal-sheathed
    (b) types MTW, RHW, RHW-2, TW, THW, THW-2, THHW, THWN, THWN-2, XHHW, XHHW-2, XHWN, XHWN-2 or ZW
    (c) of a type listed for use in wet locations
    (d) any of these

17. In general, the minimum size conductor permitted for parallel installations is _____.

    (a) 10 AWG
    (b) 4 AWG
    (c) 1 AWG
    (d) 1/0 AWG

18. Parallel conductors shall have the same _____.

    (a) length
    (b) conductor material
    (c) size in circular mil area
    (d) all of these

19. Where conductors in parallel are run in _____ raceway(s), the raceway(s) shall have the same electrical characteristics.

    (a) separate
    (b) similar
    (c) the same
    (d) different

20. Where there are no adjustment or correction factors required, the service conductors for a rated service of _____ supplying the entire load associated with an individual dwelling unit, Table 310.12(A) shall be permitted to be applied.

    (a) 100A
    (b) 200A
    (c) 400A
    (d) all of these

21. Where there are no adjustment or correction factors required, the feeder conductors rated between 100A and _____ supplying the entire load associated with an individual dwelling unit, Table 310.12(A) shall be permitted to be applied..

    (a) 150A
    (b) 200A
    (c) 300A
    (d) 400A

22. No conductor shall be used where its _____ temperature exceeds that designated for the type of insulated conductor involved.

    (a) operating
    (b) ambient
    (c) highest
    (d) lowest

23. The _____ rating of a conductor is the maximum temperature, at any location along its length, which the conductor can withstand over a prolonged period of time without serious degradation.

    (a) ampacity
    (b) temperature
    (c) conductivity
    (d) short-circuit

24. There are four principal determinants of conductor operating temperature, one of which is _____ generated internally in the conductor as the result of load current flow, including fundamental and harmonic currents.

    (a) friction
    (b) magnetism
    (c) heat
    (d) compatibility

25. In accordance with Article 310, temperature correction and adjustment factors are permitted to be applied to the ampacity for the temperature rating of the _____, if the corrected and adjusted ampacity does not exceed the ampacity for the temperature rating of the termination in accordance with 110.14(C).

    (a) conductor
    (b) feeder
    (c) service
    (d) termination

Article 310 | Conductors for General Wiring

26. For raceways exposed to direct sunlight on or above rooftops where the distance above the roof to the bottom of the raceway or cable is less than _____, a temperature adder of 60°F shall be added to the outdoor temperature to determine the ambient temperature correction factor.

    (a) ¼ in.
    (b) ⅓ in.
    (c) ½ in.
    (d) ¾ in.

27. Type _____ insulated conductors shall not be subject to ampacity adjustment where installed exposed to direct sunlight on a rooftop.

    (a) THW-2
    (b) XHHW-2
    (c) THWN-2
    (d) RHW-2

28. Conductor adjustment factors shall not apply to conductors in raceways having a length not exceeding _____.

    (a) 12 in.
    (b) 24 in.
    (c) 36 in.
    (d) 48 in.

29. Where six current-carrying conductors are run in the same conduit, the ampacity of each conductor shall be adjusted to _____ of its ampacity.

    (a) 40 percent
    (b) 60 percent
    (c) 80 percent
    (d) 90 percent

30. A raceway contains two three-phase, 4-wire circuits where the neutrals carry only the unbalanced current from the other conductors. The ampacity adjustment factor for these conductors is _____.

    (a) 70 percent
    (b) 80 percent
    (c) 90 percent
    (d) 100 percent

31. A(An) _____ conductor that carries only the unbalanced current from other conductors of the same circuit shall not be required to be counted when applying the provisions of 310.15(C)(1).

    (a) neutral
    (b) ungrounded
    (c) grounding
    (d) bonded

32. In a 3-wire circuit consisting of two phase conductors and the neutral conductor of a 4-wire, three-phase, wye-connected system, the neutral conductor shall _____ when applying the provisions of 310.15(C)(1).

    (a) be counted
    (b) not be counted
    (c) be reduced
    (d) be ignored

33. On a 4-wire, three-phase wye circuit where the major portion of the neutral load consists of _____ loads, the neutral conductor shall be considered a current-carrying conductor.

    (a) 240V
    (b) 277V
    (c) nonlinear
    (d) linear

34. For the purposes of ampacity adjustment, when determining the number of current-carrying conductors, a grounding or bonding conductor _____ be counted when applying the provisions of 310.15(C)(1).

    (a) shall not
    (b) shall
    (c) is permitted to
    (d) can

35. The minimum size THHN conductor for a 150A noncontinuous load is _____.

    (a) 1 AWG
    (b) 1/0 AWG
    (c) 2/0 AWG
    (d) 3/0 AWG

36. The minimum conductor size required for a 60A load if the terminals are rated 75°C is _____ THW copper.

    (a) 2 AWG
    (b) 4 AWG
    (c) 6 AWG
    (d) 8 AWG

37. The minimum size THW service-entrance conductors for a 200A commercial service is _____.

    (a) 2/0 AWG
    (b) 3/0 AWG
    (c) 4/0 AWG
    (d) 250 KCMIL

38. The maximum allowable ampacity for each of 6 THW conductors in a raceway is _____.

    (a) 55A
    (b) 65A
    (c) 70A
    (d) 80A

Notes

ARTICLE 312

CABINETS, CUTOUT BOXES, AND METER SOCKET ENCLOSURES

Introduction to Article 312—Cabinets, Cutout Boxes, and Meter Socket Enclosures

Article 312 covers the installation and construction specifications for cabinets for panelboards, cutout boxes for disconnects, and meter socket enclosures. Notice that these rules cover the cabinets and enclosures that contain electrical equipment such as panel boards—not the equipment itself. Some topics covered in this material include:

- Damp and Wet Locations
- Repairing Noncombustible Surfaces
- Deflection of Conductors
- Space in Enclosures
- Screws or Other Fasteners

This article consists of two parts:

- Part I. General
- Part II. Construction Specifications

Please use the 2023 *Code* book to answer the following questions.

1. The ampacities specified in Table 310.16 apply to _____.
   (a) conductors rated 60°C, 75°C, or 90°C
   (b) wiring installed in an ambient temperature of 86°F
   (c) where there is not more than three current-carrying conductors
   (d) all of these

2. Article _____ covers the installation and construction specifications of cabinets, cutout boxes, and meter socket enclosures.
   (a) 300
   (b) 310
   (c) 312
   (d) 314

Article 312 | Cabinets, Cutout Boxes, and Meter Socket Enclosures

3. Cabinets, cutout boxes, and meter socket enclosures installed in wet locations shall be _____.

    (a) waterproof
    (b) raintight
    (c) weatherproof
    (d) watertight

4. In walls constructed of wood or other _____ material, electrical cabinets shall be flush with the finished surface or project therefrom.

    (a) nonconductive
    (b) porous
    (c) fibrous
    (d) combustible

5. Noncombustible surfaces that are broken or incomplete shall be repaired so there will be no gaps or open spaces greater than _____ at the edge of a cabinet or cutout box employing a flush-type cover.

    (a) 1/32 in.
    (b) 1/16 in.
    (c) 1/8 in.
    (d) 1/4 in.

6. Where cable is used, each cable shall be _____ to the cabinet, cutout box, or meter socket enclosure.

    (a) secured
    (b) supported
    (c) strapped
    (d) stapled

7. Nonmetallic-sheathed cables can enter the top of surface-mounted cabinets, cutout boxes, and meter socket enclosures through nonflexible raceways not less than 18 in. and not more than _____ in length if all of the required conditions are met.

    (a) 3 ft
    (b) 10 ft
    (c) 25 ft
    (d) 100 ft

8. The minimum wire-bending space and gutter width at terminals for 4/0 AWG entering an enclosure is _____.

    (a) 4 in.
    (b) 6 in.
    (c) 7 in.
    (d) 8 in.

9. The minimum wire-bending space and gutter width at terminals for 500 kcmil entering an enclosure is _____.

    (a) 4 in.
    (b) 6 in.
    (c) 7 in.
    (d) 8 in.

10. The wiring space within enclosures for _____ and overcurrent devices shall be permitted for other wiring and equipment subject to limitations for specific equipment in accordance with Article 312.

    (a) receptacles
    (b) luminaires
    (c) signs
    (d) switches

11. Enclosures for switches or overcurrent devices are allowed to have conductors feeding through where the wiring space at any cross section is not filled to more than _____ of the cross-sectional area of the space.

    (a) 20 percent
    (b) 30 percent
    (c) 40 percent
    (d) 60 percent

12. Cabinets, cutout boxes, and meter socket enclosures can be used for conductors feeding through, spliced, or tapping off to other enclosures, switches, or overcurrent devices where _____.

    (a) the total area of the conductors at any cross section does not exceed 40 percent of the cross-sectional area of that space
    (b) the total area of conductors, splices, and taps installed at any cross section does not exceed 75 percent of the cross-sectional area of that space
    (c) a warning label on the enclosure identifies the closest disconnecting means for any feed-through conductors
    (d) all of these

13. Screws or other fasteners installed in the field that enter wiring spaces of cabinets and cutout boxes shall be as provided by or specified by the manufacturer or _____.

    (a) screws shall be machine type
    (b) other fasteners shall have blunt ends
    (c) screws or other fasteners shall extend no more than ¼ in. into the enclosure unless the end is protected with an approved means
    (d) any of these

14. Screws or other fasteners installed in the field that enter wiring spaces of cabinets and cutout boxes shall be permitted to extend into the enclosure not more than ⁷⁄₁₆ in. if located within _____ of an enclosure wall.

    (a) ⅛ in.
    (b) ¼ in.
    (c) ⅜ in.
    (d) ½ in.

Notes

ARTICLE 314 — BOXES, CONDUIT BODIES, AND HANDHOLE ENCLOSURES

Introduction to Article 314—Boxes, Conduit Bodies, and Handhole Enclosures

This article contains the installation requirements for outlet and device boxes, pull and junction boxes, conduit bodies, and handhole enclosures. Some topics covered in this material include:

- Round, Nonmetallic, and Metal Boxes
- Screws and Fasteners
- Number of Conductors in a Box or Conduit Body
- Conductor and Cables Entering Boxes
- Boxes Enclosing Devices or Equipment
- Surface- and Flush-Mounted Installations
- Repairing Noncombustible Surfaces Around Boxes
- Depth and Dimensions of Boxes
- Covers and Canopies
- Outlet Box, Pull Box, Junction Box, and Conduit Body Rules
- Accessibility

Article 314 consists of four parts:

- Part I. General
- Part II. Installation
- Part III. Use on Systems over 1000 Volts, Nominal (not covered in this material)
- Part IV. Construction Specifications

Article 314 | Boxes, Conduit Bodies, and Handhole Enclosures

Please use the 2023 *Code* book to answer the following questions.

1. The installation and use of all boxes and conduit bodies used as outlet, device, junction, or pull boxes, depending on their use, and handhole enclosures, are covered within _____.

    (a) Article 110
    (b) Article 200
    (c) Article 300
    (d) Article 314

2. Nonmetallic boxes can be used with _____.

    (a) nonmetallic sheaths
    (b) nonmetallic raceways
    (c) flexible cords
    (d) all of these

3. Where internal _____ means are provided between all entries, nonmetallic boxes shall be permitted to be used with metal raceways or metal-armored cables.

    (a) grounding
    (b) bonding
    (c) connecting
    (d) splicing

4. Metal boxes shall be _____ in accordance with Article 250.

    (a) grounded
    (b) bonded
    (c) secured
    (d) grounded and bonded

5. Screws or other fasteners installed in the field that enter wiring spaces of outlet, device, pull, or junction boxes, shall be permitted to be longer than specified in 314.5(3) through (6) if the end of the screw is protected with _____ means.

    (a) a listed
    (b) an approved
    (c) an identified
    (d) any of these

6. Screws or other fasteners installed in the field that enter wiring spaces of outlet and device boxes shall be as provided by or specified by the manufacturer or shall _____.

    (a) have blunt ends
    (b) extend no more than 3⁄8 in. if attaching a cover
    (c) extend no more than 5⁄16 in. if penetrating a cover
    (d) all of these

7. Screws or other fasteners installed in the field that enter wiring spaces penetrating a wall of a pull or junction box exceeding 100 cu in. shall extend no more than 1⁄4 in., or more than 7⁄16 in. if located within _____ of cabinets and cutout boxes of an adjacent box wall.

    (a) 1⁄8 in.
    (b) 1⁄4 in.
    (c) 3⁄8 in.
    (d) 1⁄2 in.

8. Screws or other fasteners installed in the field that enter wiring spaces penetrating a wall of a pull or junction box not exceeding 100 cu in. and not covered in 314.23(B)(1) shall be made _____.

    (a) within 1⁄8 in. of the box interior
    (b) within 1⁄4 in. of the box interior
    (c) within 3⁄8 in. of the box interior
    (d) flush with the box interior

9. In accordance with Article 314, screws or other fasteners installed in the field that enter wiring spaces penetrating the wall of a conduit body shall be made _____.

    (a) within 1⁄8 in. of the conduit body
    (b) within 1⁄4 in. of the conduit body
    (c) within 3⁄8 in. of the conduit body
    (d) flush with the conduit body

10. Boxes, conduit bodies, and fittings installed in wet locations shall be listed for use in _____ locations.

    (a) wet
    (b) damp
    (c) dry
    (d) corrosive

11. Boxes and conduit bodies shall be of an approved size to provide free space for all enclosed _____.

    (a) conductors
    (b) splices
    (c) terminations
    (d) all of these

12. According to the *NEC*, the volume of a 3 in. × 2 in. × 2 in. device box for conductor fill is _____.

    (a) 8 cu in.
    (b) 10 cu in.
    (c) 12 cu in.
    (d) 14 cu in.

13. A metal box sized _____ can accommodate nine 12 AWG conductors.

    (a) 4 in. × 4 in. × 1¼ in.
    (b) 3¾ in. × 2 in. × 3 in.
    (c) 3¾ in. × 2 in. × 3-½ in.
    (d) none of these

14. The number of 12 AWG THWN-2 conductors permitted in a 4 in. × 4 in. × 1½ in. box is _____.

    (a) 7
    (b) 9
    (c) 11
    (d) 13

15. The total volume occupied by two internal cable clamps, six 12 AWG conductors, and a single-pole switch is _____.

    (a) 2.00 cu in.
    (b) 4.50 cu in.
    (c) 14.50 cu in.
    (d) 20.25 cu in.

16. When counting the number of conductors in a box, a conductor running through the box with an unbroken loop or coil not less than twice the minimum length required for free conductors shall be counted as _____ double volume(s) allowance.

    (a) one
    (b) two
    (c) three
    (d) four

17. Equipment grounding conductor(s), and not more than _____ fixture wire(s) smaller than 14 AWG is(are) permitted to be omitted from the calculations where they enter the box from a domed luminaire or similar canopy and terminate within that box.

    (a) one
    (b) two
    (c) three
    (d) four

18. Where one or more internal cable clamps are present in the box, a single volume allowance shall be made based on the _____ present in the box.

    (a) largest conductor
    (b) smallest conductor
    (c) average conductor size
    (d) number of devices

19. Where a luminaire stud or hickey is present in the box, _____ volume allowance shall be made for each type of fitting, based on the largest conductor present in the box.

    (a) a single
    (b) a double
    (c) a ¼
    (d) no additional

20. For the purposes of determining box fill, each device or utilization equipment in the box which is wider than a single device box counts as two volume allowances for each _____ required for the mounting.

    (a) in.
    (b) ft
    (c) gang
    (d) box

21. A device or utilization equipment wider than a single 2 in. device box shall have _____ volume allowance provided for each gang required for mounting.

    (a) a single
    (b) a double
    (c) a ¼
    (d) no additional

Article 314 | Boxes, Conduit Bodies, and Handhole Enclosures

22. Where up to four equipment grounding conductors enter a box, _____ volume allowance in accordance with Table 314.16(b) shall be made based on the largest equipment grounding conductor entering the box.

    (a) a single
    (b) a double
    (c) a ¼
    (d) no additional

23. Conduit bodies that are durably and legibly marked by the manufacturer with their _____ can contain splices, taps, or devices.

    (a) volume
    (b) size
    (c) rating
    (d) capacity

24. Where cable assemblies with nonmetallic sheaths are used, the sheath shall extend not less than _____ inside the box and beyond any cable clamp.

    (a) ¼ in.
    (b) ⅜ in.
    (c) ½ in.
    (d) ¾ in.

25. In installations within noncombustible walls or ceilings, the front edge of a box, plaster ring, extension ring, or listed extender employing a flush-type cover, shall be set back not more than _____ from the finished surface.

    (a) ⅛ in.
    (b) ¼ in.
    (c) ⅜ in.
    (d) ½ in.

26. In installations within walls or ceilings constructed of wood or other combustible surface material, boxes, plaster rings, extension rings, or listed extenders shall _____.

    (a) extend to the finished surface or project therefrom
    (b) not be permitted
    (c) be fire rated
    (d) be set back no more than ¼ in.

27. Noncombustible surfaces that are broken or incomplete around boxes employing a flush-type cover shall be repaired so there will be no gaps or open spaces larger than _____ at the edge of the box.

    (a) 1/16 in.
    (b) ⅛ in.
    (c) ¼ in.
    (d) ½ in.

28. Surface extensions shall be made by mounting and _____ securing an extension ring over the box, unless otherwise permitted.

    (a) mechanically
    (b) electrically
    (c) physically
    (d) solidly

29. An outlet box or enclosure mounted on a building or other surface shall be _____.

    (a) rigidly and securely fastened in place
    (b) supported by cables that protrude from the box
    (c) supported by cable entries from the top and permitted to rest against the supporting surface
    (d) permitted to be supported by the raceway(s) terminating at the box

30. In accordance with Article 314, metal braces used for the support of boxes shall be protected against _____.

    (a) corrosion
    (b) weather
    (c) rain
    (d) snow

31. A wood brace used for supporting a box for structural mounting shall have a cross-section not less than nominal _____.

    (a) 1 in. × 2 in.
    (b) 2 in. × 2 in.
    (c) 2 in. × 3 in.
    (d) 2 in. × 4 in.

32. When mounting an enclosure in a finished surface, the enclosure shall be _____ secured to the surface by clamps, anchors, or fittings identified for the application.

    (a) temporarily
    (b) partially
    (c) never
    (d) rigidly

33. Outlet boxes can be secured to suspended-ceiling framing members by mechanical means such as _____, or by other means identified for use with the suspended-ceiling framing member(s).

    (a) bolts
    (b) screws
    (c) rivets
    (d) any of these

34. Support wire(s) used for enclosure support in suspended ceilings shall be fastened at _____ so as to be taut within the ceiling cavity.

    (a) each end
    (b) each corner
    (c) each ceiling support
    (d) the ceiling grid

35. Enclosures not over 100 cu in. having threaded entries and not containing a device shall be considered to be supported where _____ or more conduits are threaded wrenchtight into the enclosure and each conduit is secured within 3 ft of the enclosure.

    (a) one
    (b) two
    (c) three
    (d) four

36. Two intermediate metal or rigid metal conduits threaded wrenchtight into an enclosure can be used to support an outlet box containing devices or luminaires if each raceway is supported within _____ of the box.

    (a) 12 in.
    (b) 18 in.
    (c) 24 in.
    (d) 36 in.

37. A pendant box shall be supported from a multiconductor cord or cable in an approved manner that protects the conductors against strain. A connection to a box equipped with a hub shall be made with a(an) _____ cord grip attachment fitting marked for use with a threaded hub.

    (a) approved
    (b) listed
    (c) marked
    (d) identified

38. Boxes used at luminaire outlets on a vertical surface shall be marked on the interior of the box to indicate the maximum weight of the luminaire that is permitted to be supported by the box if other than _____.

    (a) 6 lb
    (b) 12 lb
    (c) 35 lb
    (d) 50 lb

39. A vertically mounted luminaire weighing not more than _____ can be supported to a device box or plaster ring with no fewer than two No. 6 or larger screws.

    (a) 4 lb
    (b) 6 lb
    (c) 8 lb
    (d) 10 lb

40. Boxes used at luminaire or lampholder outlets in a ceiling shall be designed so that a luminaire or lampholder can be attached and the boxes shall be required to support a luminaire weighing a minimum of _____.

    (a) 20 lb
    (b) 30 lb
    (c) 40 lb
    (d) 50 lb

41. A luminaire that weighs more than _____ can be supported by an outlet box that is listed for the weight of the luminaire.

    (a) 20 lb
    (b) 30 lb
    (c) 40 lb
    (d) 50 lb

Article 314 | Boxes, Conduit Bodies, and Handhole Enclosures

42. Floor boxes _____ specifically for the application shall be used for receptacles located in the floor.

    (a) identified
    (b) listed
    (c) approved
    (d) designed

43. Listed outlet boxes to support ceiling-suspended fans that weigh more than _____ shall have the maximum allowable weight marked on the box.

    (a) 35 lb
    (b) 50 lb
    (c) 60 lb
    (d) 70 lb

44. Outlet boxes mounted in the ceilings of habitable rooms _____, in a location acceptable for the future installation of a ceiling-suspended (paddle) fan, shall be listed for the support of ceiling-suspended paddle fans.

    (a) used for childcare
    (b) of guest suites
    (c) of dwelling occupancies
    (d) of apartments

45. Utilization equipment weighing not more than 6 lb can be supported to any box or plaster ring secured to a box, provided the equipment is secured with at least two _____ or larger screws.

    (a) No. 6
    (b) No. 8
    (c) No. 10
    (d) No. 12

46. In straight pulls of 2-in. raceways, the length of the pull box shall be a minimum of _____ the trade diameter of the 2-in. raceway.

    (a) 8 times
    (b) 7 times
    (c) 5 times
    (d) 10 times

47. The minimum distance from the raceway entry to the opposite wall of a pull or junction box for a U pull with two 3-in. raceways is _____.

    (a) 16 in.
    (b) 15 in.
    (c) 18 in.
    (d) 21 in.

48. Where splices, angle, or U pulls are made, the distance between each raceway entry inside the box and the opposite wall of the box may not be less than _____ the trade size of the largest raceway.

    (a) six times
    (b) eight times
    (c) ten times
    (d) twelve times

49. The minimum depth required for a pull box in a wet location that has a 3½ in. raceway with three 400 kcmil XHHW compact aluminum conductors entering the wall opposite a removable cover is _____.

    (a) 6 in.
    (b) 7 in.
    (c) 21 in.
    (d) 28 in.

50. Where a raceway or cable entry is in the wall of a box or conduit body opposite a removable cover, the distance from that wall to the cover shall be permitted to comply with the distance required for _____ wire(s) per terminal in accordance with Table 312.6(A).

    (a) one
    (b) two
    (c) three
    (d) four

51. Pull boxes or junction boxes with any dimension over _____ shall have all conductors cabled or racked in an approved manner.

    (a) 3 ft
    (b) 6 ft
    (c) 9 ft
    (d) 12 ft

52. Underground _____ shall be installed so they are accessible without excavating sidewalks, paving, earth, or other substance that is to be used to establish the finished grade.

    (a) boxes and handhole enclosures
    (b) conduit bodies
    (c) handhole enclosures
    (d) none of these

53. Handhole enclosures shall be designed and installed to withstand _____.

    (a) 600 lb of pressure
    (b) 3000 lb of pressure
    (c) 6000 lb of pressure
    (d) all loads likely to be imposed on them

54. Underground raceways and cable assemblies entering a handhole enclosure shall extend into the enclosure, but they are not required to be _____.

    (a) bonded
    (b) insulated
    (c) mechanically connected to the enclosure
    (d) electrically connected to the enclosure

55. Conductors, splices, or terminations in a handhole enclosure shall be listed as suitable for _____.

    (a) wet locations
    (b) damp locations
    (c) direct burial in the earth
    (d) exterior use

56. Handhole enclosure covers shall have an identifying mark or logo that prominently identifies the function of the enclosure, such as "_____."

    (a) danger
    (b) utility
    (c) high voltage
    (d) electric

57. Handhole enclosure covers shall require the use of tools to open, or they shall weigh over _____.

    (a) 45 lb
    (b) 70 lb
    (c) 100 lb
    (d) 200 lb

Notes

ARTICLE 320 ARMORED CABLE (TYPE AC)

Introduction to Article 320—Armored Cable (Type AC)

Article 320 covers the use, installation, and construction specifications of armored cable (Type AC). AC cable is an assembly of up to four phase conductors and one neutral insulated conductor, sizes 14 AWG through 1 AWG, individually wrapped in a moisture-resistant, fire-retardant paper contained within a flexible spiral metal sheath. Some topics covered in this material include:

- Listing Requirements
- Uses Permitted
- Uses Not Permitted
- Installation in Accessible Roof Spaces
- Bending Radius
- Securing and Supporting
- Ampacity
- Construction
- Marking

This article consists of three parts:

- Part I. General
- Part II. Installation
- Part III. Construction Specifications

Please use the 2023 *Code* book to answer the following questions.

1. Article _____ covers the use, installation, and construction specifications for armored cable, Type AC.

    (a) 300
    (b) 310
    (c) 320
    (d) 334

2. Type AC cable and associated fittings shall be _____.

    (a) identified
    (b) approved
    (c) listed
    (d) labeled

Article 320 | Armored Cable (Type AC)

3. Type AC cable is permitted in _____.

   (a) wet locations
   (b) corrosive conditions
   (c) damp locations
   (d) cable trays

4. Armored cable shall not be installed _____.

   (a) in damp or wet locations
   (b) where subject to physical damage
   (c) where exposed to corrosive conditions
   (d) all of these

5. Exposed runs of Type AC cable can be installed on the underside of joists where supported at each joist and located so it is not subject to physical damage.

   (a) physical damage
   (b) severe damage
   (c) minor damage
   (d) any of these

6. Type AC cable installed through, or parallel to, framing members shall be protected against physical damage from penetration by _____.

   (a) screws
   (b) nails
   (c) screws or nails
   (d) none of these

7. Where Type AC cable is run across the top of a framing member(s) in an attic space not accessible by permanently installed stairs or ladders, guard strip protection shall only be required within _____ of the scuttle hole or attic entrance.

   (a) 3 ft
   (b) 4 ft
   (c) 5 ft
   (d) 6 ft

8. The radius of the curve of the inner edge of any bend shall not be less than _____ for Type AC cable.

   (a) five times the largest conductor within the cable
   (b) three times the diameter of the cable
   (c) five times the diameter of the cable
   (d) six times the outside diameter of the conductors

9. Type AC cable shall be supported and/or secured by _____.

   (a) staples or straps
   (b) cable ties listed and identified for securement and support
   (c) Type AC cable fittings
   (d) any of these

10. Type AC cable fittings shall not be permitted as a means of cable support.

    (a) True
    (b) False

11. Type AC cable shall be secured at intervals not exceeding 4½ ft and within _____ of every outlet box, cabinet, conduit body, or fitting.

    (a) 6 in.
    (b) 8 in.
    (c) 10 in.
    (d) 12 in.

12. Horizontal runs of Type AC cable installed in wooden or metal framing members or similar supporting means shall be considered supported and secured where such support does not exceed _____ intervals.

    (a) 2-ft
    (b) 3-ft
    (c) 4½-ft
    (d) 6-ft

13. Armored cable used to connect recessed luminaires or equipment within an accessible ceiling can be unsupported and unsecured for lengths up to _____.

    (a) 2 ft
    (b) 3 ft
    (c) 4½ ft
    (d) 6 ft

14. Type AC cable installed in thermal insulation shall have conductors that are rated at 90°C. The ampacity of the cable in this application shall not exceed that of a _____ rated conductor.

    (a) 60°C
    (b) 75°C
    (c) 90°C
    (d) 100°C

15. Type AC cable shall provide an adequate path for _____ to act as an equipment grounding conductor.

    (a) fault current
    (b) short-circuit current
    (c) overcurrent
    (d) arcing current

Notes

ARTICLE 330

METAL-CLAD CABLE (TYPE MC)

Introduction to Article 330—Metal-Clad Cable (Type MC)

This article covers the use, installation, and construction specifications of metal-clad cable (Type MC). Type MC cable is an assembly of any number of insulated conductors, 18 AWG through 2000 kcmil, with an overall polypropylene wrap enclosed in a metal sheath of either corrugated or smooth copper or aluminum tubing, or in spiral interlocked steel or aluminum. Some topics covered in this material include:

- Listing Requirements
- Uses Permitted
- Uses Not Permitted
- Installation in Accessible Roof Spaces
- Bending Radius
- Securing and Supporting
- Ampacity
- Construction
- Marking

Article 330 consists of three parts:

- Part I. General
- Part II. Installation
- Part III. Construction Specifications

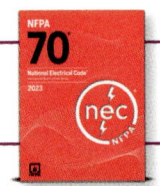

Please use the 2023 *Code* book to answer the following questions.

1. Article _____ covers the use, installation, and construction specifications of metal-clad cable, Type MC.

    (a) 300
    (b) 310
    (c) 320
    (d) 330

2. Type MC cable shall be listed and fittings used for connecting Type MC cable to boxes, cabinets, or other equipment shall _____.

    (a) be nonmetallic only
    (b) be listed and identified for such use
    (c) be listed and identified as weatherproof
    (d) include anti-shorting bushings

Article 330 | Metal-Clad Cable (Type MC)

3. Type MC cable shall be permitted for _____.
   (a) branch circuits
   (b) feeders
   (c) services
   (d) any of these

4. Type MC cable is permitted for use in damp or wet locations where a corrosion-resistant jacket is provided over the metallic covering and _____.
   (a) the metallic covering is impervious to moisture.
   (b) a jacket resistant to moisture is provided under the metal covering.
   (c) the insulated conductors under the metallic covering are listed for use in wet locations.
   (d) any of these

5. Type MC cable shall not be used _____.
   (a) where subject to physical damage
   (b) direct buried in the earth or embedded in concrete unless identified for direct burial
   (c) exposed to cinder fills, strong chlorides, caustic alkalis, or vapors of chlorine or of hydrochloric acids
   (d) all of these

6. Exposed runs of Type MC cable, except as provided in 300.11(B), shall closely follow the surface of the _____.
   (a) building finish
   (b) running boards
   (c) underside of joists
   (d) any of these

7. Type MC cable installed through, or parallel to, framing members shall be protected against physical damage from penetration by screws or nails by _____ separation or protected by a suitable metal plate.
   (a) 1¼ in.
   (b) 1½ in.
   (c) 3¼ in.
   (d) 3½ in.

8. Smooth-sheath Type MC cable with an external diameter not greater than ¾ in. shall have a bending radius not less than _____ times the external diameter of the cable.
   (a) five
   (b) ten
   (c) twelve
   (d) thirteen

9. Bends made in interlocked or corrugated sheath Type MC cable shall have a radius of at least _____ times the external diameter of the metallic sheath.
   (a) five
   (b) seven
   (c) ten
   (d) twelve

10. Type MC cable shall be supported and secured by staples; cable ties _____ for securement and support; straps, hangers, or similar fittings; or other approved means designed and installed so as not to damage the cable.
    (a) listed and identified
    (b) marked or labeled
    (c) installed and approved
    (d) any of these

11. Type MC cable fittings shall be permitted as a means of cable support.
    (a) True
    (b) False

12. Unless otherwise permitted in the *Code*, Type MC cable shall be secured at intervals not exceeding _____.
    (a) 3 ft
    (b) 4 ft
    (c) 6 ft
    (d) 8 ft

13. Type MC cable containing four or fewer conductors, sized no larger than 10 AWG, shall be secured within _____ of every box, cabinet, fitting, or other cable termination.
    (a) 8 in.
    (b) 12 in.
    (c) 18 in.
    (d) 24 in.

14. Unless otherwise permitted in the *Code*, Type MC cable installed horizontally through wooden or metal framing members is considered secured and supported where such support does not exceed _____ intervals.

    (a) 3-ft
    (b) 4-ft
    (c) 6-ft
    (d) 8-ft

15. Type MC cable can be unsupported and unsecured where the cable is _____.

    (a) fished between access points through concealed spaces in finished buildings or structures
    (b) not more than 2 ft in length at terminals where flexibility is necessary
    (c) not more than 8 ft from the last point of support within an accessible ceiling
    (d) installed in attic spaces

Notes

ARTICLE 334

NONMETALLIC-SHEATHED CABLE (TYPE NM)

Introduction to Article 334—Nonmetallic-Sheathed Cable (Type NM)

Article 334 covers the use, installation, and construction specifications of nonmetallic-sheathed cable (Type NM). Type NM cable is an assembly of insulated conductors and an insulated or bare equipment grounding conductor, 14 AWG through 2AWG, with an overall nonmetallic flame-retardant sheath. This type of cable provides limited physical protection for the conductors inside the sheath, so its uses are limited by the building construction type. Its low cost and relative ease of installation makes it a common wiring method for residential and light commercial applications. Some topics covered in this material include:

- Listing Requirements
- Uses Permitted
- Uses Not Permitted
- Exposed Work
- Installation in Accessible Roof Spaces
- Bending Radius
- Securing and Supporting
- Ampacity
- Construction
- Marking

This article consists of three parts:

- Part I. General
- Part II. Installation
- Part III. Construction Specifications

Article 334 | Nonmetallic-Sheathed Cable (Type NM)

Please use the 2023 *Code* book to answer the following questions.

1. Type NM cable and associated fittings shall be _____.
   (a) marked
   (b) approved
   (c) identified
   (d) listed

2. Type NM and Type NMC cables are permitted in _____, except as prohibited in 334.12.
   (a) one- and two-family dwellings and their attached/detached garages and storage buildings
   (b) multifamily dwellings and their detached garages permitted to be of Types III, IV, and V construction
   (c) other structures permitted to be of Types III, IV, and V construction
   (d) any of these

3. Type NM cable can be installed in multifamily dwellings and their detached garages permitted to be of Type(s) _____ construction.
   (a) III
   (b) IV
   (c) V
   (d) all of these

4. Type NM cable shall not be permitted to be installed _____ in dropped or suspended ceilings in other than one- and two-family and multifamily dwellings.
   (a) concealed
   (b) exposed
   (c) open
   (d) hidden

5. Type NM cable shall not be used _____.
   (a) in other than dwelling units
   (b) in the air void of masonry block not subject to excessive moisture
   (c) for exposed work
   (d) embedded in poured cement, concrete, or aggregate

6. Type NM cable shall closely follow the _____ of the building finish or running boards when run exposed.
   (a) surface
   (b) edges
   (c) corners
   (d) none of these

7. Type NM cable shall be protected from physical damage by _____.
   (a) EMT
   (b) Schedule 80 PVC conduit
   (c) RMC
   (d) any of these

8. Where conduit or tubing is used for the protection from physical damage of Type NM cable, it shall be provided with a bushing or adapter that provides protection from abrasion at the point the cable _____ the raceway.
   (a) enters and exits
   (b) leaves and comes into
   (c) begins and ends
   (d) none of these

9. Where Type NM cable is run at angles with joists in unfinished basements and crawl spaces, it is permissible to secure cables not smaller than _____ conductors directly to the lower edges of the joist.
   (a) three, 6 AWG
   (b) four, 8 AWG
   (c) four, 10 AWG
   (d) two 6 AWG or three 8 AWG

10. Type NM cable on a wall of an unfinished basement installed in a listed raceway shall have a _____ installed at the point where the cable enters the raceway.
    (a) suitable insulating bushing or adapter
    (b) sealing fitting
    (c) bonding bushing
    (d) junction box

11. Grommets or bushings for the protection of Type NM cable installed through or parallel to framing members shall be _____ for the purpose.

    (a) marked
    (b) approved
    (c) identified
    (d) listed

12. The sheath on nonmetallic-sheathed cable shall extend not less than _____ beyond any cable clamp or cable entry.

    (a) 1/8 in.
    (b) 1/4 in.
    (c) 3/8 in.
    (d) 1/2 in.

13. When Type NM cable is run across the top of a floor joist in an attic without permanent ladders or stairs, guard strips within _____ of the scuttle hole or attic entrance shall protect the cable.

    (a) 3 ft
    (b) 4 ft
    (c) 5 ft
    (d) 6 ft

14. The radius of the curve of the inner edge of any bend during or after installation of Type NM cable shall not be less than _____ the diameter of the cable or the major diameter dimension of the cable for flat cables.

    (a) 5 times
    (b) 6 times
    (c) 7 times
    (d) 8 times

15. Type NM cable can be supported and secured by _____.

    (a) staples
    (b) cable ties listed and identified for securement and support
    (c) straps
    (d) any of these

16. Flat Type NM cables shall not be stapled on edge.

    (a) True
    (b) False

17. Nonmetallic-sheathed cable shall be permitted to be unsupported where the cable is _____.

    (a) fished between access points through concealed spaces in finished buildings or structures
    (b) not more than 6 ft from the last point of cable support to the point of connection to a luminaire within an accessible ceiling in one-, two-, or multifamily dwellings
    (c) between framing members and exterior masonry walls
    (d) where installed in attics

18. A box is not required for Type NM cable where used with _____.

    (a) self-contained switches
    (b) self-contained receptacles
    (c) listed nonmetallic-sheathed cable interconnector devices
    (d) any of these

19. The 90°C rating shall be permitted to be used for ampacity adjustment and correction calculations for Type NM cable, provided the final calculated ampacity does not exceed that of a _____ rated conductor.

    (a) 60°C
    (b) 75°C
    (c) 90°C
    (d) 104°C

20. Where more than two NM cables are installed through the same bored hole in wood framing that is to be sealed with _____, the ampacity of each conductor shall be adjusted.

    (a) thermal insulation
    (b) caulk
    (c) sealing foam
    (d) any of these

21. For Types NM and NMC cable, the _____ rating shall be permitted to be used for ampacity adjustment and correction calculations, provided the final calculated ampacity does not exceed that of a 60°C rated conductor.

    (a) 60°C
    (b) 75°C
    (c) 90°C
    (d) 104°C

Article 334 | Nonmetallic-Sheathed Cable (Type NM)

22. In addition to the insulated conductors, Type NM cable shall have a(an) _____ equipment grounding conductor.

   (a) insulated
   (b) bare
   (c) covered
   (d) any of these

ARTICLE 336
POWER AND CONTROL TRAY CABLE (TYPE TC)

Introduction to Article 336—Power and Control Tray Cable (Type TC)

This article covers the use and installation of power and control tray cable (Type TC). Type TC cable is flexible, inexpensive, and easily installed making it an attractive wiring method for industrial applications and for generators. Some topics covered in this material include:

- Listing Requirements
- Uses Permitted
- Uses Not Permitted
- Exposed Work
- Bending Radius
- Ampacity
- Construction
- Marking

Article 336 consists of three parts:

- Part I. General
- Part II. Installation
- Part III. Construction Specifications

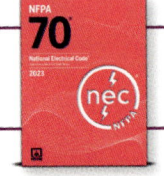

Please use the 2023 *Code* book to answer the following questions.

1. Article _____ covers the use, installation, and construction specifications for power and control tray cable, Type TC.

    (a) 326
    (b) 330
    (c) 334
    (d) 336

2. Type TC cable and associated fittings shall be _____.

    (a) identified
    (b) approved
    (c) listed
    (d) labeled

Article 336 | Power and Control Tray Cable (Type TC)

3. Type TC cable can be used _____.
   (a) for power, lighting, control, and signal circuits
   (b) in cable trays including those with mechanically discontinuous segments up to 1 ft
   (c) for Class 1 control circuits as permitted in Parts II and III of Article 725
   (d) all of these

4. Type TC-ER-JP cable shall be permitted for _____ in one- and two-family dwelling units.
   (a) branch circuits
   (b) feeders
   (c) branch circuits and feeders
   (d) service conductors

5. Where Type TC-ER-JP cable is used to connect a generator and associated equipment having terminals rated _____ or higher, the cable shall not be limited in ampacity by 334.80 or 340.80.
   (a) 60°C
   (b) 75°C
   (c) 90°C
   (d) 100°C

6. Type TC cable shall be permitted to be direct buried, where _____ for such use.
   (a) identified
   (b) approved
   (c) listed
   (d) labeled

7. Type TC cable shall be permitted for use in hazardous (classified) locations where specifically _____ by other articles in this *Code*.
   (a) required
   (b) permitted
   (c) approved
   (d) identified

8. Which of following statements about power and control tray cable is incorrect?
   (a) It may be used in a raceway.
   (b) It may be used for power, lighting, or control circuits.
   (c) It may be installed where it will be exposed to physical damage.
   (d) It may be used in cable trays in hazardous locations where the conditions of maintenance and supervision ensure that only qualified persons will service the installation.

9. Type TC cable shall not be used where _____.
   (a) it will be exposed to physical damage
   (b) installed outside of a raceway or cable tray system, unless permitted in 336.10(4), 336.10(7), 336.10(9), and 336.10(10)
   (c) exposed to direct rays of the sun, unless identified as sunlight resistant
   (d) all of these

10. Bends in Type TC cable shall be made so as not to damage the cable. For TC Cable larger than 1 in. and up to 2 in. in diameter, without metal shielding, the minimum bending radius shall be at least _____ times the overall diameter of the cable.
    (a) 2 times
    (b) 3 times
    (c) 5 times
    (d) 7 times

ARTICLE 338 — SERVICE-ENTRANCE CABLE (TYPES SE AND USE)

Introduction to Article 338—Service-Entrance Cable (Types SE and USE)

Article 338 covers the use, installation, and construction specifications of service-entrance cable (Types SE and USE). These cables can be a single conductor or a multiconductor assembly in sizes 14 AWG and larger for copper, and 12 AWG and larger for aluminum or copper-clad aluminum, within an overall nonmetallic outer jacket or covering. Some topics covered in this material include:

- Listing Requirements
- Uses Permitted
- Uses Not Permitted
- Bending Radius
- Construction
- Marking

This article consists of three parts:

- Part I. General
- Part II. Installation
- Part III. Construction Specifications

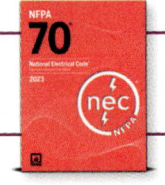

Please use the 2023 *Code* book to answer the following questions.

1. Types SE and USE cables and associated fittings shall be _____.
   (a) identified
   (b) approved
   (c) listed
   (d) labeled

2. _____ cable can be used for interior wiring as long as it complies with the installation requirements of Part II of Article 334, excluding 334.80.
   (a) Type SE
   (b) Type UF
   (c) Type MI
   (d) Type FCC

Article 338 | Service-Entrance Cable (Types SE and USE)

3. Where more than two Type SE cables are installed in contact with thermal insulation, caulk, or sealing foam without maintaining spacing between cables, the ampacity of each conductor shall be _____ in accordance with Table 310.15(C)(1).

    (a) increased
    (b) adjusted
    (c) corrected
    (d) multiplied

4. For interior installations of Type SE cable with ungrounded conductor sizes _____ and smaller, where installed in thermal insulation, the ampacity shall be in accordance with 60°C (140°F) conductor temperature rating.

    (a) 14 AWG
    (b) 12 AWG
    (c) 10 AWG
    (d) 8 AWG

5. Type USE cable is not permitted for _____ wiring.

    (a) underground
    (b) interior
    (c) aerial
    (d) aboveground installations

6. The radius of the curve of the inner edge of any bend, during or after installation, shall not be less than _____ the diameter of Types USE or SE cable.

    (a) 5 times
    (b) 7 times
    (c) 10 times
    (d) 12 times

ARTICLE 340 UNDERGROUND FEEDER AND BRANCH-CIRCUIT CABLE (TYPE UF)

Introduction to Article 340—Underground Feeder and Branch-Circuit Cable (Type UF)

This article covers the use, installation, and construction specifications of underground feeder and branch-circuit cable (Type UF). Type UF cable is an assembly of conductors in sizes 14 AWG through 4/0 AWG [340.104] covered in a moisture-, fungus-, and corrosion-resistant sheath suitable for direct burial in the Earth. The sheath of multiconductor Type UF cable is a molded plastic that encases the insulated conductors. It can be difficult to strip off the sheath without damaging the conductor insulation or cutting yourself, so be careful. Some topics covered in this material include:

- Listing Requirements
- Uses Permitted
- Uses Not Permitted
- Bending Radius
- Construction

Article 340 consists of three parts:

- Part I. General
- Part II. Installation
- Part III. Construction Specifications

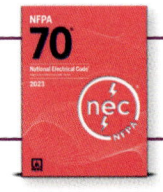

Please use the 2023 *Code* book to answer the following questions.

1. Article 340 covers the use, installation, and construction specifications for underground feeder and branch-circuit cable, Type _____.
   (a) USE
   (b) UF
   (c) UFC
   (d) NMC

2. Type UF cable and associated fittings shall be _____.
   (a) identified
   (b) approved
   (c) listed
   (d) labeled

Article 340 | Underground Feeder and Branch-Circuit Cable (Type UF)

3. The ampacity of Type UF cable shall be that of _____ conductors in accordance with 310.14.

   (a) 60°C
   (b) 75°C
   (c) 90°C
   (d) 105°C

ARTICLE 342
INTERMEDIATE METAL CONDUIT (IMC)

Introduction to Article 342—Intermediate Metal Conduit (IMC)

Article 342 covers the use, installation, and construction specifications of intermediate metal conduit (IMC) and associated fittings. IMC is a circular metal raceway that can be threaded and is available in trade sizes from ½ to 6. It has the same outside diameter as rigid metal conduit (RMC) [Article 344] but is made of a stronger metal which allows a thinner wall, making it lighter and providing a larger interior cross-sectional area for holding conductors. Some topics covered in this material include:

- Listing Requirements
- Uses Permitted
- Dissimilar Metals
- Bending, Reaming, and Threading
- Securing and Supporting
- Bushings
- Use as an Equipment Grounding Conductor
- Construction

This article consists of three parts:

- Part I. General
- Part II. Installation
- Part III. Construction Specifications

Please use the 2023 *Code* book to answer the following questions.

1. A permitted wiring method for use in underground installations is _____.

   (a) Type SE cable
   (b) Type UF cable
   (c) Type THHN in PVC conduit
   (d) Type NM in a raceway

2. Type UF cable is permitted to be installed as single-conductor cables, when all conductors of the feeder or branch circuit, including the grounded conductor and equipment grounding conductor, if any, are _____.

   (a) run in the same trench
   (b) within a nonmetallic raceway
   (c) within a metallic raceway
   (d) none of these

Article 342 | Intermediate Metal Conduit (IMC)

3. Type UF cable can be used as service entrance cable.
   (a) True
   (b) False

4. Type UF cable can be used in commercial garages.
   (a) True
   (b) False

5. Type UF cable shall not be used in _____.
   (a) motion picture studios
   (b) storage battery rooms
   (c) hoistways
   (d) all of these

6. Type UF cable shall not be used _____.
   (a) in any hazardous (classified) location except as otherwise permitted in this *Code*
   (b) embedded in poured cement, concrete, or aggregate
   (c) where exposed to direct rays of the sun, unless identified as sunlight resistant
   (d) all of these

7. Type UF cable shall not be used where subject to physical damage.
   (a) True
   (b) False

8. Article _____ covers the use, installation, and construction specifications for intermediate metal conduit (IMC) and associated fittings.
   (a) 342
   (b) 348
   (c) 352
   (d) 356

9. IMC, elbows, couplings, and fittings shall be permitted to be installed in concrete, in direct contact with the earth, in direct burial applications, or in areas subject to severe corrosive influences where protected by corrosion protection _____ for the condition.
   (a) identified
   (b) approved
   (c) listed
   (d) suitable

10. Type IMC conduit shall be permitted to be installed where subject to _____ physical damage.
    (a) severe
    (b) minor
    (c) minimal
    (d) massive

11. Where practicable, contact of dissimilar metals shall be avoided in an IMC raceway installation to prevent the possibility of _____.
    (a) corrosion
    (b) galvanic action
    (c) short circuits
    (d) ground faults

12. The total degrees of bends in a run of IMC shall not exceed _____ between pull points.
    (a) 120 degrees
    (b) 180 degrees
    (c) 270 degrees
    (d) 360 degrees

13. Where intermediate metal conduit is threaded in the field, a standard cutting die with a taper of _____ per ft shall be used.
    (a) ½ in.
    (b) ¾ in.
    (c) 1 in.
    (d) 1½ in.

14. IMC shall be secured _____.
    (a) by fastening within 3 ft of each outlet box, junction box, device box, cabinet, conduit body, or other conduit termination
    (b) within 5 ft of a box or termination fitting when structural members do not readily permit the raceway to be secured within 3 ft of the termination
    (c) except when the IMC is within 3 ft of the service head for an above-the-roof termination of a mast
    (d) any of these

15. Trade size 1 IMC run straight with threaded couplings shall be supported at intervals not exceeding _____.
    (a) 8 ft
    (b) 10 ft
    (c) 12 ft
    (d) 15 ft

16. Horizontal runs of IMC supported by openings through framing members at intervals not exceeding _____ and securely fastened within 3 ft of terminations shall be permitted.

    (a) 5 ft
    (b) 8 ft
    (c) 10 ft
    (d) 15 ft

17. Threadless couplings approved for use with IMC in wet locations shall be _____.

    (a) rainproof
    (b) listed for wet locations
    (c) moistureproof
    (d) concrete-tight

18. Running threads shall not be used on IMC for connection at _____.

    (a) couplings
    (b) terminal adapters
    (c) enclosures
    (d) threadless connectors

19. Where IMC enters a box, fitting, or other enclosure, _____ shall be provided to protect the wire from abrasion unless the design of the box, fitting, or enclosure affords equivalent protection.

    (a) a bushing
    (b) duct seal
    (c) electrical tape
    (d) seal fittings

Notes

ARTICLE 344
RIGID METAL CONDUIT (RMC)

Introduction to Article 344—Rigid Metal Conduit (RMC)

This article covers the use, installation, and construction specifications of rigid metal conduit (RMC) and associated fittings. RMC, commonly called "rigid," has long been the standard raceway used to protect conductors from physical damage and from difficult environments. This type of conduit is available in trade sizes up to 6, can be threaded, and has the same outside diameter as intermediate metal conduit but has a thicker wall. It can be made of a variety of metals including steel, aluminum, red brass, and stainless steel. Some topics covered in this material include:

- Listing Requirements
- Uses Permitted
- Dissimilar Metals
- Size
- Bending, Reaming, and Threading
- Securing and Supporting
- Bushings
- Use as an Equipment Grounding Conductor
- Construction

Article 344 consists of three parts:

- Part I. General
- Part II. Installation
- Part III. Construction Specifications

Article 344 | Rigid Metal Conduit (RMC)

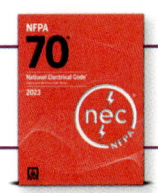

Please use the 2023 *Code* book to answer the following questions.

1. Article 344 covers the use, installation, and construction specifications for _____ conduit and associated fittings.
   (a) intermediate metal
   (b) rigid metal
   (c) electrical metallic
   (d) aluminum metal

2. RMC and fittings are permitted to be installed in concrete, in direct contact with the earth, in direct burial applications, or in areas subject to severe corrosive influences when protected by _____ approved for the condition.
   (a) ceramic
   (b) corrosion protection
   (c) backfill
   (d) a natural barrier

3. All supports, bolts, straps, screws, and so forth, associated with the installation of RMC in wet locations shall be _____.
   (a) weatherproof
   (b) made of stainless steel
   (c) made of aluminum
   (d) protected against corrosion

4. Type RMC conduit shall be permitted to be installed where subject to _____ physical damage.
   (a) severe
   (b) minor
   (c) minimal
   (d) massive

5. Stainless steel and aluminum fittings and enclosures shall be permitted to be used with galvanized steel RMC, and galvanized steel fittings and enclosures shall be permitted to be used with aluminum RMC where not subject to _____.
   (a) physical damage
   (b) severe corrosive influences
   (c) excessive moisture
   (d) all of these

6. RMC smaller than trade size _____ or larger than trade size _____ shall not be used.
   (a) ¾, 4
   (b) ½, 4
   (c) ½, 6
   (d) ¾, 6

7. The total degrees of bends in a run of RMC shall not exceed _____ between pull points.
   (a) 120 degrees
   (b) 180 degrees
   (c) 270 degrees
   (d) 360 degrees

8. Cut ends of RMC shall be _____ or otherwise finished to remove rough edges.
   (a) threaded
   (b) reamed
   (c) painted
   (d) galvanized

9. PVC-coated RMC shall be _____ in accordance with manufacturer's instructions to prevent damage to the exterior coating.
   (a) threaded
   (b) cut
   (c) bent
   (d) none of these

10. RMC shall be securely fastened within _____ of each outlet box, junction box, device box, cabinet, conduit body, or other conduit termination.
    (a) 3 ft
    (b) 4 ft
    (c) 5 ft
    (d) 6 ft

11. Where framing members do not readily permit fastening, RMC may be fastened within _____ of each outlet box, junction box, device box, cabinet, conduit body, or other conduit termination.

    (a) 3 ft
    (b) 4 ft
    (c) 5 ft
    (d) 8 ft

12. Where approved, RMC shall not be required to be securely fastened within _____ of the service head for above-the-roof termination of a mast.

    (a) 1 ft
    (b) 2 ft
    (c) 3 ft
    (d) 5 ft

13. Trade size 2 MC run straight with threaded couplings shall be supported at intervals not exceeding _____.

    (a) 10 ft
    (b) 12 ft
    (c) 14 ft
    (d) 16 ft

14. The maximum distance between supports for a vertical installation of trade size 2 RMC is _____.

    (a) 16 ft
    (b) 10 ft
    (c) 20 ft
    (d) 18 ft

15. Horizontal runs of RMC supported by openings through _____ at intervals not exceeding 10 ft and securely fastened within 3 ft of termination points shall be permitted.

    (a) walls
    (b) trusses
    (c) rafters
    (d) framing members

16. Threadless couplings and connectors used with RMC buried in masonry or concrete shall be the _____ type.

    (a) raintight
    (b) wet and damp location
    (c) nonabsorbent
    (d) concrete tight

17. Threadless couplings and connectors used with RMC in wet locations shall be _____.

    (a) listed for wet locations
    (b) listed for damp locations
    (c) nonabsorbent
    (d) weatherproof

18. Running threads shall not be used on RMC for connection at _____.

    (a) boxes
    (b) cabinets
    (c) couplings
    (d) meter sockets

19. Where RMC enters a box, fitting, or other enclosure, _____ shall be provided to protect the wire from abrasion, unless the design of the box, fitting, or enclosure affords equivalent protection.

    (a) a bushing
    (b) duct seal
    (c) electrical tape
    (d) seal fittings

Notes

ARTICLE 348
FLEXIBLE METAL CONDUIT (FMC)

Introduction to Article 348—Flexible Metal Conduit (FMC)

Article 348 covers the use, installation, and construction specifications for flexible metal conduit (FMC) and associated fittings. FMC, commonly called "flex" or sometimes "Greenfield" (after its inventor), is a raceway made a spiral interlocked steel or aluminum strip. It is primarily used where flexibility is necessary or where equipment moves, shakes, or vibrates. Some topics covered in this material include:

- Listing Requirements
- Uses Permitted
- Uses Not Permitted
- Size
- Bending and Trimming
- Securing and Supporting
- Couplings and Connectors
- Splices and Taps
- Use as an Equipment Grounding Conductor

This article consists of two parts:

- Part I. General
- Part II. Installation

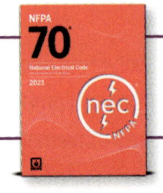

Please use the 2023 *Code* book to answer the following questions.

1. Article 348 covers the use, installation, and construction specifications for flexible metal conduit (FMC) and associated _____.
   (a) fittings
   (b) connections
   (c) terminations
   (d) devices

2. FMC shall be permitted to be used in exposed locations only.
   (a) True
   (b) False

Article 348 | Flexible Metal Conduit (FMC)

3. FMC shall not be installed _____.
   (a) in wet locations
   (b) embedded in poured concrete
   (c) where subject to physical damage
   (d) all of these

4. Bends in FMC shall be made so that the conduit is not damaged and the internal diameter of the conduit is _____.
   (a) larger than ⅜ in.
   (b) not effectively reduced
   (c) increased
   (d) larger than 1 in.

5. The total degrees of bends in a run of FMC _____ between pull points.
   (a) shall not be made
   (b) need not be limited (in degrees)
   (c) shall not exceed 360 degrees
   (d) shall not exceed 180 degrees

6. Cut ends of FMC shall be trimmed or otherwise finished to remove rough edges, except where fittings _____.
   (a) are the crimp-on type
   (b) thread into the convolutions
   (c) contain insulated throats
   (d) are listed for grounding

7. Flexible metal conduit shall be supported at intervals not exceeding _____.
   (a) 1 ft
   (b) 3 ft
   (c) 4½ ft
   (d) 6 ft

8. Cable ties used to securely fasten flexible metal conduit shall be _____ for securement and support.
   (a) approved
   (b) labeled
   (c) listed
   (d) listed and identified

9. Flexible metal conduit shall not be required to be _____ where fished between access points through concealed spaces in finished buildings or structures and supporting is impracticable.
   (a) fastened
   (b) strapped
   (c) complete
   (d) secured and supported

10. For flexible metal conduit, if flexibility is necessary after installation, unsecured lengths from the last point the raceway is securely fastened shall not exceed _____.
    (a) 3 ft for trade sizes ½ through 1¼
    (b) 4 ft for trade sizes 1½ through 2
    (c) 5 ft for trade sizes 2½ and larger
    (d) all of these

11. FMC to a luminaire or electrical equipment within an accessible ceiling is permitted to be unsupported for not more than _____ from the last point where the raceway is securely fastened, including securement and support by listed FMC fittings.
    (a) 3 ft
    (b) 5 ft
    (c) 6 ft
    (d) 8 ft

12. FMC shall be permitted to be used as _____ when installed in accordance with 250.118(5) where flexibility is not required after installation.
    (a) an equipment grounding conductor
    (b) an expansion fitting
    (c) flexible nonmetallic connectors
    (d) adjustable supports

13. For FMC, _____ shall be installed where flexibility is necessary to minimize the transmission of vibration from equipment or to provide flexibility for equipment that requires movement after installation.
    (a) an equipment grounding conductor
    (b) an expansion fitting
    (c) flexible nonmetallic connectors
    (d) adjustable supports

ARTICLE 350

LIQUIDTIGHT FLEXIBLE METAL CONDUIT (LFMC)

Introduction to Article 350—Liquidtight Flexible Metal Conduit (LFMC)

This article covers the use, installation, and construction specifications of liquidtight flexible metal conduit (LFMC) and associated fittings. LFMC, with its associated connectors and fittings, is a flexible raceway commonly available in trade size ½ and larger. It is used for connections to equipment that vibrates or must be occasionally moved. LFMC is commonly called "Sealtight®" or "liquidtight." It is similar in use and construction to flexible metal conduit but has an outer liquidtight thermoplastic covering that provides protection from liquids and some corrosive effects. Some topics covered in this material include:

- Listing Requirements
- Uses Permitted
- Uses Not Permitted
- Size
- Number of Conductors
- Bending and Trimming
- Securing and Supporting
- Couplings and Connectors
- Splices and Taps
- Grounding and Bonding

Article 350 consists of three parts:

- Part I. General
- Part II. Installation
- Part III. Construction Specifications

Article 350 | Liquidtight Flexible Metal Conduit (LFMC)

Please use the 2023 *Code* book to answer the following questions.

1. The use, installation, and construction specifications for liquidtight flexible metal conduit (LFMC) and associated fittings are covered within Article _____.
   (a) 300
   (b) 334
   (c) 350
   (d) 410

2. The use of LFMC shall be permitted for direct burial where listed and _____ for the purpose.
   (a) marked
   (b) identified
   (c) labeled
   (d) approved

3. The minimum size liquid tight flexible metal conduit is _____.
   (a) trade size ⅜
   (b) trade size ½
   (c) trade size ¾
   (d) trade size 1

4. All cut ends of LFMC conduit shall be _____ inside and outside to remove rough edges.
   (a) sanded
   (b) trimmed
   (c) brushed
   (d) any of these

5. Liquidtight flexible metal conduit shall be securely fastened by a means approved by the authority having jurisdiction within _____ of termination.
   (a) 6 in.
   (b) 10 in.
   (c) 12 in.
   (d) 10 ft

6. Where used to securely fasten LFMC, cable ties shall be _____ for securement and support.
   (a) identified
   (b) labeled
   (c) marked
   (d) listed and identified

7. LFMC shall not be required to be secured or supported where fished between access points through _____ spaces in finished buildings or structures and supporting is impractical.
   (a) concealed
   (b) exposed
   (c) hazardous (classified)
   (d) completed

8. For liquidtight flexible metal conduit, if flexibility is necessary after installation, unsecured lengths from the last point the raceway is securely fastened shall not exceed _____.
   (a) 3 ft for trade sizes ½ through 1¼
   (b) 4 ft for trade sizes 1½ through 2
   (c) 5 ft for trade sizes 2½ and larger
   (d) all of these

9. Where flexibility is not required after installation, liquidtight flexible metal conduit shall be permitted to be used as an equipment grounding conductor when installed in accordance with _____.
   (a) 250.102
   (b) 250.118(A)(5)
   (c) 250.118(A)(6)
   (d) 348.6

10. When LFMC is used to connect equipment where flexibility is necessary to minimize the transmission of vibration from equipment or for equipment requiring movement after installation, a(an) _____ conductor shall be installed.
    (a) main bonding
    (b) grounded
    (c) equipment grounding
    (d) grounding electrode

ARTICLE 352 — RIGID POLYVINYL CHLORIDE CONDUIT (PVC)

Introduction to Article 352—Rigid Polyvinyl Chloride Conduit (PVC)

Article 352 covers the use, installation, and construction specifications of polyvinyl chloride conduit (PVC) and associated fittings. PVC is a rigid nonmetallic conduit that is available in trade sizes ½ to 6. Two wall thicknesses ("schedules") are available. Schedule 40 PVC is used in most applications that are not subject to physical damage. Schedule 80 PVC, which has the same outside diameter but a thicker wall, is used where resistance to physical damage is required. This type of conduit is inexpensive, lightweight, and easily installed. It is permitted in concrete, corrosive areas, underground, and in wet locations. Some topics covered in this material include:

- Listing Requirements
- Uses Permitted
- Uses Not Permitted
- Size
- Number of Conductors
- Bending and Trimming
- Securing and Supporting
- Expansion Fittings
- Bushings and Joints
- Splices and Taps
- Grounding and Bonding

This article consists of three parts:

- Part I. General
- Part II. Installation
- Part III. Construction Specifications

Article 352 | Rigid Polyvinyl Chloride Conduit (PVC)

Please use the 2023 *Code* book to answer the following questions.

1. Article 352 covers the use, installation, and construction specifications for _____ and associated fittings.

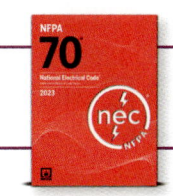

    (a) ENT
    (b) RMC
    (c) IMC
    (d) PVC

2. Extreme _____ may cause PVC conduit to become brittle, and therefore more susceptible to damage from physical contact.

    (a) sunlight
    (b) corrosive conditions
    (c) heat
    (d) cold

3. PVC conduit shall be permitted to be _____.

    (a) encased in concrete
    (b) used for the support of luminaires
    (c) installed in movie theaters
    (d) none of these

4. PVC conduit is permitted in locations subject to severe corrosive influences and where subject to chemicals for which the materials are specifically _____.

    (a) approved
    (b) identified
    (c) listed
    (d) non-hazardous

5. Schedule 40 PVC conduit shall be permitted for _____ work.

    (a) rough-in
    (b) exposed
    (c) airplane
    (d) automobile

6. Schedule _____ shall be permitted for exposed work where subject to physical damage.

    (a) 20 PVC conduit
    (b) 30 PVC conduit
    (c) 40 PVC conduit
    (d) 80 PVC conduit

7. All _____ PVC conduit fittings are suitable for connection to both Schedule 40 and Schedule 80 PVC conduit.

    (a) listed
    (b) marked
    (c) labeled
    (d) identified

8. PVC conduit shall not be used _____, unless specifically permitted.

    (a) in hazardous (classified) locations
    (b) for the support of luminaires or other equipment
    (c) where subject to physical damage unless it is Schedule 80
    (d) all of these

9. PVC smaller than trade size _____ or larger than trade size _____ shall not be used.

    (a) ½, 4
    (b) ¾, 4
    (c) ½, 6
    (d) ¾, 6

10. The number of conductors permitted in PVC conduit shall not exceed the percentage fill specified in _____.

    (a) Chapter 9, Table 1
    (b) Table 250.66
    (c) Table 310.16
    (d) 240.6

11. Field bends in PVC conduit shall be made only _____.

    (a) by hand forming the bend
    (b) with identified bending equipment
    (c) with a truck exhaust pipe
    (d) by use of an open flame torch

12. The total degrees of bends in a run of PVC shall not exceed _____ between pull points.

    (a) 120 degrees
    (b) 180 degrees
    (c) 270 degrees
    (d) 360 degrees

13. The _____ ends of PVC conduit shall be trimmed inside and outside to remove the burrs and rough edges.

    (a) cut
    (b) new
    (c) old
    (d) blunt

14. PVC conduit shall be securely fastened within _____ of each box.

    (a) ½ ft
    (b) 1 ft
    (c) 2 ft
    (d) 3 ft

15. PVC conduit trade sizes 1¼ to 2 shall be supported no greater than _____ between supports.

    (a) 3 ft
    (b) 4 ft
    (c) 5 ft
    (d) 6 ft

16. Expansion fittings for PVC conduit shall be provided to compensate for thermal expansion and contraction where the length change, in accordance with Table 352.44(A), is expected to be _____ or greater in a straight run between securely mounted items such as boxes, cabinets, elbows, or other conduit terminations.

    (a) 1/16 in.
    (b) 1/8 in.
    (c) ¼ in.
    (d) ½ in.

17. Expansion fittings for underground runs of direct buried PVC conduit emerging from the ground shall be provided above grade when required to compensate for _____.

    (a) earth settling
    (b) earth movement
    (c) frost heave
    (d) all of these

18. Where a PVC conduit enters a box, fitting, or other enclosure, a _____ or adapter shall be provided to protect the wire from abrasion unless the box, fitting, or enclosure design provides equivalent protection.

    (a) bushing
    (b) connector
    (c) coupling
    (d) insulator

19. Joints between PVC conduit, couplings, fittings, and boxes shall be made by a(an) _____ method.

    (a) listing
    (b) marking
    (c) approved
    (d) identified

20. Where equipment grounding is required, a separate grounding conductor shall be installed in Type PVC conduit except where the _____ is used to ground equipment as permitted in 250.142.

    (a) grounding jumper
    (b) grounded conductor
    (c) bonding jumper
    (d) bonded conductor

Notes

ARTICLE 356

LIQUIDTIGHT FLEXIBLE NONMETALLIC CONDUIT (LFNC)

Introduction to Article 356—Liquidtight Flexible Nonmetallic Conduit (LFNC)

This article covers the use, installation, and construction specifications of liquidtight flexible nonmetallic conduit (LFNC) and associated fittings. LFNC has an inner flexible core with an outer liquidtight, nonmetallic, sunlight-resistant jacket. It is available in trade sizes ½ to 4 and is sometimes referred to as "Carflex®." Some topics covered in this material include:

- Listing Requirements
- Uses Permitted
- Uses Not Permitted
- Size
- Number of Conductors
- Bending and Trimming
- Securing and Supporting
- Couplings and Connectors
- Grounding and Bonding

Article 356 consists of three parts:

- Part I. General
- Part II. Installation
- Part III. Construction Specifications

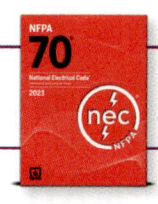

Article 356 | Liquidtight Flexible Nonmetallic Conduit (LFNC)

Please use the 2023 *Code* book to answer the following questions.

1. Article _____ covers the use, installation, and construction specifications for liquidtight flexible nonmetallic conduit (LFNC) and associated fittings.
   (a) 300
   (b) 334
   (c) 350
   (d) 356

2. When LFNC is used, and equipment grounding is required, a separate _____ shall be installed in the conduit.
   (a) grounding conductor
   (b) expansion fitting
   (c) flexible nonmetallic connector
   (d) grounded conductor

3. LFNC shall be permitted for _____.
   (a) direct burial where listed and marked for the purpose
   (b) where flexibility is required for installation, operation, or maintenance
   (c) outdoors where listed and marked for this purpose
   (d) all of these

4. LFNC shall be permitted to be used exposed or concealed in locations subject to severe _____ influences or where subject to chemicals for which the materials are specifically approved.
   (a) corrosive
   (b) wet
   (c) dry
   (d) damp

5. Extreme cold can cause some types of liquidtight flexible nonmetallic conduit to become _____ and therefore more susceptible to damage from physical contact.
   (a) stiff
   (b) larger
   (c) weak
   (d) brittle

6. Liquidtight nonmetallic flexible conduit is not permitted to be used _____.
   (a) where subject to physical damage
   (b) where ambient and conductor temperatures exceed its listing
   (c) in lengths greater than 6 ft unless approved
   (d) all of these

7. The number of conductors permitted in LFNC shall not exceed the percentage fill specified in _____.
   (a) Chapter 9, Table 1
   (b) Table 250.66
   (c) Table 310.16
   (d) 240.6

8. Bends in LFNC shall be made so that the conduit will not be damaged and the internal diameter of the conduit will not be effectively reduced. Bends can be made _____.
   (a) manually without auxiliary equipment
   (b) with bending equipment identified for the purpose
   (c) with any kind of conduit bending tool that will work
   (d) by the use of an open flame torch

9. The total degrees of bends in a run of LFNC shall not exceed _____ between pull points.
   (a) 120 degrees
   (b) 180 degrees
   (c) 270 degrees
   (d) 360 degrees

10. Cable ties used to secure and support LFNC shall be _____ for the application and for securing and supporting.
    (a) identified
    (b) labeled
    (c) listed
    (d) marked

11. Where Type LFNC conduit is installed in lengths exceeding _____, the conduit shall be securely fastened at intervals not exceeding 3 ft and within 12 in. on each side of every outlet box, junction box, cabinet, or fitting.

    (a) 2 ft
    (b) 3 ft
    (c) 6 ft
    (d) 10 ft

12. Securing or supporting of LFNC is not required where installed in lengths not exceeding _____ from the last point where the raceway is securely fastened for connections within an accessible ceiling to a luminaire(s) or other equipment.

    (a) 3 ft
    (b) 6 ft
    (c) 8 ft
    (d) 10 ft

Notes

ARTICLE 358

ELECTRICAL METALLIC TUBING (EMT)

Introduction to Article 358—Electrical Metallic Tubing (EMT)

Article 358 covers the use, installation, and construction specifications of electrical metallic tubing (EMT) and associated fittings. EMT is a lightweight metal tubing that is easy to bend, cut, and ream but it cannot be threaded. It is the most common raceway used in commercial and industrial installations. Some topics covered in this material include:

- Listing Requirements
- Uses Permitted
- Dissimilar Metals
- Size
- Number of Conductors
- Bending, Reaming, and Threading
- Securing and Supporting
- Use as an Equipment Grounding Conductor
- Construction

This article consists of three parts:

- Part I. General
- Part II. Installation
- Part III. Construction Specifications

Please use the 2023 *Code* book to answer the following questions.

1. Article _____ covers the use, installation, and construction specifications for electrical metallic tubing (EMT) and associated fittings.

   (a) 334
   (b) 350
   (c) 356
   (d) 358

2. The use of EMT shall be permitted in concrete in direct contact with the earth, in direct burial applications with fittings identified for direct burial, or in areas subject to severe _____ influences, where installed in accordance with 358.10(B).

   (a) corrosive
   (b) weather
   (c) sunlight
   (d) none of these

Article 358 | Electrical Metallic Tubing (EMT)

3. Galvanized steel and stainless steel EMT, elbows, couplings, and fittings can be installed in concrete, in direct contact with the earth, or in areas subject to severe corrosive influences where _____.

   (a) protected by corrosion protection
   (b) made of aluminum
   (c) made of stainless steel
   (d) listed for wet locations

4. When EMT is installed in wet locations, all supports, bolts, straps, and screws shall be _____.

   (a) made of aluminum
   (b) protected against corrosion
   (c) made of stainless steel
   (d) of nonmetallic materials only

5. EMT shall not be used where _____.

   (a) subject to severe physical damage or used for the support of luminaires or other equipment except conduit bodies no larger than the largest trade size of the tubing
   (b) embedded in concrete
   (c) protected from corrosion only by enamel
   (d) installed in wet locations

6. EMT smaller than trade size _____ or larger than trade size _____ shall not be used.

   (a) ¾, 4
   (b) ½, 4
   (c) ½, 6
   (d) ¾, 6

7. Raceway bends are not permitted to be made in any manner that will _____ the raceway.

   (a) damage
   (b) kink
   (c) change the internal diameter of
   (d) damage and change the internal diameter of

8. The total degrees of bends in a run of EMT shall not exceed _____ between pull points.

   (a) 120 degrees
   (b) 180 degrees
   (c) 270 degrees
   (d) 360 degrees

9. EMT run in unbroken lengths between termination points, are permitted to be securely fastened within _____ of each outlet box, junction box, device box, cabinet, conduit body, or other tubing termination where structural members do not readily permit fastening.

   (a) 1 ft
   (b) 3 ft
   (c) 5 ft
   (d) 10 ft

10. EMT shall be securely fastened in place at intervals not to exceed _____.

    (a) 4 ft
    (b) 5 ft
    (c) 8 ft
    (d) 10 ft

11. EMT run between termination points shall be securely fastened within _____ of each outlet box, junction box, device box, cabinet, conduit body, or other tubing termination.

    (a) 12 in.
    (b) 18 in.
    (c) 2 ft
    (d) 3 ft

12. EMT couplings and connectors shall be made up _____.

    (a) of metal
    (b) in accordance with industry standards
    (c) tight
    (d) to be readily accessible

13. EMT shall not be permitted as an equipment grounding conductor.

    (a) True
    (b) False

ARTICLE 362

ELECTRICAL NONMETALLIC TUBING (ENT)

Introduction to Article 362—Electrical Nonmetallic Tubing (ENT)

This article covers the use, installation, and construction specifications of electrical nonmetallic tubing (ENT) and associated fittings. ENT is a nonmetallic, pliable, corrugated, circular raceway. It is often referred to as "Smurf Pipe" or "Smurf Tube" after the cartoon characters by the same name because it was only available in blue when it was first available, but now comes in additional colors. This type of tubing is fragile and is not sunlight resistant, so it has limited uses. Some topics covered in this material include:

- Listing Requirements
- Uses Permitted
- Uses Not Permitted
- Size
- Number of Conductors
- Bending and Trimming
- Securing and Supporting
- Bushings
- Use as an Equipment Grounding Conductor

Article 362 consists of three parts:

- Part I. General
- Part II. Installation
- Part III. Construction Specifications

Article 362 | Electrical Nonmetallic Tubing (ENT)

Please use the 2023 *Code* book to answer the following questions.

1. Article _____ covers the use, installation, and construction specifications for electrical nonmetallic tubing (ENT) and associated fittings.

    (a) 358
    (b) 362
    (c) 366
    (d) 392

2. Where a building is supplied with a(an) _____ automatic fire protective system, ENT shall be permitted to be used within floors and ceilings, exposed or concealed, in buildings exceeding three floors above grade.

    (a) listed
    (b) identified
    (c) approved
    (d) NFPA 72

3. When a building is supplied with an approved automatic _____ system, ENT can be installed above any suspended ceiling.

    (a) fire protective
    (b) fire sprinkled
    (c) fire alarm
    (d) any of these

4. ENT and fittings can be _____, provided fittings identified for this purpose are used.

    (a) encased in poured concrete floors, ceilings, walls, and slabs
    (b) embedded in a concrete slab on grade where the tubing is placed on sand or approved screenings
    (c) installed in wet locations as permitted in 362.10
    (d) any of these

5. ENT is not permitted in hazardous (classified) locations, unless permitted in other articles of the *Code*.

    (a) True
    (b) False

6. ENT shall is permitted for direct earth burial.

    (a) True
    (b) False

7. ENT shall not be used where exposed to the direct rays of the sun, unless identified as _____.

    (a) high-temperature rated
    (b) sunlight resistant
    (c) Schedule 80
    (d) suitable for the application

8. The number of conductors permitted in ENT shall not exceed the percentage fill specified in _____.

    (a) Chapter 9, Table 1
    (b) Table 250.66
    (c) Table 310.16
    (d) 240.6

9. Cut ends of ENT shall be trimmed inside and _____ to remove rough edges.

    (a) outside
    (b) tapered
    (c) filed
    (d) beveled

10. ENT shall be installed as a _____ system in accordance with 300.18 and shall be securely _____ by an approved means and supported in accordance with 362.30(A) and (B).

    (a) complete
    (b) underground
    (c) overhead
    (d) none of these

11. Cable ties used to securely fasten ENT shall be _____ for the application and for securing and supporting.

    (a) identified
    (b) labeled
    (c) listed
    (d) identified and listed

12. Unbroken lengths of electric nonmetallic tubing shall not be required to be secured where fished between access points for _____ work in finished buildings or structures and securing is impractical.

    (a) concealed
    (b) exposed
    (c) hazardous
    (d) completed

13. Electrical nonmetallic tubing may extend a maximum of _____ from a fixture terminal connection without support for tap connections to lighting fixtures.

    (a) 3 ft
    (b) 5 ft
    (c) 10 ft
    (d) 2 ft

14. Where ENT enters a box, fitting, or other enclosure, a bushing or _____ shall be provided to protect the wire from abrasion unless the box, fitting, or enclosure design provides equivalent protection.

    (a) adapter
    (b) coupling
    (c) connector
    (d) insulator

15. Joints between lengths of ENT, couplings, fittings, and boxes shall be made by _____.

    (a) a qualified person
    (b) set screw fittings
    (c) an approved method
    (d) exothermic welding

16. Where ENT is the wiring method and equipment grounding is required, a _____ equipment grounding conductor shall be installed in the raceway.

    (a) separate
    (b) additional
    (c) supplemental
    (d) none of these

17. Where ENT is the wiring method and equipment grounding is required, the equipment grounding conductor shall not be required where the _____ conductor is used as part of the effective ground-fault path as permitted.

    (a) grounded
    (b) equipment grounding
    (c) ungrounded
    (d) none of these

Notes

ARTICLE 376 — METAL WIREWAYS

Introduction to Article 376—Metal Wireways

Article 376 covers the use, installation, and construction specifications of metal wireways and associated fittings. Metal wireways are commonly used where access to conductors inside a raceway is required to make terminations, splices, or taps to several devices at a single location. They are often incorrectly called "auxiliary gutters" or "gutters" in the field. Wireways and auxiliary gutters are similar in design but a wireway is a raceway [Article 100] while an auxiliary gutter [Article 366] is not—it is a supplemental enclosure for wiring. Some topics covered in this material include:

- Uses Permitted
- Uses Not Permitted
- Size And Number of Conductors
- Securing and Supporting
- Splices, Taps, and Power Distribution Blocks
- Use as an Equipment Grounding Conductor
- Construction

This article consists of three parts:

- Part I. General
- Part II. Installation
- Part III. Construction Specifications

Article 376 | Metal Wireways

Please use the 2023 *Code* book to answer the following questions.

1. Metal wireways shall not be permitted for _____.

   (a) exposed work
   (b) hazardous (classified) locations
   (c) wet locations
   (d) severe corrosive environments

2. For metal wireways, where single conductor cables comprising each phase, neutral, or grounded conductor of an alternating-current circuit are connected in parallel, the conductors shall be installed in groups consisting of not more than _____ per phase, neutral, or grounded conductor.

   (a) one conductor
   (b) two conductors
   (c) three conductors
   (d) four conductors

3. The purpose of having all parallel conductor sets installed in metal wireways within the same group, is to prevent _____ imbalance in the paralleled conductors due to inductive reactance.

   (a) current
   (b) voltage
   (c) inductive
   (d) all of these

4. No conductor larger than _____ shall be installed in a metal wireway.

   (a) 500 kcmil
   (b) 1000 kcmil
   (c) 2000 kcmil
   (d) that for which the wireway is designed

5. The sum of the cross-sectional areas of all conductors at any cross section of a metal wireway shall not exceed _____ of the interior cross-sectional area of the wireway.

   (a) 50 percent
   (b) 20 percent
   (c) 25 percent
   (d) 80 percent

6. The ampacity adjustment factors in 310.15(C)(1) shall be applied to a metal wireway only where the number of current-carrying conductors in any cross section of the wireway exceeds _____.

   (a) 30
   (b) 40
   (c) 50
   (d) 60

7. Where insulated conductors are deflected within a metal wireway, the wireway shall be sized to meet the bending requirements corresponding to _____ per terminal in Table 312.6(A).

   (a) one wire
   (b) two wires
   (c) three wires
   (d) four wires

8. Wireways shall be supported where run horizontally at each end and at intervals not to exceed _____.

   (a) 5 ft
   (b) 6 ft
   (c) 7 ft
   (d) 8 ft

9. Splices and taps are permitted within metal wireways provided they are accessible and shall not fill the wireway to more than _____ of its area at that point.

   (a) 35 percent
   (b) 40 percent
   (c) 55 percent
   (d) 75 percent

10. Power distribution blocks installed in metal wireways on the line side of the service equipment shall be marked "_____ for use on the line side of service equipment" or equivalent.

    (a) suitable
    (b) acceptable
    (c) allowed
    (d) approved

11. Power distribution blocks in metal wireways shall not have _____ live parts exposed within a(an) _____.

    (a) energized
    (b) concealed
    (c) insulated
    (d) uninsulated

12. Listed metal wireway shall be permitted _____ in accordance with 250.118(A)(13).

    (a) as an equipment grounding conductor
    (b) where subject to physical damage
    (c) for use in corrosive environments
    (d) to be installed through walls

Notes

ARTICLE 380 — MULTIOUTLET ASSEMBLIES

Introduction to Article 380—Multioutlet Assemblies

This article covers the use and installation requirements for multioutlet assemblies. A multioutlet assembly is a surface, flush, or free-standing raceway designed to hold conductors and receptacles. It can be assembled in the field or at the factory and is not required to be listed. Some topics covered in this material include:

- Uses Permitted
- Uses Not Permitted
- Insulated Conductors

Article 380 consists of two parts:

- Part I. General
- Part II. Installation

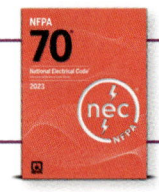

Please use the 2023 *Code* book to answer the following questions.

1. A multioutlet assembly can be installed in _____ locations.
   - (a) dry
   - (b) damp
   - (c) damp and wet
   - (d) dry and damp

2. A multioutlet assembly shall not be installed _____.
   - (a) in hoistways
   - (b) where subject to severe physical damage
   - (c) where subject to corrosive vapors
   - (d) all of these

3. Metal multioutlet assemblies can extend through (not run within) dry partitions if arrangements are made for removing the cap or cover on all _____ portions and no outlet is located within the partitions.
   - (a) exposed
   - (b) concealed
   - (c) uninsulated
   - (d) none of these

Notes

ARTICLE 386 — SURFACE METAL RACEWAYS

Introduction to Article 386—Surface Metal Raceways

Article 386 covers the use, installation, and construction specifications of surface metal raceways and associated fittings. Surface metal raceways are often used where exposed traditional raceway systems are not aesthetically pleasing and raceway concealment is not economically feasible. They come in several colors and shapes and may be referred to as "Wiremold®" in the field. Some topics covered in this material include:

- Listing Requirements
- Uses Permitted
- Uses Not Permitted
- Size And Number of Conductors
- Securing and Supporting
- Equipment Grounding Conductor Connections

This article consists of three parts:

- Part I. General
- Part II. Installation
- Part III. Construction Specifications

Please use the 2023 *Code* book to answer the following questions.

1. Article 386 covers the use, installation, and construction specifications for surface _____ and associated fittings.
   (a) nonmetallic raceways
   (b) metal raceways
   (c) metal wireways
   (d) enclosures

2. Unbroken lengths of surface metal raceways can be run through dry _____.
   (a) walls
   (b) partitions
   (c) floors
   (d) all of these

Article 386 | Surface Metal Raceways

3. Surface metal raceways shall not be used _____.
   (a) where subject to severe physical damage
   (b) where subject to corrosive vapors
   (c) in hoistways
   (d) all of these

4. The voltage between conductors in a surface metal raceway shall not exceed _____ unless the metal has a thickness of not less than 0.040 in. nominal.
   (a) 150V
   (b) 300V
   (c) 600V
   (d) 1000V

5. No conductor larger than that for which the raceway is designed shall be installed in a surface metal raceway.
   (a) True
   (b) False

6. The number of conductors or cables installed in surface metal raceways shall not _____.
   (a) exceed more than 30 percent of the inside diameter
   (b) be greater than the number for which it was designed
   (c) be more than 75 percent of the cross-sectional area
   (d) be more than that which is permitted in Table 312.6(A)

7. The ampacity adjustment factors of 310.15(C)(1) shall not apply to conductors installed in surface metal raceways where the _____.
   (a) cross-sectional area exceeds 4 sq in.
   (b) current-carrying conductors do not exceed 30 in number
   (c) total cross-sectional area of all conductors does not exceed 20 percent of the interior cross-sectional area of the raceway
   (d) all of these

8. Surface metal raceways and associated fittings shall be supported _____.
   (a) in accordance with the manufacturer's installation instructions
   (b) at intervals appropriate for the building design
   (c) at intervals not exceeding 4 ft
   (d) at intervals not exceeding 8 ft

9. Splices and taps in surface metal raceways without removable covers shall be made only in _____.
   (a) boxes
   (b) raceways
   (c) conduit bodies
   (d) none of these

10. Surface metal raceway enclosures providing a transition from other wiring methods shall have a means for connecting a(an) _____ conductor.
    (a) grounded
    (b) ungrounded
    (c) equipment grounding
    (d) all of these

ARTICLE 392 — CABLE TRAYS

Introduction to Article 392—Cable Trays

This article covers cable tray systems including ladder, ventilated trough, ventilated channel, solid bottom, and other similar structures. A cable tray system is a unit or an assembly of units or sections with associated fittings forming a structural system used to securely fasten or support cables and raceways. Some topics covered in this material include:

- Uses Permitted
- Uses Not Permitted
- Cable Tray Installation
- Conductor Installation
- Number of Conductors
- Securing and Supporting
- Expansion Splice Plates
- Grounding and Bonding
- Conductor Ampacity

This article consists of three parts:

- Part I. General
- Part II. Installation
- Part III. Construction Specifications

Article 392 | Cable Trays

Please use the 2023 *Code* book to answer the following questions.

1. Cable tray systems, including ladder, ventilated trough, ventilated channel, solid bottom, and other similar structures are covered within Article _____.

    (a) 358
    (b) 362
    (c) 366
    (d) 392

2. Cable trays can be used as a support system for _____.

    (a) service conductors, feeders, and branch circuits
    (b) communications circuits
    (c) control and signaling circuits
    (d) all of these

3. Single conductor cables and single insulated conductors used in cable trays shall be marked on the surface for use in cable trays and shall be no smaller than _____.

    (a) 1 AWG
    (b) 1/0 AWG
    (c) 2/0 AWG
    (d) 4/0 AWG

4. Cable tray systems shall not be used _____.

    (a) in hoistways
    (b) where subject to severe physical damage
    (c) in hazardous (classified) locations
    (d) in hoistways or where subject to severe physical damage

5. Cable tray systems shall be permitted to have mechanically discontinuous _____ between cable tray runs or between cable tray runs and equipment.

    (a) portions
    (b) segments
    (c) pieces
    (d) any of these

6. Each run of cable tray shall be _____ before the installation of cables.

    (a) tested for 25 ohms of resistance
    (b) insulated
    (c) completed
    (d) all of these

7. Cable trays shall be _____ except as permitted by 392.18(D).

    (a) exposed
    (b) accessible
    (c) readily accessible
    (d) exposed and accessible

8. In industrial facilities where conditions of maintenance and supervision ensure that only qualified persons will service the installation, cable tray systems can be used to support _____.

    (a) raceways
    (b) cables
    (c) boxes and conduit bodies
    (d) all of these

9. Where single conductor cables comprising each phase, neutral, or grounded conductor of a circuit are connected in parallel in a cable tray, the conductors shall be installed _____, to prevent current imbalance in the paralleled conductors due to inductive reactance.

    (a) in groups consisting of not more than three conductors per phase or neutral, or grounded conductor
    (b) in groups consisting of not more than one conductor per phase, neutral, or grounded conductor
    (c) as individual conductors securely bound to the cable tray
    (d) in separate groups

10. Cable trays shall be supported at _____ in accordance with the installation instructions.

    (a) intervals
    (b) portions
    (c) segments
    (d) any of these

11. A box is not required where conductors or cables in cable tray transition to a raceway wiring method from a _____.

    (a) cable tray
    (b) enclosure
    (c) outlet box
    (d) conduit body

12. Cable _____ made and insulated by approved methods can be located within a cable tray provided they are accessible and do not project above the side rails where the splices may be subject to physical damage.

    (a) connections
    (b) jumpers
    (c) splices
    (d) conductors

13. Steel or aluminum cable tray systems are permitted to be used as an equipment grounding conductor, provided the cable tray sections and fittings are identified as _____, among other requirements.

    (a) an equipment grounding conductor
    (b) special equipment
    (c) industrial grade
    (d) all of these

Notes

CHAPTER 4
EQUIPMENT FOR GENERAL USE

Introduction to Chapter 4—Equipment for General Use

With the first three chapters of the *NEC* behind you, this fourth one is necessary for building a solid foundation in general equipment installations. Some examples of general equipment include but are not limited to luminaires, heaters, motors, air-conditioning units, generators, and transformers. The articles in Chapter 4 help you apply the first three chapters to installations involving general equipment. You must understand the first four chapters of the *Code* to properly apply these requirements to Chapters 5, 6, and 7, and at times to Chapter 8.

Chapter 4 is arranged in the following manner:

▶ **Article 400—Flexible Cords.** Article 400 covers the general requirements, applications, and construction specifications for flexible cords.

▶ **Article 402—Fixture Wires.** This article covers the general requirements and construction specifications for fixture wires.

▶ **Article 404—Switches.** The requirements of Article 404 apply to switches of all types. These include snap (toggle) switches, dimmer switches, fan switches, knife switches, circuit breakers, and automatic switches such as time clocks, timers, and switches and circuit breakers used for disconnects.

▶ **Article 406—Receptacles and Attachment Plugs (Caps).** This article covers the rating, type, and installation of receptacles and attachment plugs. It also covers flanged surface inlets.

▶ **Article 408—Switchboards and Panelboards.** Article 408 covers specific requirements for switchboards, panelboards, and distribution boards that supply lighting and power circuits.

> **Author's Comment:**
>
> ▶ See Article 100 for the definitions of "Panelboard" and "Switchboard."

▶ **Article 410—Luminaires and Lamps.** This article contains the requirements for luminaires, lampholders, and lamps. Because of the many types and applications of luminaires, manufacturer's instructions are very important and helpful for proper installation.

▶ **Article 411—Low-Voltage Lighting.** Article 411 covers lighting systems, and their associated components, which operate at no more than 30V alternating current, or 60V direct current.

▶ **Article 422—Appliances.** This article covers electric appliances used in any occupancy.

. . .

Chapter 4 | Equipment for General Use

> **Author's Comment:**
>
> ▸ Dishwashers, water heaters, ovens, and cooktops are all appliances per the Article 100 definition. It is a very broad term covering utilization equipment that, as a unit, performs one or more functions.

▸ **Article 424—Fixed Electric Space-Heating Equipment.** Article 424 covers fixed electric equipment used for space heating. For the purpose of this article, heating equipment includes heating cable, unit heaters, boilers, central systems, and other fixed electric space-heating equipment. This article does not apply to process heating or room air-conditioning.

▸ **Article 430—Motors, Motor Circuits, and Controllers.** This article contains the specific requirements for conductor sizing, overcurrent protection, control circuit conductors, motor controllers, and disconnects. The installation requirements for motor control centers are covered in Article 430, Part VIII. This Article has fourteen parts [XIV], the most in the *Code*.

▸ **Article 440—Air-Conditioning Equipment.** Article 440 applies to electrically driven air-conditioning equipment with a motorized hermetic compressor. The requirements in this article are in addition to, or amend, those in Article 430 and others.

▸ **Article 445—Generators.** Article 445 contains the electrical installation requirements for both portable and stationary generators, both of which are required to be listed [445.6]. Installation requirements such as where they can be located, nameplate markings, conductor ampacity, and disconnects are also covered.

▸ **Article 450—Transformers.** This article covers the installation of transformers. Understanding the overcurrent protection requirements in Table 450.3(B) and the disconnect location is important to provide protection properly.

▸ **Article 480—Storage Batteries.** Article 480 covers stationary installations of storage batteries.

ARTICLE 400 FLEXIBLE CORDS

Introduction to Article 400—Flexible Cords

Article 400 covers the general requirements, applications, and construction specifications for flexible cords as contained in Table 400.4. The *NEC* does not consider flexible cords to be a wiring method like those addressed in Chapter 3 because they are not used as part of the wiring in the construction of a building. This article has four parts, but only two are within the scope of this material. Some of the topics covered here include:

- Suitability
- Types
- Ampacities
- Uses Permitted
- Uses Not Permitted
- Splices
- Overcurrent Protection
- Protection From Damage
- Construction
- Equipment Grounding Conductor

This article consists of four parts:

- Part I. General
- Part II. Construction Specifications
- Part III. Portable Cables 600V, up to 2000V, Nominal (not covered)
- Part IV. Portable Power Feeder Cables Over 2000V, Nominal (not covered)

Article 400 | Flexible Cords

Please use the 2023 *Code* book to answer the following questions.

1. Article _____ covers general requirements, applications, and construction specifications for flexible cords and flexible cables.

    (a) 300
    (b) 310
    (c) 400
    (d) 402

2. Flexible cords and flexible cables can be used for _____.

    (a) wiring of luminaires
    (b) portable and mobile signs or appliances
    (c) connection of utilization equipment to facilitate frequent interchange
    (d) all of these

3. Flexible cord sets and power-supply cords shall not be used as a substitute for _____ wiring of a structure.

    (a) temporary
    (b) fixed
    (c) concealed
    (d) permanent

4. Flexible cord sets and power-supply cords shall not be used where they are _____.

    (a) run through holes in walls, ceilings, or floors
    (b) run through doorways, windows, or similar openings
    (c) used as a substitute for the fixed wiring of a structure
    (d) all of these

5. Flexible cords, flexible cables, cord sets (extension cords), and power-supply cords are not permitted to be concealed by walls, floors, or ceilings, or above suspended or dropped ceilings.

    (a) ceilings
    (b) suspended or dropped ceilings
    (c) floors or walls
    (d) all of these

6. Unless specifically permitted in 400.10, flexible cords, flexible cables, cord sets, and power-supply cords shall not be used where subject to _____ damage.

    (a) physical
    (b) severe
    (c) harsh
    (d) minor

7. Flexible cords and flexible cables shall be connected to devices and to fittings so that tension is not transmitted to _____.

    (a) joints
    (b) terminals
    (c) joints or terminals
    (d) none of these

8. Flexible cords shall be protected by _____ where passing through holes in covers, outlet boxes, or similar enclosures.

    (a) sleeves
    (b) grommets
    (c) raceways
    (d) bushing or fittings

ARTICLE 402 — FIXTURE WIRES

Introduction to Article 402—Fixture Wires

This article covers the general requirements and construction specifications for fixture wires. Fixture wires must be of a type and size listed in Table 402.3. Some topics covered in this material include:

- Types
- Ampacities
- Minimum Size
- Identification
- Uses Permitted
- Uses Not Permitted
- Overcurrent Protection

Please use the 2023 *Code* book to answer the following questions.

1. Thermoplastic covered flexible stranded fixture wire Type TFF has an operating temperature of _____.
   - (a) 140°F
   - (b) 167°F
   - (c) 194°F
   - (d) 302°F

2. Thermoplastic covered fixture wire Type TF has an operating temperature of _____.
   - (a) 140°F
   - (b) 167°F
   - (c) 194°F
   - (d) 302°F

3. The ampacity of 18 AWG fixture wire is _____.
   - (a) 6A
   - (b) 8A
   - (c) 10A
   - (d) 14A

4. The ampacity of 14 AWG fixture wire is _____.
   - (a) 6A
   - (b) 8A
   - (c) 10A
   - (d) 17A

Article 402 | Fixture Wires

5. The ampacity of 12 AWG fixture wire is _____.
   - (a) 6A
   - (b) 8A
   - (c) 10A
   - (d) 23A

6. The smallest size fixture wire permitted by the *NEC* is _____.
   - (a) 18 AWG
   - (b) 16 AWG
   - (c) 14 AWG
   - (d) 12 AWG

7. Fixture wires shall not be used for _____ conductors, except as permitted in other articles of the *Code*.
   - (a) branch-circuit
   - (b) feeders
   - (c) service
   - (d) any of these

ARTICLE 404 SWITCHES

Introduction to Article 404—Switches

Article 404 covers all types of switches, switching devices, and circuit breakers such as snap (toggle) switches, dimmer switches, fan switches, disconnect switches, circuit breakers, and automatic switches such as those used for time clocks and timers. Some topics covered in this material include:

- Switch Connection Types
- Enclosures
- Position and Connection of Switches
- Mounting
- Circuit Breakers as Switches
- Rating and Use of Switches
- Construction Specifications

This article consists of two parts:

- Part I. General
- Part II. Construction Specifications

Please use the 2023 *Code* book to answer the following questions.

1. Article 404 covers all _____ used as switches operating at 1000V and below, unless specifically referenced elsewhere in this *Code* for higher voltages.

    (a) switches
    (b) switching devices
    (c) circuit breakers
    (d) all of these

2. Three-way and four-way switches shall be wired so that all switching is done only in the _____ circuit conductor.

    (a) ungrounded
    (b) grounded
    (c) equipment grounded
    (d) neutral

Article 404 | Switches

3. The grounded circuit conductor for the controlled lighting circuit shall be installed at the location where switches control lighting loads that are supplied by a grounded general-purpose branch circuit serving _____.

   (a) habitable rooms or occupiable spaces
   (b) attics
   (c) crawlspaces
   (d) basements

4. Switches controlling line-to-neutral lighting loads shall not be required to have a grounded conductor provided at the switch location where a switch controls a _____.

   (a) ceiling fan
   (b) bathroom exhaust fan
   (c) lighting load consisting of all fluorescent fixtures with integral disconnects for the ballasts
   (d) receptacle load

5. Switch enclosures shall not be used as _____ for conductors feeding through or tapping off to other switches or overcurrent devices unless the enclosure complies with 312.8.

   (a) junction boxes
   (b) auxiliary gutters
   (c) raceways
   (d) any of these

6. Surface-mounted switches or circuit breakers in a damp or wet location shall be enclosed in a _____ enclosure or cabinet that complies with 312.2.

   (a) weatherproof
   (b) rainproof
   (c) watertight
   (d) raintight

7. Switches shall not be installed within tub or shower spaces unless installed as part of a _____ tub or shower assembly.

   (a) listed
   (b) identified
   (c) marked
   (d) any of these

8. _____ shall indicate whether they are in the open (off) or closed (on) position.

   (a) General-use switches
   (b) Motor-circuit switches
   (c) Circuit breakers
   (d) all of these

9. All switches and circuit breakers used as switches shall be located so that they can be operated from a readily _____ place.

   (a) accessible
   (b) visible
   (c) operable
   (d) open

10. In general, switches and circuit breakers used as switches, shall be installed such that the center of the grip of the operating handle of the switch or circuit breaker, when in its highest position, is not more than _____ above the floor or working platform.

    (a) 5 ft 6 in.
    (b) 6 ft 7 in.
    (c) 7 ft 6 in.
    (d) 10 ft

11. Switches and circuit breakers installed adjacent to motors, appliances, or other equipment that they supply shall be permitted to be located _____ than 6 ft 7 in. and to be accessible by portable means.

    (a) lower
    (b) higher
    (c) no further
    (d) none of these

12. Snap switches shall not be grouped or ganged in enclosures unless the voltage between adjacent devices does not exceed _____, or unless installed with identified barriers between adjacent devices.

    (a) 100V
    (b) 200V
    (c) 300V
    (d) 400V

13. Metal faceplates for snap switches, including dimmer and similar control switches, shall be connected _____ whether or not a metal faceplate is installed.

    (a) to the grounded electrode
    (b) to the equipment grounding conductor
    (c) to the grounded conductor
    (d) to the ungrounded conductor

14. A snap switch wired under the provisions of 404.9(B) Ex 1 and located within 8 ft vertically, or _____ horizontally, of ground or exposed grounded metal objects shall be provided with a faceplate of nonconducting noncombustible material with nonmetallic attachment screws, unless the switch mounting strap or yoke is nonmetallic or the circuit is protected by a ground-fault circuit interrupter.

    (a) 3 ft
    (b) 5 ft
    (c) 7 ft
    (d) 9 ft

15. Snap switches in listed assemblies are not required to be connected to an equipment grounding conductor if _____.

    (a) the device is provided with a nonmetallic faceplate and the device is designed such that no metallic faceplate replaces the one provided
    (b) the device is equipped with a nonmetallic yoke
    (c) all parts of the device that are accessible after installation of the faceplate are manufactured of nonmetallic material
    (d) all of these

16. A snap switch with an integral nonmetallic enclosure complying with 300.15(E) shall be permitted without a _____ connection to an equipment grounding conductor.

    (a) grounding
    (b) bonding
    (c) earth
    (d) none of these

17. Flush-type general-use snap switches, dimmers, and control switches mounted in boxes that are set back of the finished surface shall be installed so that the _____ is(are) seated against the surface.

    (a) extension plaster ears
    (b) body
    (c) toggle
    (d) all of these

18. Metal enclosures for switches or circuit breakers shall be connected to a(an) _____ conductor.

    (a) grounded
    (b) grounding
    (c) equipment grounding
    (d) any of these

19. Alternating-current general-use snap switches shall only be used on ac circuits and may be used for controlling motor loads not exceeding _____ of the ampere rating of the switch at its rated voltage.

    (a) 70 percent
    (b) 80 percent
    (c) 110 percent
    (d) 125 percent

20. Snap switches directly connected to aluminum conductors and rated _____ or less shall be marked CO/ALR.

    (a) 15A
    (b) 20A
    (c) 30A
    (d) 50A

21. Terminals of 15A and 20A snap switches not marked CO/ALR shall be used with_____.

    (a) copper and copper-clad aluminum conductors only
    (b) copper conductors only
    (c) aluminum conductors only
    (d) copper-clad aluminum conductors only

22. Snap switch terminals marked _____ shall be permitted to be used with copper, aluminum, and copper-clad aluminum conductors.

    (a) CO/ALR
    (b) CU/AL
    (c) CU only
    (d) AL only

Article 404 | Switches

23. General-use dimmer switches and electronic control switches, such as timing switches and occupancy sensors, shall be used only to control _____ connected loads, such as incandescent luminaires unless, listed for the control of other loads and installed accordingly.

    (a) permanently
    (b) temporary
    (c) occasionally
    (d) none of these

24. Where in the off position, a switching device with a marked OFF position shall completely disconnect all _____ conductors of the load it controls.

    (a) grounded
    (b) ungrounded
    (c) grounding
    (d) all of these

ARTICLE 406 — RECEPTACLES, ATTACHMENT PLUGS, AND FLANGED INLETS

Introduction to Article 406—Receptacles, Attachment Plugs, and Flanged Inlets

This article covers the rating, type, and installation of receptacles, attachment plugs, and flanged inlets. There are many types of receptacles such as self-grounding, isolated ground, tamper resistant, weather resistant, GFCIs and AFCIs, energy controlled, work surface and countertop assemblies, USBs, surge protectors, and so on. Some topics covered in this material include:

- Receptacle Types and Ratings
- Mounting
- Faceplates
- Flanged Surface Devices, Cord Connectors, and Attachment Plugs
- Damp or Wet Locations
- Equipment Grounding Conductor Terminals
- Tamper-Resistant Receptacles

Please use the 2023 *Code* book to answer the following questions.

1. Article _____ covers the rating, type, and installation of receptacles, cord connectors, and attachment plugs (cord caps).
   - (a) 400
   - (b) 404
   - (c) 406
   - (d) 408

2. Receptacles rated 20A or less and designed for the direct connection of aluminum conductors shall be marked _____.
   - (a) AL
   - (b) AL/CU
   - (c) CU
   - (d) CO/ALR

3. Receptacle terminals of _____ receptacles not marked CO/ALR shall be used with copper and copper-clad aluminum conductors only.
   - (a) 15-ampere and 20-ampere
   - (b) surface-mounted
   - (c) single
   - (d) 30 ampere or greater

4. Receptacle terminals marked CO/ALR shall be permitted to be used with _____ conductors.
   - (a) aluminum
   - (b) copper
   - (c) copper-clad aluminum
   - (d) any of these

Article 406 | Receptacles, Attachment Plugs, and Flanged Inlets

5. Receptacles incorporating an isolated grounding conductor connection intended for the reduction of electromagnetic interference shall be identified by _____ located on the face of the receptacle.

    (a) the letters "IG"
    (b) a green circle
    (c) a green square
    (d) an orange triangle

6. 15A and 20A receptacles that are controlled by an automatic control device for the purpose of energy management or building automation shall be permanently marked with the word "_____."

    (a) power
    (b) controlled
    (c) energy management
    (d) any of these

7. Except as permitted for two-wire replacements as provided in 406.4(D), receptacles installed on _____ branch circuits shall be of the grounding type.

    (a) 15A and 20A
    (b) up to 30A
    (c) 125V
    (d) 250V

8. Receptacles and cord connectors that have equipment grounding conductor contacts shall have those contacts connected to _____.

    (a) the enclosure
    (b) a bonding bushing
    (c) an equipment grounding conductor
    (d) any of these

9. Where a grounding means exists in the receptacle enclosure a(an) _____ receptacle shall be used.

    (a) isolated ground-type
    (b) grounding-type
    (c) GFCI-type
    (d) dedicated-type

10. When replacing a nongrounding-type receptacle where attachment to an equipment grounding conductor does not exist in the receptacle enclosure, a _____ can be used as the replacement.

    (a) nongrounding-type receptacle
    (b) grounding receptacle
    (c) AFCI-type receptacle
    (d) Tamper-resistant receptacle

11. When nongrounding-type receptacles are replaced by GFCI-type receptacles where attachment to an equipment grounding conductor does not exist in the receptacle enclosure, _____ shall be marked "No Equipment Ground."

    (a) the receptacle
    (b) the protective device
    (c) the branch circuit
    (d) these receptacles or their cover plates

12. Where attachment to an equipment grounding conductor does not exist in the receptacle enclosure, a nongrounding-type receptacle(s) shall be permitted to be replaced with a grounding-type receptacle(s) where supplied through a ground-fault circuit interrupter and _____ shall be marked "GFCI Protected" and "No Equipment Ground," visible after installation.

    (a) the receptacle(s)
    (b) their cover plates
    (c) the branch circuit
    (d) the receptacle(s) or their cover plates

13. Where attachment to an equipment grounding conductor does not exist in the receptacle enclosure, a nongrounding-type receptacle shall be permitted to be replaced with a GFCI-type receptacle; however, some equipment or appliance manufacturers require that the _____ to the equipment or appliance includes an equipment grounding conductor.

    (a) feeder
    (b) branch circuit
    (c) small-appliance circuit
    (d) power cord

14. Ground-fault circuit-interrupter protection for receptacles shall be provided where _____ are made at receptacle outlets that are required to be so protected elsewhere in this *Code*.

    (a) maintenance
    (b) repairs
    (c) replacements
    (d) any of these

15. Where a receptacle outlet is supplied by a branch circuit that requires arc-fault circuit-interrupter protection [210.12(A),(B), or (C)], a replacement receptacle at this outlet shall be a _____.

    (a) listed outlet branch-circuit type AFCI receptacle
    (b) receptacle protected by a listed outlet branch-circuit type AFCI type receptacle
    (c) receptacle protected by a listed combination type AFCI type circuit breaker
    (d) any of these

16. Listed tamper-resistant receptacles shall be provided where replacements are made at receptacle outlets that are required to be tamper-resistant elsewhere in this *Code* except where a nongrounding-type receptacle is replaced with _____ receptacle.

    (a) an isolated
    (b) a GFCI-type
    (c) another nongrounding
    (d) any of these

17. Weather-resistant receptacles _____ where replacements are made at receptacle outlets that are required to be so protected elsewhere in the *Code*.

    (a) shall be provided
    (b) are not required
    (c) are optional
    (d) are not allowed

18. Automatically controlled receptacles shall be replaced with _____ controlled receptacles.

    (a) listed
    (b) suitably
    (c) equivalently
    (d) identified

19. Receptacles shall be provided with GFPE where replacements are made at receptacle outlets that are required to be so protected elsewhere in the *NEC*.

    (a) True
    (b) False

20. Physical protection of floor receptacles shall allow _____ equipment to be operated without damage to receptacles.

    (a) floor-cleaning
    (b) service
    (c) high ampacity
    (d) fixed

21. All 125-volt, single-phase, 15- and 20-ampere floor receptacles installed in food courts and waiting spaces of passenger transportation facilities where food or drinks are allowed shall be _____.

    (a) listed for corrosive environments
    (b) GFCI protected
    (c) listed for wet locations
    (d) tamper-resistant

22. Receptacles mounted in boxes set back from the finished surface shall be installed such that the mounting _____ of the receptacle is(are) held rigidly at the finished surface.

    (a) screws
    (b) yoke or strap
    (c) cover plate
    (d) grounding clip

23. Receptacles mounted in boxes flush with the finished surface or projecting beyond it shall be installed so that the mounting yoke or strap of the receptacle is held rigidly against the _____.

    (a) box or box cover
    (b) faceplate
    (c) finished surface
    (d) bonding connection

24. Receptacles mounted to and supported by a cover shall be secured by more than _____ screw(s) unless listed and identified for securing by a single screw.

    (a) one
    (b) two
    (c) three
    (d) four

25. After installation, receptacle faces shall be flush with or project from faceplates of insulating material and shall project a minimum of _____ from metal faceplates.

    (a) 0.015 in.
    (b) 0.020 in.
    (c) 0.125 in.
    (d) 0.250 in.

Article 406 | Receptacles, Attachment Plugs, and Flanged Inlets

26. Receptacle assemblies for installation in countertop surfaces shall be _____ for countertop applications.

    (a) identified
    (b) labeled
    (c) listed
    (d) approved

27. Receptacle assemblies and _____ receptacle assemblies listed for work surface or countertop applications shall be permitted to be installed in work surfaces.

    (a) AFCI
    (b) GFCI
    (c) current-limiting
    (d) all of these

28. Receptacles in or on countertop surfaces or work surfaces shall not be installed _____, unless listed for countertop or work surface applications.

    (a) in the sides of cabinets
    (b) in a face-up position
    (c) on GFCI circuits
    (d) on the kitchen small-appliance circuit

29. Receptacles shall not be grouped or ganged in enclosures unless the voltage between adjacent devices does not exceed _____.

    (a) 100V
    (b) 200V
    (c) 300V
    (d) 400V

30. Attachment plugs and cord connectors shall be listed and marked with the _____.

    (a) manufacturer's name or identification
    (b) voltage rating
    (c) amperage rating
    (d) all of these

31. An outdoor receptacle in a location protected from the weather shall be installed in an enclosure that is weatherproof when the receptacle is _____.

    (a) covered
    (b) enclosed
    (c) protected
    (d) recessed in the finished surface

32. A receptacle is considered to be in a location protected from the weather when located under roofed open porches, canopies, marquees, and the like, where it will not be subjected to _____.

    (a) spray from a hose
    (b) a direct lightning hit
    (c) beating rain or water runoff
    (d) falling or wind-blown debris

33. Where required for receptacles in damp or wet locations, _____ covers of outlet box hoods shall be able to open at least 90°, or fully open if the cover is not designed to open 90° from the closed to open position, after installation.

    (a) flush
    (b) hinged
    (c) surface mounted
    (d) any of these

34. Receptacles of _____, 125V and 250V installed in a wet location shall have an enclosure that is weatherproof whether or not the attachment plug cap is inserted.

    (a) 15A and 20A
    (b) 30A and less
    (c) up to 50A
    (d) up to 100A

35. Where 15A and 20A receptacles are installed in a wet location, the outlet box _____ shall be listed and identified as extra-duty use.

    (a) sleeve
    (b) hood
    (c) threaded entry
    (d) mounting

36. Where 15A and 20A receptacles are installed in a wet location, hinged covers of outlet box hoods shall be able to open at least _____, or fully open if the cover is not designed to open 90° from the closed to open position, after installation.

    (a) 90°
    (b) 120°
    (c) 180°
    (d) 360°

37. All 15A and 20A, 125V and 250V nonlocking-type receptacles shall be listed and so identified as the _____ type.

   (a) weatherproof
   (b) weather-resistant
   (c) raintight
   (d) waterproof

38. A 30A, 208V receptacle installed in a wet location shall be listed weather-resistant type, and where the product intended to be plugged into it is not attended while in use, shall have an enclosure that is _____ with the attachment plug cap inserted or removed.

   (a) weatherproof
   (b) rainproof
   (c) raintight
   (d) any of these

39. Receptacles shall not be installed within a zone measured _____ horizontally from any outside edge of the bathtub or shower stall, including the space outside the bathtub or shower stall space below the zone, and 8 ft vertically above the top of the bathtub rim or shower stall threshold.

   (a) 3 ft
   (b) 4 ft
   (c) 5 ft
   (d) 6 ft

40. Receptacles shall not be installed inside of the tub or shower or within a zone measured 3 ft horizontally from any outside edge of the bathtub or shower stall. Receptacles installed where a hydromassage bathtub is _____ with the supply receptacle accessible only through a service access opening shall be permitted.

   (a) rated 20A or less
   (b) rated 30A or less
   (c) cord-and plug-connected
   (d) less than 125V

41. In bathrooms with less than the required zone, the receptacle required by 210.52(D) can be installed _____ the bathtub rim or shower stall threshold on the farthest wall within the room.

   (a) opposite
   (b) vertically in
   (c) horizontally in
   (d) any of these

42. In a dwelling unit, a _____ receptacle shall be permitted for an electronic toilet or an electronic bidet seat. The receptacle shall be readily accessible and cannot be located in the space between the toilet and the bathtub or shower.

   (a) duplex
   (b) single
   (c) quad
   (d) any of these

43. All nonlocking type 125V and 250V, 15A and 20A receptacles installed in _____ shall be listed as tamper resistant.

   (a) dwelling units
   (b) boathouses
   (c) mobile homes
   (d) all of these

44. Where tamper-resistant receptacles are required, receptacles located more than _____ above the floor shall not be required to be tamper resistant.

   (a) 4 ft
   (b) 5 ft
   (c) 5½ ft
   (d) 6 ft 7 in.

45. Nonlocking-type 15A and 20A, 125V and 250V receptacles in a dwelling unit shall be listed as tamper resistant except _____.

   (a) receptacles located more than 8½ ft above the floor
   (b) receptacles that are part of an appliance
   (c) receptacles that are part of a luminaire
   (d) receptacles that are part of a luminaire or appliance

46. Nonlocking-type 125V and 250V, 15A and 20A receptacles installed in _____ shall be listed as tamper resistant.

   (a) guest rooms and guest suites of hotels and motels
   (b) childcare facilities
   (c) preschools and elementary education facilities
   (d) all of these

47. Nongrounding 15A and 20A, 125V and 250V receptacles used for replacements as permitted in 406.4(D)(2)(A) shall not be required to be listed as tamper resistant.

   (a) True
   (b) False

Notes

ARTICLE 408 — SWITCHBOARDS AND PANELBOARDS

Introduction to Article 408—Switchboards and Panelboards

Article 408 covers the specific requirements for switchboards and panelboards that control power and lighting circuits. Since these rules address the equipment at the heart of the premises electrical system, take some time to become familiar with them. Some topics covered in this material include:

- Support and Arrangement of Busbars And Conductors
- Circuit Identification
- Clearance From Conductors Entering Enclosures
- Short-Circuit Current Ratings
- Unused Openings
- Replacement Panelboards
- Damp or Wet Locations
- Locations
- Energy Management Systems
- Enclosures
- Grounding and Grounded Conductor Terminations
- Orientation

This article consists of four parts:

- Part I. General
- Part II. Switchboards and Switchgear
- Part III. Panelboards
- Part IV. Construction Specifications

Author's Comment:

- The slang term in the electrical field for a panelboard is "the guts." The requirements for panelboards are contained in Article 408.

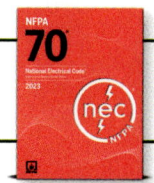

Article 408 | Switchboards and Panelboards

Please use the 2023 *Code* book to answer the following questions.

1. All 15A and 20A, 125V and 250V nonlocking-type receptacles within clinics, medical and dental offices, and outpatient facilities in _____ shall be listed as tamper resistant.
   (a) business offices accessible to the general public spaces
   (b) lobbies, and waiting spaces
   (c) spaces of nursing homes and limited care facilities covered in 517.10(B)(2)
   (d) all of these

2. Nonlocking-type 125V and 250V, 15A and 20A receptacles installed in _____ shall be listed as tamper resistant.
   (a) places of awaiting transportation
   (b) gymnasiums, skating rinks, and auditoriums
   (c) dormitory units
   (d) all of these

3. Nonlocking-type 125V and 250V, 15A and 20A receptacles installed in _____ shall be listed as tamper resistant.
   (a) residential care/assisted living facilities
   (b) social and substance abuse rehabilitation facilities
   (c) group homes
   (d) all of these

4. Nonlocking-type 125V and 250V, 15A and 20A receptacles installed in _____ shall be listed as tamper resistant.
   (a) foster care facilities
   (b) nursing homes
   (c) psychiatric hospitals
   (d) all of these

5. Nonlocking-type 125V and 250V, 15A and 20A _____ installed in areas of agricultural buildings accessible to the general public and any common areas, shall be listed as tamper resistant.
   (a) receptacles
   (b) switches
   (c) overcurrent devices
   (d) none of these

6. Nonlocking-type 125V and 250V, 15A and 20A receptacles installed in areas of agricultural buildings converted to hospitality areas shall be listed as tamper resistant. These areas can include _____.
   (a) petting zoos
   (b) stables
   (c) buildings used for recreation or educational purposes
   (d) any of these

7. Article 408 covers _____.
   (a) switchboards
   (b) switchgear
   (c) panelboards
   (d) all of these

8. Panelboards supplied by a three-phase, 4-wire, delta-connected system shall have the phase with the higher voltage-to-ground connected to the _____ phase.
   (a) A
   (b) B
   (c) C
   (d) any of these

9. A switchboard, switchgear, or panelboard containing a 4-wire, _____ system where the midpoint of one phase winding is grounded, shall be legibly and permanently field-marked to caution that one phase has a higher voltage-to-ground.
   (a) wye-connected
   (b) delta-connected
   (c) solidly grounded
   (d) ungrounded

10. Every panelboard circuit and circuit _____ shall be provided with a legible and permanent description.
    (a) location
    (b) installation
    (c) manufacturer
    (d) modification

11. Every panelboard circuit and circuit modification shall be provided with a legible and permanent description that is clear, evident, and specific to the purpose or use of each circuit including _____ positions with an unused overcurrent device.

    (a) spare
    (b) random
    (c) blank
    (d) special

12. Every panelboard circuit and circuit modification shall be provided with a legible and permanent description that is not dependent on _____ conditions of occupancy.

    (a) special
    (b) transient
    (c) random
    (d) any of these

13. Every panelboard circuit and circuit modification shall be provided with a legible and permanent description that is described with a degree of detail and clarity that is unlikely to result in confusion between circuits and is clear in explaining _____.

    (a) abbreviations and symbols
    (b) trademarks
    (c) listings
    (d) installer information and dates

14. All switchboards, switchgear, and panelboards supplied by a feeder(s) in _____ shall be permanently marked to indicate the identification and physical location where the power supply originates.

    (a) other than one- or two-family dwellings
    (b) all dwelling units
    (c) all nondwelling units
    (d) all dwelling units and all nondwelling units

15. The source of supply label required for switchboards, switchgear, and panelboards [408.4(B)] shall be permanently affixed, of sufficient durability to withstand the environment involved, and cannot be handwritten.

    (a) True
    (b) False

16. Conduits and raceways, including end fittings, shall not rise more than _____ above the bottom of a switchboard enclosure.

    (a) 3 in.
    (b) 4 in.
    (c) 5 in.
    (d) 6 in.

17. Panelboards for other than one- and two-family dwellings shall have a short-circuit current rating not less than the _____.

    (a) equipment rated current
    (b) available fault current
    (c) overcurrent protection rated current
    (d) ground-fault protection current

18. Unused openings for circuit breakers and switches in switchboards and panelboards shall be closed using _____, or other approved means that provide protection substantially equivalent to the wall of the enclosure.

    (a) duct seal and tape
    (b) identified closures
    (c) exothermic welding
    (d) sheet metal

19. Where a replacement panelboard is not listed for the specific enclosure and the available fault current is 10,000A or less, the completed work shall be _____.

    (a) field labeled
    (b) identified for the application
    (c) approved only by special permission of the AHJ
    (d) not be used

20. For other than a totally enclosed switchboard, a space shall be provided between the top of the switchboard and any combustible ceiling that is not less than _____.

    (a) 3 ft
    (b) 6 ft
    (c) 6 ft 6 in.
    (d) 3 ft 6 in.

21. Each section of switchboard or switchgear equipment that requires rear or side access to make field connections shall be so marked by _____ on the front.

    (a) the installer
    (b) the manufacturer
    (c) field evaluation
    (d) the electrical inspector

Article 408 | Switchboards and Panelboards

22. A panelboard shall be protected by an overcurrent device within the panelboard, or at any point on the _____ side of the panelboard.

    (a) load
    (b) supply
    (c) branch circuit
    (d) any of these

23. Where a panelboard is supplied through a transformer, the overcurrent protection shall be located _____.

    (a) at the main distribution panel
    (b) on the primary side of the transformer
    (c) on the secondary side of the transformer
    (d) on either the primary or secondary side of the transformer

24. Plug-in-type back-fed circuit breakers used to terminate field-installed ungrounded supply conductors shall be _____ by an additional fastener that requires more than a pull to release.

    (a) grounded
    (b) secured in place
    (c) shunt tripped
    (d) current-limited

25. Panelboards shall be mounted in cabinets, cutout boxes, or identified enclosures and where the available fault current is greater than _____, the panelboard and enclosure combination shall be evaluated for the application.

    (a) 5000A
    (b) 10,000A
    (c) 12,500A
    (d) 22,500A

26. Panelboard cabinets and panelboard frames, if of metal, shall be in physical contact with each other and shall be connected to a(an) _____.

    (a) equipment grounding conductor
    (b) grounding electrode conductor
    (c) steel building structure
    (d) separate ground rod

27. When separate equipment grounding conductors are provided in panelboards, a _____ shall be secured inside the cabinet.

    (a) grounded conductor
    (b) terminal lug
    (c) terminal bar
    (d) bonding jumper

28. Each _____ conductor shall terminate within the panelboard at an individual terminal that is not used for another conductor.

    (a) grounded
    (b) ungrounded
    (c) grounding
    (d) all of these

29. Panelboards _____ be installed in the face-up or face-down position.

    (a) shall not
    (b) are permitted to
    (c) listed for such purpose may
    (d) approved for such use may

ARTICLE 410 LUMINAIRES

Introduction to Article 410—Luminaires

This article covers luminaires, lampholders, lamps, decorative lighting products, lighting accessories for temporary seasonal and holiday use, portable flexible lighting products, and the wiring and equipment of such products and lighting installations. Article 410 is massive. It contains 84 sections divided into 17 parts. Several of these parts and their corresponding sections are not within the scope of this material. Some of the topics that are covered here include:

- Clothes Closets, Show Windows, and Cove Lighting
- LED Luminaires
- Cord-Connected Luminaires
- Luminaires Used as Raceways
- Damp or Wet Locations
- Recessed Luminaires
- Track Lighting and Decorative Lighting
- HID Lighting
- Horticultural and Germicidal Lighting

Article 410 consists of 17 parts:

- Part I. General
- Part II. Luminaire Locations
- Part III. Luminaire Outlet Boxes, Canopies, and Pans
- Part IV. Luminaire Supports
- Part V. Grounding
- Part VI. Wiring of Luminaires
- Part VII. Construction of Luminaires
- Part VIII. Installation of Lampholders
- Part IX. Lamps and Auxiliary Equipment
- Part X. Special Provisions for Flush and Recessed Luminaires
- Part XI. Construction of Flush and Recessed Luminaires
- Part XII. Special Provisions for Electric-Discharge Lighting Systems of 1000V or Less
- Part XIII. Special Provisions for Electric-Discharge Lighting Systems of More Than 1000V
- Part XIV. Lighting Track
- Part XV. Decorative Lighting and Similar Accessories
- Part XVI. Special Provisions for Horticultural Lighting Equipment
- Part XVII. Special Provisions for Germicidal Irradiation Luminaires

Article 410 | Luminaires

Please use the 2023 *Code* book to answer the following questions.

1. Article 410 covers luminaires, portable luminaires, lampholders, pendants, incandescent filament lamps, arc lamps, electric-discharge lamps, and _____, and the wiring and equipment forming part of such products and lighting installations.

   (a) decorative lighting products
   (b) lighting accessories for temporary seasonal and holiday use
   (c) portable flexible lighting products
   (d) all of these

2. All luminaires, lampholders, and retrofit kits shall be _____.

   (a) listed
   (b) approved
   (c) labeled
   (d) listed or labeled

3. Luminaires _____ "suitable for wet locations" shall be permitted to be used in a damp location.

   (a) marked
   (b) listed
   (c) identified
   (d) approved as

4. No parts of cord-connected luminaires, chain-, cable-, or cord-suspended luminaires, lighting track, pendants, or paddle fans with a light kit, shall be located within a zone measured 3 ft horizontally and _____ vertically from the top of the bathtub rim or shower stall threshold.

   (a) 4 ft
   (b) 6 ft
   (c) 8 ft
   (d) 12 ft

5. Luminaires located where subject to bathroom shower spray shall be marked suitable for _____ locations.

   (a) damp
   (b) wet
   (c) outdoor
   (d) wet or outdoor

6. Luminaires installed under roof decking where subject to physical damage shall be installed and supported so there is not less than _____ measured from the lowest surface of the roof decking to the top of the luminaire.

   (a) 1 in.
   (b) 1¼ in.
   (c) 1½ in.
   (d) 2 in.

7. Where luminaires are installed under metal-corrugated sheet roof decking, the 1½ in. spacing is not required where metal-corrugated sheet roof decking is covered with a minimum thickness _____ concrete slab, measured from the top of the corrugated roofing.

   (a) ½ in.
   (b) 1 in.
   (c) 1½ in.
   (d) 2 in.

8. Where luminaires are installed in a clothes closet, the clothes-closet storage space shall be the volume bounded by the sides and back closet walls and planes extending from the closet floor vertically to a height of _____ or to the highest clothes hanging rod.

   (a) 5½ ft
   (b) 6 ft
   (c) 6 ft 7 in.
   (d) 7 ft

9. A _____ type luminaire can be installed in a clothes closet storage space.

   (a) surface-mounted or recessed incandescent luminaire or LED luminaire with completely enclosed light source
   (b) surface-mounted or recessed fluorescent luminaire
   (c) surface-mounted fluorescent or LED luminaire identified as suitable for clothes closets
   (d) any of these

10. Incandescent luminaires with _____ enclosed lamps and pendant luminaires or lampholders shall not be permitted in clothes closet storage spaces.

    (a) open
    (b) partially
    (c) open or partially
    (d) any of these

11. Surface-mounted fluorescent luminaires in clothes closet storage spaces are permitted on the wall above the door or on the ceiling, provided there is a minimum clearance of _____ from the storage space.

    (a) 3 in.
    (b) 6 in.
    (c) 8 in.
    (d) 12 in.

12. In clothes closet storage spaces, recessed incandescent or LED luminaires with a completely enclosed light source can be installed in the wall or the ceiling, provided there is a minimum clearance of _____ from the storage space.

    (a) 3 in.
    (b) 6 in.
    (c) 8 in.
    (d) 12 in.

13. Surface-mounted fluorescent or LED luminaires shall be permitted to be installed within the clothes closet storage space where _____ for this use.

    (a) identified
    (b) listed
    (c) approved
    (d) none of these

14. Electric-discharge and LED luminaires supported independently of the outlet box shall be connected to the branch circuit through _____.

    (a) metal or nonmetallic raceways
    (b) Type MC, AC, MI, or NM cable
    (c) flexible cords
    (d) any of these

15. Electric-discharge and LED luminaires surface mounted over concealed outlet, pull, or junction boxes and designed not to be supported solely by the outlet box shall be provided with suitable openings in the _____ of the luminaire to provide access to the wiring in the box.

    (a) back
    (b) front
    (c) side
    (d) cover

16. A pole supporting luminaires shall have a handhole not less than _____ with a cover suitable for use in wet locations to provide access to the supply terminations within the pole or pole base.

    (a) 2 in. × 2 in.
    (b) 2 in. × 4 in.
    (c) 4 in. × 4 in.
    (d) 4 in. × 6 in.

17. Metal raceways shall be bonded to the metal pole supporting luminaires with a(an) _____.

    (a) grounding electrode
    (b) grounded conductor
    (c) equipment grounding conductor
    (d) any of these

18. Luminaires attached to the framing members of a suspended ceiling shall be secured to the framing member(s) by mechanical means such as _____.

    (a) bolts
    (b) screws
    (c) rivets
    (d) any of these

19. Luminaires shall be _____ to an equipment grounding conductor.

    (a) securely connected
    (b) clamped
    (c) mechanically connected
    (d) none of these

Article 410 | Luminaires

20. Replacement luminaires are not required to be connected to an equipment grounding conductor if no equipment grounding conductor exists at the outlet box and the luminaire is _____.

    (a) more than 20 years old
    (b) mounted to the box using nonmetallic fittings and screws
    (c) mounted more than 6 ft above the floor
    (d) GFCI protected

21. An electric-discharge or LED luminaire can be cord connected provided the luminaire is located _____ the outlet, the cord is visible for its entire length except at terminations, and the cord is not subject to strain or physical damage.

    (a) within
    (b) directly below
    (c) directly above
    (d) adjacent to

22. For existing installed fluorescent or LED luminaires that utilize double-ended lamps and contain ballast(s) or LED driver(s) without disconnecting means, a(an) _____ shall be installed at the time a ballast or LED driver is added or replaced.

    (a) disconnecting means
    (b) supplemental overcurrent protective device
    (c) ground-fault for equipment device
    (d) energy code-compliant ballast

23. In indoor locations other than dwellings and associated accessory structures, fluorescent or LED luminaires that utilize double-ended lamps and contain ballast(s) or LED driver(s) that can be serviced in place shall not require a disconnecting means where luminaires _____.

    (a) are installed in hazardous (classified) location(s)
    (b) provide emergency illumination required in 700.16
    (c) are cord-and-plug-connected
    (d) all of these

24. In indoor locations other than dwellings and associated accessory structures, fluorescent or LED luminaires that utilize double-ended lamps and contain ballast(s) or LED driver(s) that can be serviced in place shall not require a disconnecting means where _____.

    (a) more than one luminaire is installed in the building area and not connected to a multiwire branch circuit
    (b) the design of the installation includes a disconnecting means
    (c) the building area will not be left in total darkness should only one disconnect be opened
    (d) all of these

25. When connected to _____ branch circuits, the disconnecting means for fluorescent or LED luminaires shall simultaneously break all the supply conductors to the ballast or driver, including the grounded conductor.

    (a) multiwire
    (b) individual
    (c) dedicated
    (d) series-parallel

26. The disconnecting means for fluorescent or LED luminaires that utilize double-ended lamps shall be located so as to be accessible to _____ before servicing or maintaining the ballast.

    (a) maintenance personnel
    (b) qualified persons
    (c) service technicians
    (d) manufacturer representatives

27. Where recessed luminaires are installed, adjacent combustible materials shall not be subject to temperatures in excess of _____.

    (a) 60°C
    (b) 75°C
    (c) 90°C
    (d) 110°C

28. A recessed luminaire that is not identified for contact with insulation shall have all recessed parts spaced not less than _____ from combustible materials.

    (a) ½ in.
    (b) ⅝ in.
    (c) ¾ in.
    (d) 1 in.

29. Recessed luminaires that are identified to be in contact with insulation are designated _____.

    (a) Type BC
    (b) Type BI
    (c) Type CI
    (d) Type IC

30. Thermal insulation shall not be installed above a recessed luminaire or within _____ of the recessed luminaire's enclosure or wiring compartment unless the luminaire is identified as Type IC.

    (a) 1 in.
    (b) 1¼ in.
    (c) 1½ in.
    (d) 3 in.

31. Lighting track fittings can be equipped with general-purpose receptacles.

    (a) True
    (b) False

32. The connected load on lighting track is permitted to exceed the rating of the track under certain conditions.

    (a) True
    (b) False

33. Track lighting shall not be installed _____.

    (a) where likely to be subjected to physical damage
    (b) in wet or damp locations
    (c) where concealed
    (d) all of these

34. Lighting track shall not be installed less than _____ above the finished floor except where protected from physical damage or where the track operates at less than 30V rms open-circuit voltage.

    (a) 4 ft
    (b) 5 ft
    (c) 5½ ft
    (d) 6 ft

35. Lighting track shall not be installed within the zone measured 3 ft horizontally and _____ vertically from the top of the bathtub rim or shower stall threshold.

    (a) 2 ft
    (b) 3 ft
    (c) 4 ft
    (d) 8 ft

36. Lighting track shall have two supports for a single section of _____ or shorter in length and each individual section of not more than 4 ft attached to it shall have one additional support unless the track is identified for supports at greater intervals.

    (a) 2 ft
    (b) 4 ft
    (c) 6 ft
    (d) 8 ft

37. Lighting equipment _____ for horticultural use is designed to provide a spectral characteristic needed for the growth of plants and can also provide supplemental general illumination within the growing environment.

    (a) identified
    (b) labeled
    (c) marked
    (d) listed

38. Lighting equipment _____ for horticultural use shall be installed and used in accordance with the manufacturer's installation instructions and installation markings on the equipment as required by that listing.

    (a) labeled
    (b) designed
    (c) identified
    (d) suitable

39. Flexible cord shall only be permitted when provided as part of listed lighting equipment identified for horticultural use for _____.

    (a) connecting a horticultural lighting luminaire directly to a branch circuit outlet
    (b) interconnecting horticultural lighting luminaires
    (c) connecting a horticultural lighting luminaire to a remote power source
    (d) any of these

Article 410 | Luminaires

40. Lighting equipment identified for horticultural use employing flexible cord(s) with one or more separable connector(s) or attachment plug(s) shall be supplied by lighting outlets protected by a listed _____.

    (a) AFCI
    (b) GFPE
    (c) GFCI
    (d) SPD

ARTICLE 411 — LOW-VOLTAGE LIGHTING

Introduction to Article 411—Low-Voltage Lighting

Article 411 covers low-voltage lighting systems and associated components. Low-voltage lighting is often used for landscaping, lighting under kitchen cabinets, and display lighting in commercial establishments, art galleries, and museums. Do not let the half-page size of this article give you the impression that low-voltage lighting is not important. These systems are limited in their voltage, but the current rating can be as high as 25A which creates a potential source of fire. Some topics covered in this material include:

- Listing Requirements
- Voltage Limits

Please use the 2023 *Code* book to answer the following questions.

1. Article 411 covers _____ lighting systems and their associated components.

    (a) low voltage
    (b) medium voltage
    (c) horticultural
    (d) solar

2. Listed low-voltage lighting systems or a lighting system assembled from listed parts shall be permitted to be reconditioned.

    (a) True
    (b) False

3. Low-voltage lighting systems shall be listed for use as part of the same identified lighting system or assembled from _____ parts.

    (a) listed
    (b) identified
    (c) labeled
    (d) marked

4. Where wet contact is likely to occur, the operating voltage of low-voltage lighting systems and their associated components shall not exceed _____ or 30V dc.

    (a) 12V ac
    (b) 15V ac
    (c) 24V ac
    (d) 30V ac

5. The output circuits of the power system for low-voltage lighting systems shall be rated for _____ maximum under all load conditions.

    (a) 15A
    (b) 20A
    (c) 25A
    (d) 30A

Article 411 | Low-Voltage Lighting

6. Low-voltage lighting system conductors can be concealed or extended through _____.

    (a) walls
    (b) floors
    (c) ceilings
    (d) any of these

7. Low-voltage lighting systems shall be installed not less than _____ horizontally from the nearest edge of the water in pools, spas, fountains, or similar locations, unless permitted by Article 680.

    (a) 5 ft
    (b) 6 ft
    (c) 10 ft
    (d) 20 ft

8. Low-voltage lighting system transformers shall be supplied from a maximum _____ branch circuit.

    (a) 15A
    (b) 20A
    (c) 25A
    (d) 30A

ARTICLE 422 APPLIANCES

Introduction to Article 422—Appliances

This article covers electric appliances that are fastened in place, permanently connected, or cord-and-plug-connected in any occupancy. Some topics covered in this material include:

- Disconnect Requirements
- Cord-and-Plug Connections

Article 422 consists of five parts:

- Part I. General
- Part II. Installation
- Part III. Disconnecting Means
- Part IV. Construction
- Part V. Marking

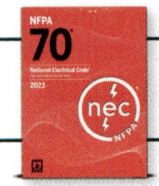

Please use the 2023 *Code* book to answer the following questions.

1. Each appliance shall have a means to _____ disconnect all ungrounded circuit conductors.

    (a) sequentially
    (b) automatically
    (c) simultaneously
    (d) all of these

2. The ampacities of individual branch-circuit conductors for appliances shall not be less than the marked rating of the _____.

    (a) receptacle outlet
    (b) appliance
    (c) overcurrent protective device
    (d) power cord

3. If a branch circuit supplies a single nonmotor-operated appliance, the rating of overcurrent protection shall not exceed _____ if the overcurrent protection rating is not marked and the appliance is rated 13.30A or less.

    (a) 15A
    (b) 20A
    (c) 25A
    (d) 30A

Article 422 | Appliances

4. If a branch circuit supplies a single nonmotor-operated appliance, the rating of overcurrent protection shall not exceed _____ of the appliance rated current if the overcurrent protection rating is not marked and the appliance is rated over 13.30A.

   (a) 100 percent
   (b) 125 percent
   (c) 150 percent
   (d) 160 percent

5. An appliance with central heating equipment, other than fixed electric space-heating equipment, shall be supplied by a(an) _____ branch circuit.

   (a) multiwire
   (b) individual
   (c) multipurpose
   (d) small-appliance

6. The branch-circuit overcurrent device and conductors for a fixed storage-type water heater appliance that has a capacity of 120 gallons or less shall have an ampere rating not less than _____ of the ampere rating of the water heater.

   (a) 80 percent
   (b) 115 percent
   (c) 125 percent
   (d) 150 percent

7. Flexible cord for appliances is permitted to _____.

   (a) connect appliances to facilitate their frequent interchange
   (b) prevent the transmission of noise
   (c) facilitate the removal or disconnection of appliances that are fastened in place for maintenance or repair and the appliance is intended or identified for flexible cord connection
   (d) any of these

8. A waste disposer can be cord-and-plug-connected; the cord shall not be less than 18 in. or more than _____ in length.

   (a) 30 in.
   (b) 36 in.
   (c) 42 in.
   (d) 48 in.

9. Where a waste disposer is cord-and-plug-connected, the receptacles shall be _____ to protect against physical damage to the flexible cord.

   (a) located
   (b) shielded
   (c) guarded
   (d) any of these

10. The flexible cord for a(an) in-sink waste disposer shall have an equipment grounding conductor and terminate with a _____ attachment plug.

    (a) 3-wire
    (b) 4-wire
    (c) nongrounding-type
    (d) grounding-type

11. The length of the flexible cord for a trash compactor shall not be less than 3 ft or exceed _____ in length, measured from the face of the attachment plug to the plane of the rear of the appliance.

    (a) 2 ft
    (b) 4 ft
    (c) 6 ft
    (d) 8 ft

12. The length of the flexible cord for a built-in dishwasher shall not be less than 3 ft or exceed _____ in length, measured from the face of the attachment plug to the plane of the rear of the appliance.

    (a) 6½ ft
    (b) 7 ft
    (c) 7½ ft
    (d) 8 ft

13. Receptacles for built-in dishwashers and trash compactors shall be located so as to protect against physical damage to the _____.

    (a) flexible cord
    (b) cord cap
    (c) appliance
    (d) receptacle

14. Where a built-in trash compactor is to be cord-and-plug connected the receptacle shall be located _____ occupied by the appliance.

    (a) in the space
    (b) adjacent to the space
    (c) directly above the space
    (d) in the space or adjacent to the space

15. Where the flexible cord for a built-in trash compactor or dishwasher passes through an opening, it shall be protected against damage by a(an) _____.

    (a) bushing
    (b) grommet
    (c) approved means
    (d) any of these

16. Wall-mounted ovens and counter-mounted cooking units shall be permitted to be connected with a flexible cord identified as _____ for the purpose.

    (a) listed
    (b) manufactured
    (c) suitable
    (d) sufficient

17. Range hoods shall be permitted to be cord-and-plug-connected with a flexible cord identified as suitable for use on range hoods in the installation instructions of the appliance manufacturer provided _____.

    (a) the length of the cord is not less than 18 in. and not over 4 ft
    (b) receptacles are located to protect against physical damage to the flexible cord
    (c) the receptacle is supplied by an individual branch circuit
    (d) all of these

18. No metal parts of ceiling-suspended (paddle) fans in bathrooms and shower spaces shall be located within a zone measured _____ horizontally and 8 ft vertically from the top of the bathtub rim or shower stall threshold.

    (a) 2 ft
    (b) 2½ ft
    (c) 3 ft
    (d) 4 ft

19. For permanently connected appliances rated at not over _____ or ⅛ hp, the branch-circuit overcurrent device shall be permitted to serve as the disconnecting means where the switch or circuit breaker is within sight from the appliance or is capable of being locked in the open position.

    (a) 75 VA
    (b) 150 VA
    (c) 225 VA
    (d) 300 VA

20. For permanently connected appliances rated over _____, the branch-circuit switch or circuit breaker can serve as the disconnecting means where the switch or circuit breaker is within sight from the appliance or is capable of being locked in the open position.

    (a) 200 VA
    (b) 300 VA
    (c) 400 VA
    (d) 500 VA

21. For permanently connected motor-operated appliances with motors rated over _____, a switch or circuit breaker located within sight from the motor-operated appliance or capable of being locked in the open position can serve as the appliance disconnect.

    (a) ⅛ hp
    (b) ¼ hp
    (c) 15A
    (d) 1 kW

22. For cord-and-plug- (or attachment fitting-) connected appliances, a(an) _____ plug (or attachment fitting) and receptacle combination shall be permitted to serve as the disconnecting means.

    (a) labeled
    (b) accessible
    (c) metal enclosed
    (d) none of these

Notes

ARTICLE 424 — FIXED ELECTRIC SPACE-HEATING EQUIPMENT

Introduction to Article 424—Fixed Electric Space-Heating Equipment

Article 424 contains the installation requirements for fixed electrical equipment used for space heating such as heating cables, unit heaters, boilers (such as those used for radiant heating), central heating systems, or fixed electric space-heating equipment. This article has ten parts, several of which fall outside the scope of this material and will not be covered. Some topics that are covered include:

- Branch Circuits
- Supply Conductors
- Disconnecting Means
- Overcurrent Protection
- Marking of Equipment
- Heating Cables and Duct Heaters

Article 424 consists of ten parts:

- Part I. General
- Part II. Installation
- Part III. Control and Protection of Fixed Electric Space-Heating Equipment
- Part IV. Marking of Heating Equipment
- Part V. Electric Space-Heating Cables
- Part VI. Duct Heaters
- Part VII. Resistance-Type Boilers
- Part VIII. Electrode-Type Boilers
- Part IX. Electric Radiant Heating Panels and Heating Panel Sets
- Part X. Low-Voltage Fixed Electric Space-Heating Equipment

Article 424 | Fixed Electric Space-Heating Equipment

Please use the 2023 *Code* book to answer the following questions.

1. Article _____ covers fixed electric equipment used for space heating including heating cables, unit heaters, boilers, central heating systems, or other fixed electric space-heating equipment.

    (a) 410
    (b) 422
    (c) 424
    (d) 440

2. The branch-circuit conductor(s) ampacity shall not be less than _____ of the load of the fixed electric space-heating equipment and any associated motor(s).

    (a) 80 percent
    (b) 110 percent
    (c) 125 percent
    (d) 150 percent

3. Means shall be provided to simultaneously disconnect the _____ of all fixed electric space-heating equipment from all ungrounded conductors.

    (a) heater
    (b) motor controller(s)
    (c) supplementary overcurrent device(s)
    (d) all of these

4. Duct heater controller equipment shall have a disconnecting means installed within _____ the controller except as allowed by 424.19(A).

    (a) 25 ft of
    (b) sight from
    (c) the side of
    (d) none of these

ARTICLE 430 — MOTOR CIRCUITS, CONTROLLERS, AND ADJUSTABLE-SPEED DRIVES

Introduction to Article 430—Motor Circuits, Controllers, and Adjustable-Speed Drives

This article contains the specific rules for conductor sizing, overcurrent protection, control circuit conductors, controllers, and disconnects for electric motors. This massive and complex article is divided into fourteen parts, many of which fall outside the scope of this material and will not be covered. Some topics that are covered include:

- Conductor Sizing
- Overload Protection
- Branch-Circuit, Feeder Short-Circuit and Ground-Fault Protection
- Motor Control Circuits and Controllers
- Motor Control Centers
- Disconnecting Means
- Adjustable-Speed Drives
- Full-Load Current Tables

Article 430 consists of fourteen parts:

- Part I. General
- Part II. Motor Circuit Conductors
- Part III. Motor and Branch-Circuit Overload Protection
- Part IV. Motor Branch-Circuit Short-Circuit and Ground-Fault Protection
- Part V. Motor Feeder Short-Circuit and Ground-Fault Protection
- Part VI. Motor Control Circuits
- Part VII. Motor Controllers
- Part VIII. Motor Control Centers
- Part IX. Disconnecting Means
- Part X. Adjustable-Speed Drive Systems
- Part XI. Over 1000V, Nominal
- Part XII. Protection of Live Parts—All Voltages
- Part XIII. Grounding—All Voltages
- Part XIV. Tables

Article 430 | Motor Circuits, Controllers, and Adjustable-Speed Drives

Please use the 2023 *Code* book to answer the following questions.

1. Article _____ covers motors, motor branch-circuit and feeder conductors and their protection, motor overload protection, motor control circuits, motor controllers, and motor control centers.

    (a) 410
    (b) 430
    (c) 440
    (d) 450

2. For general motor applications, the *NEC* table values for full load current values shall be used instead of the actual current rating marked on the motor nameplate when determining overload protection.

    (a) True
    (b) False

3. The motor full-load currents listed in Tables 430.247 through 430.250 shall be used to determine the _____.

    (a) ampacity of motor circuit conductors
    (b) current ratings of switches
    (c) current rating for short-circuit and ground-fault protective devices
    (d) all of these

4. For general motor applications, separate motor overload protection shall be based on _____.

    (a) *NEC* Tables 430.248 and 430.250
    (b) the manufacturer's instructions
    (c) the motor disconnect current rating
    (d) the motor nameplate current rating

5. Motors shall be located so that adequate _____ is provided and so that maintenance, such as lubrication of bearings and replacing of brushes, can be readily accomplished.

    (a) space
    (b) ventilation
    (c) protection
    (d) all of these

6. Branch-circuit conductors supplying a single continuous-duty motor shall have an ampacity not less than _____ rating.

    (a) 125 percent of the motor's nameplate current
    (b) 125 percent of the motor's full-load current
    (c) 125 percent of the motor's full locked-rotor
    (d) 80 percent of the motor's full-load current

7. Conductors supplying several motors shall have an ampacity not less than _____ of the full-load current rating of the highest rated motor, plus the sum of the full-load current ratings of all other motors in the group.

    (a) 80 percent
    (b) 100 percent
    (c) 125 percent
    (d) 150 percent

8. Overload devices are intended to protect motors, motor control apparatus, and motor branch-circuit conductors against _____.

    (a) excessive heating due to motor overloads
    (b) excessive heating due to failure to start
    (c) short circuits and ground faults
    (d) excessive heating due to motor overloads and excessive heating due to failure to start

9. Each motor used in a continuous-duty application and rated more than 1 hp shall be protected against overload. The overload device for motors with a marked temperature rise of 40°C or less shall be rated at no more than _____ of the motor nameplate full-load current rating.

    (a) 100 percent
    (b) 115 percent
    (c) 125 percent
    (d) 140 percent

10. A separate overload device used to protect continuous-duty motors rated more than 1 hp shall be selected to trip at no more than _____ of the motor nameplate full-load current rating if marked with a service factor of 1.15 or greater.

    (a) 100 percent
    (b) 115 percent
    (c) 125 percent
    (d) 140 percent

11. Part IV of Article 430 specifies devices intended to protect _____ against overcurrent due to short circuits or ground faults.

    (a) motor branch-circuit conductors
    (b) motor control apparatus
    (c) motors
    (d) all of these

12. Short-circuit and ground-fault protection for a branch-circuit to which a motor or motor-operated appliance is connected shall be capable of carrying the _____ current of the motor.

    (a) ampacity
    (b) time delay
    (c) thermal protection
    (d) starting

13. Where the motor short-circuit and ground-fault protection devices determined by Table 430.52(C)(1) do not correspond to the standard sizes or ratings, a _____ rating that does not exceed the next _____ standard ampere rating is permitted.

    (a) higher
    (b) lower
    (c) smaller
    (d) larger

14. The maximum dual-element time-delay fuse branch-circuit protection for a single-phase motor is _____ of the appropriate full-load current rating found in Table 430.248.

    (a) 100 percent
    (b) 115 percent
    (c) 125 percent
    (d) 175 percent

15. The maximum rating or setting of an inverse time breaker used as the motor branch-circuit short-circuit and ground-fault protective device for a single-phase motor is _____ of the full-load current given in Table 430.248.

    (a) 100 percent
    (b) 115 percent
    (c) 125 percent
    (d) 250 percent

16. Motor branch-circuit short-circuit and ground-fault protection and motor overload protection _____ be combined in a single protective device where the rating of the device provides the required overload protection.

    (a) shall be permitted to
    (b) shall not be permitted to
    (c) shall be
    (d) shall not

17. A feeder supplying a fixed motor load(s) shall have a protective device with a rating or setting _____ branch-circuit short-circuit and ground-fault protective device for any motor in the group, plus the sum of the full-load currents of the other motors of the group.

    (a) not greater than the largest rating or setting of the
    (b) 125 percent of the largest rating of any
    (c) equal to the largest rating of any
    (d) at least 80 percent of the

18. A motor control circuit is tapped from the load side of the motor short-circuit protective device. The control circuit conductors are 14 AWG, the conductors require only short-circuit protection, and do not extend beyond the motor control equipment enclosure. The maximum overcurrent protection permitted for this motor control circuit is _____.

    (a) 15A
    (b) 20A
    (c) 50A
    (d) 100A

19. The maximum rating of the overcurrent protective device for 14 AWG motor control wiring that extends beyond the enclosure is _____.

    (a) 15A
    (b) 20A
    (c) 45A
    (d) 100A

20. Motor control circuit conductors that extend beyond the motor control equipment enclosure shall have short-circuit and ground-fault protection sized not greater than _____ of the value specified in Table 310.16 for 60°C conductors.

    (a) 100 percent
    (b) 160 percent
    (c) 300 percent
    (d) 400 percent

21. Motor control circuits shall be arranged so they will be disconnected from all sources of supply when the disconnecting means is in the _____ position.

    (a) open
    (b) closed
    (c) on
    (d) off

22. Motor controllers shall have horsepower ratings at the application voltage _____ the horsepower rating of the motor.

    (a) not lower than
    (b) not higher than
    (c) equal to
    (d) six times

23. A _____ rated in amperes is permitted as a controller for all motors.

    (a) branch-circuit inverse time circuit breaker or molded case switch
    (b) dual-element time-delay fuse
    (c) snap switch
    (d) GFCI-protected device

24. For stationary motors of 2 hp or less and 300V or less on ac circuits, the motor controller can be an ac-rated only general-use snap switch where the motor full-load current rating is not more than _____ of the rating of the switch.

    (a) 50 percent
    (b) 60 percent
    (c) 70 percent
    (d) 80 percent

25. A motor controller shall not be installed where the available fault current exceeds the motor controller's _____ current rating.

    (a) full-load
    (b) overload
    (c) short-circuit
    (d) disconnect

26. An individual disconnecting means shall be provided for each motor controller and be located _____ from the controller location.

    (a) in sight
    (b) within 3 ft
    (c) within 10 ft
    (d) within 25 ft

27. A _____ shall be located in sight from the motor location and the driven machinery location.

    (a) controller
    (b) protective device
    (c) disconnecting means
    (d) all of these

28. Where more than one motor disconnecting means is provided in the same motor branch circuit, at least one of the disconnecting means shall be _____.

    (a) readily accessible
    (b) accessible
    (c) within sight
    (d) within 25 ft

29. If a motor disconnecting means is a motor-circuit switch, it shall be rated in _____.

    (a) horsepower
    (b) watts
    (c) amperes
    (d) locked-rotor current

30. A motor disconnecting means can be a listed _____.

    (a) molded case circuit breaker
    (b) motor-circuit switch rated in horsepower
    (c) molded case switch
    (d) any of these

31. A branch-circuit overcurrent device can serve as the disconnecting means for a stationary motor of _____ or less.

    (a) ⅛ hp
    (b) ¼ hp
    (c) ⅓ hp
    (d) ½ hp

32. A horsepower-rated _____ having a horsepower rating not less than the motor rating is permitted to serve as the disconnecting means.

    (a) attachment plug and receptacle
    (b) flanged surface inlet and cord connector
    (c) attachment plug and cord connector
    (d) any of these

33. The full-load current of a 115V, 1 hp single-phase ac motor is _____.

    (a) 12A
    (b) 14A
    (c) 16A
    (d) 20A

34. The full-load current of a 230V, 1.50 hp single-phase ac motor is _____.

    (a) 10A
    (b) 12A
    (c) 14A
    (d) 16A

35. The full-load current of a three-phase 208V, 2 hp motor is _____.

    (a) 7.50A
    (b) 12A
    (c) 14A
    (d) 16A

36. The full-load current of a three-phase 208V, 7.50 hp motor is _____.

    (a) 19A
    (b) 22A
    (c) 24.20A
    (d) 38A

37. The full-load current of a three-phase 230V, 10 hp motor is _____.

    (a) 19A
    (b) 22A
    (c) 28A
    (d) 38A

38. The full-load current of a three-phase 460V, 15 hp motor is _____.

    (a) 19A
    (b) 21A
    (c) 29A
    (d) 42A

Notes

ARTICLE 440 AIR-CONDITIONING EQUIPMENT

Introduction to Article 440—Air-Conditioning Equipment

Article 440 applies to hermetic refrigerant motor-compressors, such as those used for pool heat pumps and HVAC equipment. In most cases the manufacturer has worked out all the details and identifies the minimum conductor ampacity, maximum overcurrent protective device rating, and other information (such as running-load amperes) on the nameplate, so the rules covered in this material deal with what the installer needs to know. Some topics covered in this material include:

- Ampacity and Rating of Conductors
- Single Machines
- Cord-and-Plug Connections
- Circuit Conductors and Protection
- Multi-Motor Equipment
- Equipment Grounding Conductor

This article consists of seven parts:

- Part I. General
- Part II. Disconnecting Means
- Part III. Branch-Circuit Short-Circuit and Ground-Fault Protection
- Part IV. Circuit Conductors
- Part V. Controllers for Motor-Compressors
- Part VI. Motor-Compressor and Branch-Circuit Overload Protection
- Part VII. Room Air Conditioners

Article 440 | Air-Conditioning Equipment

Please use the 2023 *Code* book to answer the following questions.

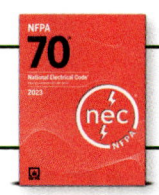

1. Article _____ applies to electric motor-driven air-conditioning and refrigerating equipment that has a hermetic refrigerant motor-compressor.

    (a) 440
    (b) 442
    (c) 450
    (d) 460

2. An air-conditioning multi-motor equipment has a nameplate that indicates a minimum circuit ampacity of 30A and a maximum overcurrent protective device of 60A. The smallest THWN-2 conductors permitted are _____.

    (a) 14 AWG
    (b) 12 AWG
    (c) 10 AWG
    (d) 8 AWG

3. An air-conditioning multi-motor equipment nameplate shows that the minimum supply circuit ampacity as 24A and the maximum circuit breaker size as 40A. The smallest conductor contained in Type NM cable permitted for this circuit is _____.

    (a) 10 AWG Type NM cable
    (b) 12 AWG Type NM cable
    (c) 14 AWG Type NM cable
    (d) 8 AWG Type NM cable

4. Air-conditioning and refrigeration equipment shall not be installed within a zone measured _____ horizontally from any outside edge of the bathtub or shower stall.

    (a) 2 ft
    (b) 3 ft
    (c) 4 ft
    (d) 6 ft

5. Where air-conditioning and refrigeration equipment is installed outdoors on a roof, a(an) _____ conductor of the wire type shall be installed in outdoor portions of metallic raceway systems that use compression-type fittings.

    (a) equipment grounding
    (b) grounding
    (c) equipment bonding
    (d) bonding

6. Where an air-conditioning or refrigeration equipment disconnecting means is readily accessible to _____, any enclosure door or hinged cover of a disconnecting means enclosure that exposes energized parts when open shall require a tool to open or be capable of being locked.

    (a) unqualified persons
    (b) qualified person
    (c) service personnel
    (d) maintenance personnel

7. The disconnecting means for air-conditioning and refrigerating equipment shall be readily accessible and _____ from the air-conditioning or refrigerating equipment.

    (a) visible
    (b) 10 ft
    (c) 20 ft
    (d) within sight

8. An individual motor-compressor protective device having a rating or setting not exceeding _____ of the motor-compressor rated-load current or branch-circuit selection current, whichever is greater, is permitted.

    (a) 115 percent
    (b) 125 percent
    (c) 175 percent
    (d) 225 percent

ARTICLE 445 GENERATORS

Introduction to Article 445—Generators

This article contains the installation and other requirements for generators and generator sets. Rules located here include such things as where generators can be installed, nameplate markings, conductor ampacity, transference of power, and disconnect requirements. Some topics covered in this material include:

- Installation Locations
- Marking
- Overcurrent Protection
- Conductor Ampacity
- Disconnecting Means and Emergency Shutdown
- Portable Generators

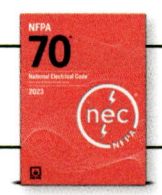

Please use the 2023 *Code* book to answer the following questions.

1. Article _____ contains installation and other requirements for generators.
   - (a) 430
   - (b) 445
   - (c) 450
   - (d) 455

2. Stationary generators shall be _____.
   - (a) marked
   - (b) labeled
   - (c) identified
   - (d) listed

3. Nameplates or manufacturer's instructions shall provide information as listed in 445.11(1) through (5) for all generators rated more than _____.
   - (a) 12 kW
   - (b) 15 kW
   - (c) 18 kW
   - (d) 20 kW

4. The ampacity of the conductors from the generator output terminals to the overcurrent protection shall not be less than _____ of the nameplate current rating of the generator.
   - (a) 75 percent
   - (b) 115 percent
   - (c) 125 percent
   - (d) 140 percent

Article 445 | Generators

5. For other than cord-and-plug-connected portable generators, an emergency shutdown device for a dwelling unit shall be located _____ at a readily accessible location.

   (a) inside the dwelling unit
   (b) outside the dwelling unit
   (c) within sight of the generator
   (d) inside or outside the dwelling unit

ARTICLE 450 TRANSFORMERS

Introduction to Article 450—Transformers

Article 450 covers the installation requirements for transformers supplying power and lighting loads. Those types of transformers not covered by these rules are listed in the "Scope" section of this article. While the *NEC* does not provide design criteria for transformers, it does give an extensive set of rules to ensure a properly selected transformer can be installed and perform as intended by the designer. Several sections of this article fall outside the scope of this material and will not be covered. Some covered topics include:

- Overcurrent Protection
- Ventilation
- Grounding and Bonding
- Accessibility
- Disconnect Requirements
- Transformer Types

This article consists of three parts:

- Part I. General
- Part II. Installation
- Part III. Transformer Vaults

Please use the 2023 *Code* book to answer the following questions.

1. Article 450 covers the installation of all _____.
   (a) motors and motor control centers
   (b) refrigeration and air-conditioning equipment
   (c) transformers
   (d) generators

2. Transformers with ventilating openings shall be installed so that the ventilating openings are _____.
   (a) a minimum 18 in. above the floor
   (b) not blocked by walls or obstructions
   (c) aesthetically located
   (d) vented to the exterior of the building

Article 450 | Transformers

3. Transformer top surfaces that are horizontal and readily accessible shall be marked _____.

   (a) to warn of high surface temperature(s)
   (b) with the arc-flash boundary
   (c) to prohibit storage
   (d) all of these

4. The equipment grounding conductor terminal bar of a dry-type transformer shall be bonded to the enclosure in accordance with 250.12 and shall not be installed on or over any _____.

   (a) ungrounded conductor terminations
   (b) transformer coils or windings
   (c) vented portion of the enclosure
   (d) all of these

5. Dry-type transformers 1000V nominal or less and not exceeding _____ that are installed in hollow spaces of buildings and not permanently closed in by the structure, shall not be required to be readily accessible.

   (a) 10 kVA
   (b) 25 kVA
   (c) 50 kVA
   (d) 112.50 kVA

6. Transformers, other than Class 2 or Class 3 transformers, shall have a disconnecting means located either in sight of the transformer or in a remote location. Where located in a remote location, the disconnecting means shall be lockable open in accordance with 110.25 and _____.

   (a) its location shall be field marked on the transformer
   (b) accessible only to qualified persons
   (c) placed in supervisory locations
   (d) none of these

ARTICLE 480 — STATIONARY STANDBY BATTERIES

Introduction to Article 480—Stationary Standby Batteries

The provisions of this article apply to all installations of stationary standby batteries having a capacity greater than 1 kWh. That is a small battery capacity and, with the many improvements in technology, these systems are much more common than they were just a few years ago. Systems such as uninterruptible power supplies, emergency power and lighting systems, and stand-alone power systems are a few of the many applications for this article. All of these types of battery systems involve highly specialized areas of knowledge found in standards other than the *NEC*. Some topics covered in this material include:

- Battery and Cell Terminations
- Overcurrent Protection
- Support Systems
- Locations
- Ventilation
- Interconnection

 Please use the 2023 *Code* book to answer the following questions.

1. The provisions of Article _____ apply to all installations of stationary standby batteries having a capacity of greater than 1 kWh.

    (a) 450
    (b) 460
    (c) 470
    (d) 480

2. Where mating dissimilar metals, antioxidant material suitable for the battery connection shall be used where _____ by the battery manufacturer's installation and instruction manual.

    (a) documented
    (b) required
    (c) recommended
    (d) the antioxidant is supplied

Article 480 | Stationary Standby Batteries

3. Electrical _____ to a storage battery, and the cable(s) between cells on separate levels or racks, shall not put mechanical strain on the battery terminals.

    (a) connections
    (b) continuity
    (c) conductivity
    (d) accessibility

4. Conductors are commonly _____ to eliminate stress on storage battery terminations.

    (a) prefabricated
    (b) preinsulated
    (c) preformed
    (d) pre-evaluated

5. The terminals of all storage battery cells or multicell units shall be readily accessible for _____ where required by the equipment design.

    (a) readings
    (b) inspections
    (c) cleaning
    (d) all of these

6. Metallic structures for battery support systems shall be provided with nonconducting support members for the cells or shall be constructed with a continuous _____ material and paint alone shall not be considered as an insulating material.

    (a) insulating
    (b) conductive
    (c) semiconductive
    (d) none of these

7. Provisions appropriate to the storage battery technology shall be made for sufficient diffusion and ventilation of gases from the battery, if present, to prevent the accumulation of a(an) _____ mixture.

    (a) explosive
    (b) noxious
    (c) toxic
    (d) chemical

FINAL EXAM A

STRAIGHT ORDER

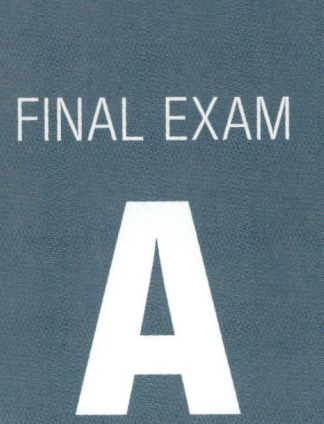

 Please use the 2023 *Code* book to answer the following questions.

1. Chapters 5, 6, and 7 of the *NEC* apply to _____ and may supplement or modify the requirements contained in Chapters 1 through 7.
   (a) special occupancies
   (b) special equipment
   (c) special conditions
   (d) all of these

2. Capable of being reached quickly for operation, renewal, or inspections without climbing over or under obstructions, removing obstacles, resorting to portable ladders, or the use of tools (other than keys) is known as "_____."
   (a) accessible (as applied to equipment)
   (b) accessible (as applied to wiring methods)
   (c) accessible, readily (readily accessible)
   (d) all of these

3. A "_____" consists of two or more ungrounded conductors that have a voltage between them, and a neutral conductor that has equal voltage between it and each ungrounded conductor of the circuit and that is connected to the neutral conductor of the system.
   (a) multi-phase branch circuit
   (b) three-phase lighting supply circuit
   (c) poly-phase branch circuit
   (d) multiwire branch circuit

4. A separate portion of a conduit or tubing system that provides access through a removable cover(s) to the interior of the system at a junction of two or more sections of the system or at a terminal point of the system defines the term "_____."
   (a) junction box
   (b) accessible raceway
   (c) conduit body
   (d) cutout box

5. A _____ is a single unit that provides complete and independent living facilities for one or more persons, including permanent provisions for living, sleeping, cooking, and sanitation.
   (a) one-family dwelling
   (b) two-family dwelling
   (c) dwelling unit
   (d) multifamily dwelling

6. A generator is a machine that converts mechanical energy into electrical energy by means of a _____ and alternator and/or inverter.
   (a) converter
   (b) rectifier
   (c) prime mover
   (d) turbine

1st Printing | Understanding the 2023 National Electrical Code Workbook, Articles 90-480 | MikeHolt.com | 235

Straight Order | Final Exam A

7. A conductor used to connect the system grounded conductor, or the equipment to a grounding electrode or to a point on the grounding electrode system, is called the "_____ conductor."

   (a) main grounding
   (b) common main
   (c) equipment grounding
   (d) grounding electrode

8. Equipment, materials, or services included in a list published by an organization that is acceptable to the authority having jurisdiction defines the term "_____."

   (a) booked
   (b) a digest
   (c) a manifest
   (d) listed

9. A "_____" is the machine that supplies the mechanical horsepower to a generator.

   (a) prime mover
   (b) motor
   (c) capacitor
   (d) starter

10. "Underground service conductors" are the underground conductors between the service point and the first point of connection to the service-entrance conductors in a terminal box, meter, or other enclosure, _____ the building wall.

    (a) inside or outside
    (b) concealed within
    (c) above
    (d) below

11. "_____" is a pliable corrugated raceway of circular cross section, with integral or associated couplings, connectors, and fittings that are listed for the installation of electrical conductors.

    (a) PVC
    (b) ENT
    (c) RMC
    (d) IMC

12. Conductor sizes are expressed in American Wire Gauge (AWG) or in _____.

    (a) inches
    (b) circular mils
    (c) square inches
    (d) cubic inches

13. Connection of conductors to terminal parts shall ensure a mechanically secure electrical connection without damaging the conductors and shall be made by means of _____.

    (a) solder lugs
    (b) pressure connectors
    (c) splices to flexible leads
    (d) any of these

14. Equipment enclosures for circuit breakers or fuses applied in compliance with the series combination ratings marked on the equipment by the manufacturer in accordance with 240.86(B) shall be _____ to indicate the equipment has been applied with a series combination rating.

    (a) legibly marked in the field
    (b) inspected and tagged
    (c) installed
    (d) listed

15. The width of the working space shall be not be less than _____ wide, or the width of the equipment, whichever is greater.

    (a) 15 in.
    (b) 30 in.
    (c) 40 in.
    (d) 60 in.

16. Enclosure Type 3X for switchboards, switchgear, or panelboards located outdoors are suitable in locations subject to _____.

    (a) rain
    (b) windblown dust
    (c) corrosive agents
    (d) any of these

17. Receptacles shall have the terminal intended for connection to the grounded conductor identified by a metal or metal coating that is white or silver in color or by the word, "_____."

    (a) green
    (b) white
    (c) silver
    (d) neutral

18. Factory-installed receptacles mounted internally to bathroom _____ assemblies shall not require GFCI protection unless required by the installation instructions or listing.

    (a) surface-mounted luminaire
    (b) exhaust fan
    (c) electric baseboard heat
    (d) all of these

19. In other than dwelling units, all single-phase receptacles rated 150V to ground or less, 50A or less and three-phase receptacles rated 150V to ground or less, 100A or less installed in indoor _____ or wet locations shall be GFCI protected.

    (a) dry
    (b) damp
    (c) humid
    (d) rainy

20. At least _____ or more 120V, 20A branch circuit(s) shall be provided to supply dwelling unit bathroom(s) receptacle outlet(s).

    (a) one
    (b) two
    (c) three
    (d) four

21. The total rating of utilization equipment fastened in place shall not exceed _____ of the rating of a 20A multiple outlet branch circuit.

    (a) 25 percent
    (b) 50 percent
    (c) 80 percent
    (d) 100 percent

22. An appliance receptacle outlet installed for a specific appliance shall be installed within _____ of the intended location of the appliance.

    (a) sight
    (b) 3 ft
    (c) 6 ft
    (d) the length of the cord

23. In dwelling units, the required bathroom receptacle outlet can be installed on the side or face of the sink cabinet if not more than _____ below the top of the sink or sink countertop.

    (a) 12 in.
    (b) 18 in.
    (c) 20 in.
    (d) 24 in.

24. The required heating, air-conditioning, and refrigeration equipment receptacle outlet can be connected to the _____ side of the equipment disconnecting means.

    (a) line
    (b) load
    (c) high
    (d) low

25. In a dwelling unit, dimmer control of lighting outlets for interior stairways installed in accordance with 210.70(A)(2)(3) shall not be permitted unless the listed control devices can provide dimming control _____ at each control location for the interior stairway illumination.

    (a) for illumination
    (b) for emergency lighting
    (c) to maximum brightness
    (d) for effective lighting

26. Feeder and service loads for fixed electric space-heating loads shall be calculated at _____ of the total connected load.

    (a) 80 percent
    (b) 100 percent
    (c) 125 percent
    (d) 200 percent

27. There shall be no reduction in the size of the neutral or grounded conductor on _____ loads supplied from a 4-wire, wye-connected, three-phase system.

    (a) dwelling unit
    (b) hospital
    (c) nonlinear
    (d) motel

28. The minimum clearance for overhead feeder conductors not exceeding 1000V that pass over public streets, alleys, roads, and parking areas subject to truck traffic is _____.

    (a) 10 ft
    (b) 12 ft
    (c) 15 ft
    (d) 18 ft

29. In accordance with Article 225—Outside Branch Circuits and Feeders, there shall be no more than _____ switches or circuit breakers to serve as the disconnecting means for a building supplied by a feeder.

    (a) two
    (b) four
    (c) six
    (d) eight

30. SPD's required by 225.42(A), shall be installed _____ the distribution equipment that is connected to the load side of the feeder and contains branch circuit overcurrent protective device(s).

    (a) in or adjacent to
    (b) within 3 ft of
    (c) within 10 ft of
    (d) within sight of

31. Overhead service conductors shall not be installed beneath openings through which materials may be moved, such as openings in farm and commercial buildings, and shall not be installed where they obstruct _____ these building openings.

    (a) entrance to
    (b) egress from
    (c) access to
    (d) a safe descent from

32. Where conduits are used as service masts, hubs shall be _____ for use with service-entrance equipment.

    (a) identified
    (b) approved
    (c) of a heavy-duty type
    (d) listed

33. Where exposed to the weather, raceways enclosing service-entrance conductors shall be _____ for use in wet locations and arranged to drain.

    (a) approved or listed
    (b) listed and identified
    (c) suitable
    (d) listed and labeled

34. The surge-protective device (SPD) required for a dwelling unit shall be _____.

    (a) Type 1 or 2
    (b) Type 2 or 3
    (c) Type 3
    (d) Type 4

35. One- and two-family dwelling emergency disconnecting means are permitted to be a listed disconnect switch or circuit breaker that is marked _____ for use as service equipment, but not marked as suitable only for use as service equipment, installed on the supply side of each service disconnect.

    (a) suitable
    (b) appropriate
    (c) ready
    (d) none of these

36. Fixture wire is permitted to be tapped to the branch-circuit conductor in accordance with which of the following?

    (a) 15A or 20A circuits—18 AWG, up to 50 ft of run length
    (b) 15A or 20A circuits—16 AWG, up to 100 ft of run length
    (c) 20A circuits—14 AWG and larger
    (d) all of these

37. When feeder taps not over 10 ft long leave the enclosure in which the tap is made, the ampacity of the tap conductors cannot be less than _____ of the rating of the device protecting the feeder.

    (a) one-tenth
    (b) one-fifth
    (c) one-half
    (d) two-thirds

38. A circuit breaker with a _____ voltage rating, such as 240V or 480V, can be used where the nominal voltage between any two conductors does not exceed the circuit-breaker voltage rating.

    (a) straight
    (b) slash
    (c) high
    (d) low

39. General requirements for grounding and bonding of electrical installations and the location of grounding connections are within the scope of _____.

    (a) Article 110
    (b) Article 200
    (c) Article 250
    (d) Article 680

40. Ungrounded alternating-current systems from 50V to 1000V or less that are not required to be grounded in accordance with 250.21(B) shall have _____.

    (a) ground detectors installed for ac systems operating at not less than 100V and at 1000V or less
    (b) the ground detection sensing equipment connected as far as practicable to where the system receives its supply
    (c) ground detectors installed for ac systems operating at not less than 120V and at 1000V or less, and have the ground detection sensing equipment connected as close as practicable to where the system receives its supply
    (d) ground-fault protection for equipment

41. A grounded conductor shall not be connected to normally noncurrent-carrying metal parts of equipment on the _____ side of the system bonding jumper of a separately derived system except as otherwise permitted.

    (a) supply
    (b) grounded
    (c) high-voltage
    (d) load

42. A grounding electrode system and grounding electrode conductor at a building or structure shall not be required if only a _____ supplies the building or structure.

    (a) 4-wire service
    (b) single or multiwire branch circuit
    (c) 3-wire service
    (d) any of these

43. Grounding electrodes of the rod type less than _____ in diameter shall be listed.

    (a) ½ in.
    (b) ⅝ in.
    (c) ¾ in.
    (d) 1 in.

44. Where bonding jumper(s) are used to connect the grounding electrodes together to form the grounding electrode system, _____ is not permitted to be used as a conductor to interconnect the electrodes.

    (a) rebar
    (b) structural steel
    (c) a grounding plate
    (d) none of these

45. The common grounding electrode conductor shall be sized in accordance with 250.66, based on the sum of the circular mil area of the _____ ungrounded conductor(s) of each set of conductors that supplies the disconnecting means.

    (a) smallest
    (b) largest
    (c) color of the
    (d) material of the

46. The largest sized grounding electrode conductor to a rod, pipe, or plate electrode required for a 400A service with 500 kcmil conductors is _____.

    (a) 8 AWG
    (b) 6 AWG
    (c) 1/0 AWG
    (d) 4/0 AWG aluminum

47. Metal enclosures and raceways for other than service conductors shall be connected to the _____ conductor.

    (a) neutral
    (b) equipment grounding
    (c) ungrounded
    (d) grounded

48. Where ungrounded supply conductors are paralleled in two or more raceways, the bonding jumper for each raceway shall be based on the size of the _____ in each raceway.

    (a) overcurrent protection for conductors
    (b) grounded conductors
    (c) largest ungrounded supply conductors
    (d) sum of all conductors

49. Lightning protection system ground terminals _____ bonded to the building or structure grounding electrode system.

    (a) shall be
    (b) shall not be
    (c) shall be permitted to be
    (d) shall be effectively

50. If the ungrounded conductors are increased in size for any reason other than as required in 310.15(B) or 310.15(C), wire-type equipment grounding conductors shall be increased in size proportionately to the increase in _____ of the ungrounded conductors.

    (a) ampacity
    (b) circular mil area
    (c) diameter
    (d) temperature rating

51. Receptacle yokes or contact devices designed and _____ as self-grounding can, in conjunction with the supporting screws, establish the equipment bonding between the device yoke and a flush-type box.

    (a) approved
    (b) advertised
    (c) listed
    (d) installed

52. Where a cable or raceway-type wiring method is installed through bored holes in joists, rafters, or wood members, the holes shall be bored so that the edge of the hole is _____ the edges of the wood member.

    (a) not less than 1¼ in. from
    (b) immediately adjacent to
    (c) not less than 1/16 in. from
    (d) 90° away from

53. Electrical metallic tubing that is directly buried under a two-family dwelling driveway shall have at least _____ of cover.

    (a) 6 in.
    (b) 12 in.
    (c) 18 in.
    (d) 24 in.

54. Backfill used for underground wiring shall not damage _____ or prevent adequate compaction of fill or contribute to corrosion.

    (a) raceways
    (b) cables
    (c) conductors
    (d) any of these

55. A(An) _____, with an integral bushed opening shall be used at the end of a conduit or other raceway that terminates underground where the conductors or cables emerge as a direct burial wiring method.

    (a) splice kit
    (b) connector
    (c) adapter
    (d) bushing or terminal fitting

56. Raceways may be used as a means of support where the raceway contains power-supply conductors for electrically controlled equipment and is used to _____ Class 2 or Class 3 circuit conductors or cables that are solely for the purpose of connection to the equipment control circuits.

    (a) support
    (b) secure
    (c) strap
    (d) none of these

57. Conductors carrying alternating current installed in ferrous metal raceways or enclosures shall be arranged so as to avoid heating the surrounding ferrous metal by induction. To accomplish this, the _____ conductor(s) shall be grouped together.

    (a) phase
    (b) grounded
    (c) equipment grounding
    (d) all of these

58. The minimum size copper conductor permitted for voltage ratings up to 2000V is _____.

    (a) 14 AWG
    (b) 12 AWG
    (c) 10 AWG
    (d) 8 AWG

59. Insulated conductors and cables used in _____ shall be Types FEP, FEPB, MTW, PFA, RHH, RHW, RHW-2, SA, THHN, THW, THW-2, THHW, THWN, THWN-2, TW, XHH, XHHW, XHHW-2, XHHN, XHWN, XHWN-2, Z, or ZW.

    (a) dry and damp locations
    (b) dry locations
    (c) damp locations
    (d) wet and damp locations

60. Where six current-carrying conductors are run in the same conduit, the ampacity of each conductor shall be adjusted to _____ of its ampacity.

    (a) 40 percent
    (b) 60 percent
    (c) 80 percent
    (d) 90 percent

61. In walls constructed of wood or other _____ material, electrical cabinets shall be flush with the finished surface or project therefrom.

    (a) nonconductive
    (b) porous
    (c) fibrous
    (d) combustible

62. Where internal _____ means are provided between all entries, nonmetallic boxes shall be permitted to be used with metal raceways or metal-armored cables.

    (a) grounding
    (b) bonding
    (c) connecting
    (d) splicing

63. Equipment grounding conductor(s), and not more than _____ fixture wire(s) smaller than 14 AWG is(are) permitted to be omitted from the calculations where they enter the box from a domed luminaire or similar canopy and terminate within that box.

    (a) one
    (b) two
    (c) three
    (d) four

64. A wood brace used for supporting a box for structural mounting shall have a cross-section not less than nominal _____.

    (a) 1 in. × 2 in.
    (b) 2 in. × 2 in.
    (c) 2 in. × 3 in.
    (d) 2 in. × 4 in.

65. Utilization equipment weighing not more than 6 lb can be supported to any box or plaster ring secured to a box, provided the equipment is secured with at least two _____ or larger screws.

    (a) No. 6
    (b) No. 8
    (c) No. 10
    (d) No. 12

66. Article _____ covers the use, installation, and construction specifications for armored cable, Type AC.

    (a) 300
    (b) 310
    (c) 320
    (d) 334

67. Type AC cable shall provide an adequate path for _____ to act as an equipment grounding conductor.

    (a) fault current
    (b) short-circuit current
    (c) overcurrent
    (d) arcing current

68. Type MC cable containing four or fewer conductors, sized no larger than 10 AWG, shall be secured within _____ of every box, cabinet, fitting, or other cable termination.

    (a) 8 in.
    (b) 12 in.
    (c) 18 in.
    (d) 24 in.

69. Grommets or bushings for the protection of Type NM cable installed through or parallel to framing members shall be _____ for the purpose.

    (a) marked
    (b) approved
    (c) identified
    (d) listed

70. Type TC cable and associated fittings shall be _____.

    (a) identified
    (b) approved
    (c) listed
    (d) labeled

71. Type USE cable is not permitted for _____ wiring.

    (a) underground
    (b) interior
    (c) aerial
    (d) aboveground installations

72. Article _____ covers the use, installation, and construction specifications for intermediate metal conduit (IMC) and associated fittings.

    (a) 342
    (b) 348
    (c) 352
    (d) 356

73. RMC and fittings are permitted to be installed in concrete, in direct contact with the earth, in direct burial applications, or in areas subject to severe corrosive influences when protected by _____ approved for the condition.

    (a) ceramic
    (b) corrosion protection
    (c) backfill
    (d) a natural barrier

74. Threadless couplings and connectors used with RMC buried in masonry or concrete shall be the _____ type.

    (a) raintight
    (b) wet and damp location
    (c) nonabsorbent
    (d) concrete tight

75. For flexible metal conduit, if flexibility is necessary after installation, unsecured lengths from the last point the raceway is securely fastened shall not exceed _____.

    (a) 3 ft for trade sizes ½ through 1¼
    (b) 4 ft for trade sizes 1½ through 2
    (c) 5 ft for trade sizes 2½ and larger
    (d) all of these

76. When LFMC is used to connect equipment where flexibility is necessary to minimize the transmission of vibration from equipment or for equipment requiring movement after installation, a(an) _____ conductor shall be installed.

    (a) main bonding
    (b) grounded
    (c) equipment grounding
    (d) grounding electrode

77. The _____ ends of PVC conduit shall be trimmed inside and outside to remove the burrs and rough edges.

    (a) cut
    (b) new
    (c) old
    (d) blunt

78. Liquidtight nonmetallic flexible conduit is not permitted to be used _____.

    (a) where subject to physical damage
    (b) where ambient and conductor temperatures exceed its listing
    (c) in lengths greater than 6 ft unless approved
    (d) all of these

79. Raceway bends are not permitted to be made in any manner that will _____ the raceway.

    (a) damage
    (b) kink
    (c) change the internal diameter of
    (d) damage and change the internal diameter of

80. ENT shall not be used where exposed to the direct rays of the sun, unless identified as _____.

    (a) high-temperature rated
    (b) sunlight resistant
    (c) Schedule 80
    (d) suitable for the application

81. The purpose of having all parallel conductor sets installed in metal wireways within the same group, is to prevent _____ imbalance in the paralleled conductors due to inductive reactance.

    (a) current
    (b) voltage
    (c) inductive
    (d) all of these

82. Single conductor cables and single insulated conductors used in cable trays shall be marked on the surface for use in cable trays and shall be no smaller than _____.

    (a) 1 AWG
    (b) 1/0 AWG
    (c) 2/0 AWG
    (d) 4/0 AWG

83. Flexible cords and flexible cables can be used for _____.

    (a) wiring of luminaires
    (b) portable and mobile signs or appliances
    (c) connection of utilization equipment to facilitate frequent interchange
    (d) all of these

84. Fixture wires shall not be used for _____ conductors, except as permitted in other articles of the *Code*.

    (a) branch-circuit
    (b) feeders
    (c) service
    (d) any of these

85. Metal faceplates for snap switches, including dimmer and similar control switches, shall be connected _____ whether or not a metal faceplate is installed.

    (a) to the grounded electrode
    (b) to the equipment grounding conductor
    (c) to the grounded conductor
    (d) to the ungrounded conductor

86. Receptacles rated 20A or less and designed for the direct connection of aluminum conductors shall be marked _____.

    (a) AL
    (b) AL/CU
    (c) CU
    (d) CO/ALR

87. Listed tamper-resistant receptacles shall be provided where replacements are made at receptacle outlets that are required to be tamper-resistant elsewhere in this *Code* except where a nongrounding-type receptacle is replaced with _____ receptacle.

    (a) an isolated
    (b) a GFCI-type
    (c) another nongrounding
    (d) any of these

88. Attachment plugs and cord connectors shall be listed and marked with the _____.

    (a) manufacturer's name or identification
    (b) voltage rating
    (c) amperage rating
    (d) all of these

89. Where tamper-resistant receptacles are required, receptacles located more than _____ above the floor shall not be required to be tamper resistant.

    (a) 4 ft
    (b) 5 ft
    (c) 5½ ft
    (d) 6 ft 7 in.

90. Every panelboard circuit and circuit _____ shall be provided with a legible and permanent description.

    (a) location
    (b) installation
    (c) manufacturer
    (d) modification

91. Plug-in-type back-fed circuit breakers used to terminate field-installed ungrounded supply conductors shall be _____ by an additional fastener that requires more than a pull to release.

    (a) grounded
    (b) secured in place
    (c) shunt tripped
    (d) current-limited

92. Where luminaires are installed in a clothes closet, the clothes-closet storage space shall be the volume bounded by the sides and back closet walls and planes extending from the closet floor vertically to a height of _____ or to the highest clothes' hanging rod.

    (a) 5½ ft
    (b) 6 ft
    (c) 6 ft 7 in.
    (d) 7 ft

93. For existing installed fluorescent or LED luminaires that utilize double-ended lamps and contain ballast(s) or LED driver(s) without disconnecting means, a(an) _____ shall be installed at the time a ballast or LED driver is added or replaced.

    (a) disconnecting means
    (b) supplemental overcurrent protective device
    (c) ground-fault for equipment device
    (d) energy code-compliant ballast

94. Lighting track shall have two supports for a single section of _____ or shorter in length and each individual section of not more than 4 ft attached to it shall have one additional support unless the track is identified for supports at greater intervals.

    (a) 2 ft
    (b) 4 ft
    (c) 6 ft
    (d) 8 ft

95. Where a built-in trash compactor is to be cord-and-plug connected the receptacle shall be located _____ occupied by the appliance.

    (a) in the space
    (b) adjacent to the space
    (c) directly above the space
    (d) in the space or adjacent to the space

96. Means shall be provided to simultaneously disconnect the _____ of all fixed electric space-heating equipment from all ungrounded conductors.

    (a) heater
    (b) motor controller(s)
    (c) supplementary overcurrent device(s)
    (d) all of these

97. The maximum dual-element time-delay fuse branch-circuit protection for a single-phase motor is _____ of the appropriate full-load current rating found in Table 430.248.

    (a) 100 percent
    (b) 115 percent
    (c) 125 percent
    (d) 175 percent

98. Where more than one motor disconnecting means is provided in the same motor branch circuit, at least one of the disconnecting means shall be _____.

    (a) readily accessible
    (b) accessible
    (c) within sight
    (d) within 25 ft

99. An air-conditioning multi-motor equipment nameplate shows that the minimum supply circuit ampacity as 24A and the maximum circuit breaker size as 40A. The smallest conductor contained in Type NM cable permitted for this circuit is _____.

    (a) 10 AWG Type NM cable
    (b) 12 AWG Type NM cable
    (c) 14 AWG Type NM cable
    (d) 8 AWG Type NM cable

100. Transformers with ventilating openings shall be installed so that the ventilating openings are _____.

    (a) a minimum 18 in. above the floor
    (b) not blocked by walls or obstructions
    (c) aesthetically located
    (d) vented to the exterior of the building

FINAL EXAM B

RANDOM ORDER

Please use the 2023 *Code* book to answer the following questions.

1. A motor control circuit is tapped from the load side of the motor short-circuit protective device. The control circuit conductors are 14 AWG, the conductors require only short-circuit protection, and do not extend beyond the motor control equipment enclosure. The maximum overcurrent protection permitted for this motor control circuit is _____.

   (a) 15A
   (b) 20A
   (c) 50A
   (d) 100A

2. Thermoplastic covered flexible stranded fixture wire Type TFF has an operating temperature of _____.

   (a) 140°F
   (b) 167°F
   (c) 194°F
   (d) 302°F

3. The rating of any one cord-and plug-connected utilization equipment on a 15A, 120V branch circuit shall not exceed _____.

   (a) 12A
   (b) 15A
   (c) 16A
   (d) 20A

4. A conductor installed on the supply side of a service or within a service equipment enclosure, or for a separately derived system, to ensure the required electrical conductivity between metal parts required to be electrically connected is known as the "_____."

   (a) supply-side bonding jumper
   (b) ungrounded conductor
   (c) electrical supply source
   (d) grounding electrode conductor

5. Installations used to export electric power from vehicles to premises wiring or for _____ current flow is covered by the *NEC*.

   (a) emergency
   (b) primary
   (c) bidirectional
   (d) secondary

6. Outlets supplying luminaires shall be calculated based on the maximum _____ rating of the equipment.

   (a) power
   (b) True power
   (c) voltage
   (d) volt-ampere

7. Feeder grounded conductors not connected to an overcurrent device can be sized at _____ of the continuous and noncontinuous load.

   (a) 80 percent
   (b) 100 percent
   (c) 125 percent
   (d) 150 percent

8. Where direct-buried conductors and cables emerge from grade, they shall be protected by enclosures or raceways to a point at least _____ above finished grade.

   (a) 3 ft
   (b) 6 ft
   (c) 8 ft
   (d) 10 ft

9. Except as permitted for two-wire replacements as provided in 406.4(D), receptacles installed on _____ branch circuits shall be of the grounding type.

   (a) 15A and 20A
   (b) up to 30A
   (c) 125V
   (d) 250V

10. The vertical clearance of final spans of overhead service conductors above, or within _____ measured horizontally of platforms, projections, or surfaces that will permit personal contact shall be maintained.

    (a) 3 ft
    (b) 4 ft
    (c) 5 ft
    (d) 6 ft

11. A ground ring encircling the building or structure can be used as a grounding electrode when the _____.

    (a) ring is in direct contact with the earth
    (b) ring consists of at least 20 ft of bare copper conductor
    (c) bare copper conductor is not smaller than 2 AWG
    (d) all of these

12. Surge-protective devices shall be _____.

    (a) listed
    (b) identified
    (c) marked
    (d) labeled

13. Insulated conductors and cables used in _____ shall be any of the types identified in this *Code*.

    (a) dry and damp locations
    (b) dry locations
    (c) damp locations
    (d) wet and damp locations

14. The use, installation, and construction specifications for liquidtight flexible metal conduit (LFMC) and associated fittings are covered within Article _____.

    (a) 300
    (b) 334
    (c) 350
    (d) 410

15. An electrode encased by at least 2 in. of concrete, located horizontally near the bottom or vertically and within that portion of a concrete foundation or footing that is in direct contact with the earth, is permitted as a grounding electrode when it consists of a bare copper conductor not smaller than _____.

    (a) 8 AWG
    (b) 6 AWG
    (c) 4 AWG
    (d) 1/0 AWG

16. A _____ is an accommodation with two or more contiguous rooms comprising a compartment that provides living, sleeping, sanitary, and storage facilities.

    (a) guest room
    (b) guest suite
    (c) dwelling unit
    (d) single-family dwelling

17. Type MC cable is permitted for use in damp or wet locations where a corrosion-resistant jacket is provided over the metallic covering and _____.

    (a) the metallic covering is impervious to moisture.
    (b) a jacket resistant to moisture is provided under the metal covering.
    (c) the insulated conductors under the metallic covering are listed for use in wet locations.
    (d) any of these

18. The connected load on lighting track is permitted to exceed the rating of the track under certain conditions.

    (a) True
    (b) False

19. Electric-discharge and LED luminaires supported independently of the outlet box shall be connected to the branch circuit through _____.

    (a) metal or nonmetallic raceways
    (b) Type MC, AC, MI, or NM cable
    (c) flexible cords
    (d) any of these

20. A demand factor of _____ applies to a multifamily dwelling with ten units if the optional calculation method is used.

    (a) 43 percent
    (b) 50 percent
    (c) 60 percent
    (d) 75 percent

21. In dwelling unit bathrooms, not less than one 15A or 20A, 125V receptacle outlet shall be installed within _____ of the outside edge of each bathroom basin.

    (a) 2 ft
    (b) 3 ft
    (c) 4 ft
    (d) 5 ft

22. A panelboard shall be protected by an overcurrent device within the panelboard, or at any point on the _____ side of the panelboard.

    (a) load
    (b) supply
    (c) branch circuit
    (d) any of these

23. Unbroken lengths of surface metal raceways can be run through dry _____.

    (a) walls
    (b) partitions
    (c) floors
    (d) all of these

24. Type UF cable shall not be used _____.

    (a) in any hazardous (classified) location except as otherwise permitted in this Code
    (b) embedded in poured cement, concrete, or aggregate
    (c) where exposed to direct rays of the sun, unless identified as sunlight resistant
    (d) all of these

25. Receptacles shall not be grouped or ganged in enclosures unless the voltage between adjacent devices does not exceed _____.

    (a) 100V
    (b) 200V
    (c) 300V
    (d) 400V

26. All luminaires, lampholders, and retrofit kits shall be _____.

    (a) listed
    (b) approved
    (c) labeled
    (d) listed or labeled

27. The building structural steel bonding jumper size for a 400A service supplied with 500 kcmil conductors is _____.

    (a) 6 AWG
    (b) 3 AWG
    (c) 2 AWG
    (d) 1/0 AWG

28. A building or structure shall be supplied by a maximum of _____ service(s), unless specifically permitted otherwise.

    (a) one
    (b) two
    (c) three
    (d) four

29. Where luminaires are installed under metal-corrugated sheet roof decking, the 1½ in. spacing is not required where metal-corrugated sheet roof decking is covered with a minimum thickness _____ concrete slab, measured from the top of the corrugated roofing.

    (a) ½ in.
    (b) 1 in.
    (c) 1½ in.
    (d) 2 in.

30. Metal raceways, cable armor, and other metal enclosures shall be _____ joined together into a continuous electric conductor so as to provide effective electrical continuity.

    (a) electrically
    (b) permanently
    (c) metallically
    (d) physically

31. Cut ends of ENT shall be trimmed inside and _____ to remove rough edges.

    (a) outside
    (b) tapered
    (c) filed
    (d) beveled

32. ENT is not permitted in hazardous (classified) locations, unless permitted in other articles of the *Code*.

    (a) True
    (b) False

33. Meter sockets supplied by and under the exclusive control of an electric utility shall not be required to be _____.

    (a) approved
    (b) rated
    (c) listed
    (d) all of these

34. The total degrees of bends in a run of EMT shall not exceed _____ between pull points.

    (a) 120 degrees
    (b) 180 degrees
    (c) 270 degrees
    (d) 360 degrees

35. If an energy management system (EMS) is used to limit the current to a feeder or service, the set point value of the EMS shall be considered _____.

    (a) at 80 percent
    (b) at 90 percent
    (c) at 100 percent
    (d) a continuous load

36. Cable wiring methods shall not be used as a means of support for _____.

    (a) other cables
    (b) raceways
    (c) nonelectrical equipment
    (d) any of these

37. Type IMC conduit shall be permitted to be installed where subject to _____ physical damage.

    (a) severe
    (b) minor
    (c) minimal
    (d) massive

38. The minimum clearance for overhead service conductors that pass over public streets, alleys, roads, parking areas subject to truck traffic is _____.

    (a) 10 ft
    (b) 12 ft
    (c) 15 ft
    (d) 18 ft

39. For the purposes of ampacity adjustment, when determining the number of current-carrying conductors, a grounding or bonding conductor _____ be counted when applying the provisions of 310.15(C)(1).

    (a) shall not
    (b) shall
    (c) is permitted to
    (d) can

40. A snap switch with an integral nonmetallic enclosure complying with 300.15(E) shall be permitted without a _____ connection to an equipment grounding conductor.

    (a) grounding
    (b) bonding
    (c) earth
    (d) none of these

41. General requirements for the examination and approval, installation and use, access to and spaces about electrical conductors and equipment; enclosures intended for personnel entry; and tunnel installations are within the scope of _____.

    (a) Article 800
    (b) Article 300
    (c) Article 110
    (d) Annex J

42. Receptacles shall be provided with GFPE where replacements are made at receptacle outlets that are required to be so protected elsewhere in the *NEC*.

    (a) True
    (b) False

43. The surge-protective device (SPD) required for a dwelling unit shall be an integral part of the service equipment or be located immediately adjacent thereto.

    (a) True
    (b) False

44. A _____ surge-protective device is permitted to be connected on either the line or load side of a service disconnect overcurrent device.

    (a) Type 1
    (b) Type 2
    (c) Type 3
    (d) Type 4

45. Floor boxes _____ specifically for the application shall be used for receptacles located in the floor.

    (a) identified
    (b) listed
    (c) approved
    (d) designed

46. Extreme _____ may cause PVC conduit to become brittle, and therefore more susceptible to damage from physical contact.

    (a) sunlight
    (b) corrosive conditions
    (c) heat
    (d) cold

47. All conductors of the same circuit, including the grounded and equipment grounding conductors and bonding conductors shall be contained within the same _____, unless otherwise permitted elsewhere in the *Code*.

    (a) raceway
    (b) conduit body
    (c) trench
    (d) all of these

48. For one- and two-family dwelling unit service conductors, an emergency disconnecting means shall be installed in a readily accessible _____ location.

    (a) indoor
    (b) outdoor
    (c) indoor or outdoor
    (d) enclosed

49. Where equipment grounding is required, a separate grounding conductor shall be installed in Type PVC conduit except where the _____ is used to ground equipment as permitted in 250.142.

    (a) grounding jumper
    (b) grounded conductor
    (c) bonding jumper
    (d) bonded conductor

50. Where ENT is the wiring method and equipment grounding is required, the equipment grounding conductor shall not be required where the _____ conductor is used as part of the effective ground-fault path as permitted.

    (a) grounded
    (b) equipment grounding
    (c) ungrounded
    (d) none of these

51. The _____ of Type AC cable is recognized as an equipment grounding conductor.

    (a) armor
    (b) cover
    (c) sheath
    (d) any of these

52. All nonlocking type 125V and 250V, 15A and 20A receptacles installed in _____ shall be listed as tamper resistant.
    (a) dwelling units
    (b) boathouses
    (c) mobile homes
    (d) all of these

53. The flexible cord for a(an) in-sink waste disposer shall have an equipment grounding conductor and terminate with a _____ attachment plug.
    (a) 3-wire
    (b) 4-wire
    (c) nongrounding-type
    (d) grounding-type

54. Where mating dissimilar metals, antioxidant material suitable for the battery connection shall be used where _____ by the battery manufacturer's installation and instruction manual.
    (a) documented
    (b) required
    (c) recommended
    (d) the antioxidant is supplied

55. Cabinets, cutout boxes, and meter socket enclosures installed in wet locations shall be _____.
    (a) waterproof
    (b) raintight
    (c) weatherproof
    (d) watertight

56. Conduits or raceways through which moisture might contact live parts shall be _____ at either or both ends.
    (a) crimped
    (b) taped
    (c) bushed
    (d) sealed or plugged

57. The minimum working space on a circuit for equipment operating at 120V to ground, with exposed live parts on one side and no live or grounded parts on the other side of the working space, is _____.
    (a) 1 ft
    (b) 3 ft
    (c) 4 ft
    (d) 6 ft

58. The total volume occupied by two internal cable clamps, six 12 AWG conductors, and a single-pole switch is _____.
    (a) 2.00 cu in.
    (b) 4.50 cu in.
    (c) 14.50 cu in.
    (d) 20.25 cu in.

59. For dwellings, all outdoor outlets, other than those covered in 210.8(A) Ex 1, and supplied by single-phase branch circuits rated 150V or less to ground, _____, shall be provided with GFCI protection.
    (a) 15A or more
    (b) 20A or less
    (c) 30A or less
    (d) 50A or less

60. Where more than two Type SE cables are installed in contact with thermal insulation, caulk, or sealing foam without maintaining spacing between cables, the ampacity of each conductor shall be _____ in accordance with Table 310.15(C)(1).
    (a) increased
    (b) adjusted
    (c) corrected
    (d) multiplied

61. Receptacles mounted to and supported by a cover shall be secured by more than _____ screw(s) unless listed and identified for securing by a single screw.
    (a) one
    (b) two
    (c) three
    (d) four

62. For dwelling unit load calculations in accordance Article 220, a load of not less than _____ for each 2-wire small-appliance branch circuit shall be applied.
    (a) 1000 VA
    (b) 1200 VA
    (c) 1500 VA
    (d) 2000 VA

63. Nameplates or manufacturer's instructions shall provide information as listed in 445.11(1) through (5) for all generators rated more than _____.

    (a) 12 kW
    (b) 15 kW
    (c) 18 kW
    (d) 20 kW

64. Cable trays shall be supported at _____ in accordance with the installation instructions.

    (a) intervals
    (b) portions
    (c) segments
    (d) any of these

65. Receptacles incorporating an isolated grounding conductor connection intended for the reduction of electromagnetic interference shall be identified by _____ located on the face of the receptacle.

    (a) the letters "IG"
    (b) a green circle
    (c) a green square
    (d) an orange triangle

66. In order for a metal underground water pipe to be used as a grounding electrode, it shall be in direct contact with the earth for _____.

    (a) 5 ft
    (b) 10 ft or more
    (c) less than 10 ft
    (d) 20 ft or more

67. The installation and use of all boxes and conduit bodies used as outlet, device, junction, or pull boxes, depending on their use, and handhole enclosures, are covered within _____.

    (a) Article 110
    (b) Article 200
    (c) Article 300
    (d) Article 314

68. In other than dwelling units, GFCI protection is required for receptacles installed in _____.

    (a) kitchens
    (b) unfinished areas of basements
    (c) laundry areas
    (d) all of these

69. Type UF cable shall not be used in _____.

    (a) motion picture studios
    (b) storage battery rooms
    (c) hoistways
    (d) all of these

70. Each _____ service conductor shall have overload protection.

    (a) overhead
    (b) underground
    (c) ungrounded
    (d) individual

71. Underground service conductors that supply power to limited loads of a single branch circuit shall not be smaller than _____.

    (a) 14 AWG copper
    (b) 14 AWG aluminum
    (c) 12 AWG copper
    (d) 12 AWG aluminum

72. Thermal insulation shall not be installed above a recessed luminaire or within _____ of the recessed luminaire's enclosure or wiring compartment unless the luminaire is identified as Type IC.

    (a) 1 in.
    (b) 1¼ in.
    (c) 1½ in.
    (d) 3 in.

73. When modifications to the electrical installation occur that affect the available fault current at the service, the available fault current shall be verified or _____ as necessary to ensure the service equipment ratings are sufficient for the available fault current at the line terminals of the equipment.

    (a) recalculated
    (b) increased
    (c) decreased
    (d) adjusted

74. All cut ends of LFMC conduit shall be _____ inside and outside to remove rough edges.

    (a) sanded
    (b) trimmed
    (c) brushed
    (d) any of these

75. Article _____ covers fixed electric equipment used for space heating including heating cables, unit heaters, boilers, central heating systems, or other fixed electric space-heating equipment.

    (a) 410
    (b) 422
    (c) 424
    (d) 440

76. ENT and fittings can be _____, provided fittings identified for this purpose are used.

    (a) encased in poured concrete floors, ceilings, walls, and slabs
    (b) embedded in a concrete slab on grade where the tubing is placed on sand or approved screenings
    (c) installed in wet locations as permitted in 362.10
    (d) any of these

77. Where attachment to an equipment grounding conductor does not exist in the receptacle enclosure, a nongrounding-type receptacle shall be permitted to be replaced with a GFCI-type receptacle; however, some equipment or appliance manufacturers require that the _____ to the equipment or appliance includes an equipment grounding conductor.

    (a) feeder
    (b) branch circuit
    (c) small-appliance circuit
    (d) power cord

78. Ground clamps and fittings that are exposed to physical damage shall be enclosed in _____ or equivalent protective covering.

    (a) metal or wood
    (b) wood or rubber
    (c) concrete
    (d) metal or plastic

79. Parallel conductors shall have the same _____.

    (a) length
    (b) conductor material
    (c) size in circular mil area
    (d) all of these

80. Replacement luminaires are not required to be connected to an equipment grounding conductor if no equipment grounding conductor exists at the outlet box and the luminaire is _____.

    (a) more than 20 years old
    (b) mounted to the box using nonmetallic fittings and screws
    (c) mounted more than 6 ft above the floor
    (d) GFCI protected

81. Mechanical continuity of raceways, cable armors, and cable sheaths as required by 300.12 does not apply to _____.

    (a) Type MI Cable
    (b) Type MC Cable
    (c) short sections of raceways used for support or protection of cable assemblies
    (d) any of these

82. Type NM cable shall not be used _____.

    (a) in other than dwelling units
    (b) in the air void of masonry block not subject to excessive moisture
    (c) for exposed work
    (d) embedded in poured cement, concrete, or aggregate

83. Where the voltage between conductors does not exceed 300, a reduction in clearance above only the overhanging portion of the roof to not less than _____ shall be permitted if not more than 6 ft of overhead service conductors, pass above the roof overhang 4 ft horizontally.

    (a) 12 in.
    (b) 18 in.
    (c) 2 ft
    (d) 5 ft

84. Where multiple outside feeder conductors to a building originate in the same panelboard, switchboard, or other distribution equipment, and each feeder terminates in a single disconnecting means, not more than _____ feeders are permitted to be run to the building.

    (a) two
    (b) four
    (c) six
    (d) eight

85. Overcurrent protective devices shall not be located _____.
    (a) where exposed to physical damage
    (b) near easily ignitible materials, such as in clothes closets
    (c) in bathrooms, showering facilities, or locker rooms with showering facilities
    (d) all of these

86. A grounding electrode conductor, sized in accordance with _____, shall be used to connect the equipment grounding conductors, the service-equipment enclosures, and, if the system is grounded, the grounded service conductor to the grounding electrode(s).
    (a) 250.66
    (b) 250.102(C)(1)
    (c) 250.122
    (d) 310.16

87. A pole supporting luminaires shall have a handhole not less than _____ with a cover suitable for use in wet locations to provide access to the supply terminations within the pole or pole base.
    (a) 2 in. × 2 in.
    (b) 2 in. × 4 in.
    (c) 4 in. × 4 in.
    (d) 4 in. × 6 in.

88. Where framing members do not readily permit fastening, RMC may be fastened within _____ of each outlet box, junction box, device box, cabinet, conduit body, or other conduit termination.
    (a) 3 ft
    (b) 4 ft
    (c) 5 ft
    (d) 8 ft

89. Alternating-current circuits of less than 50V shall be grounded if supplied by a transformer whose supply system exceeds _____.
    (a) 150V to ground
    (b) 300V to ground
    (c) 600V to ground
    (d) 1000V to ground

90. Unless otherwise specified, for purposes of calculating branch-circuit and feeder loads, _____ system voltages of 120V, 120/240V, 208Y/120V, 240V, 347V, 480Y/277V, 480V, 600Y/347V, and 600V shall be used.
    (a) nominal
    (b) separately derived
    (c) utility
    (d) secondary

91. Nonlocking-type 15A and 20A, 125V and 250V receptacles in a dwelling unit shall be listed as tamper resistant except _____.
    (a) receptacles located more than 8½ ft above the floor
    (b) receptacles that are part of an appliance
    (c) receptacles that are part of a luminaire
    (d) receptacles that are part of a luminaire or appliance

92. Underground service conductors shall have _____.
    (a) adequate mechanical strength
    (b) no splices
    (c) 90°C conductors
    (d) sufficient ampacity for the loads calculated

93. If installed _____ a building or structure, a metal piping system that is likely to become energized shall be bonded.
    (a) in
    (b) on
    (c) under
    (d) in or on

94. The circuit supplying _____ shall include an equipment grounding conductor. The frame of the appliance shall be connected to the equipment grounding conductor in the manner specified by 250.134 or 250.138.
    (a) electric ranges or clothes dryers
    (b) electric wall mounted ovens
    (c) electric counter-mounted cooking units
    (d) any of these

95. Receptacle terminals marked CO/ALR shall be permitted to be used with _____ conductors.
    (a) aluminum
    (b) copper
    (c) copper-clad aluminum
    (d) any of these

96. A "surface metal raceway" is a metal raceway that is intended to be mounted to the surface of a structure, with associated couplings, connectors, boxes, and fittings for the _____ of electrical conductors.

    (a) installation
    (b) protection
    (c) routing
    (d) enclosure

97. Horizontal runs of IMC supported by openings through framing members at intervals not exceeding _____ and securely fastened within 3 ft of terminations shall be permitted.

    (a) 5 ft
    (b) 8 ft
    (c) 10 ft
    (d) 15 ft

98. "Bonded" is defined as _____ to establish electrical continuity and conductivity.

    (a) isolated
    (b) guarded
    (c) connected
    (d) separated

99. One or more metal in-ground support structure(s) in direct contact with the earth vertically for _____ or more, with or without concrete encasement, is permitted to be a grounding electrode in accordance with 250.52.

    (a) 4 ft
    (b) 6 ft
    (c) 8 ft
    (d) 10 ft

100. Where a service _____ enters a building or structure, it shall be sealed in accordance with 300.5(G) and 300.7(A).

    (a) raceway
    (b) cable assembly
    (c) cable tray
    (d) any of these

WHAT'S THE NEXT STEP?

Follow the wheel and see how to take your career to the next level

Never stop learning...

To be a success, you have to remain current, relevant, and marketable. Your individual success is a function of your education and the key is continuous self-improvement, even if just a little each day. Here is a great map to make sure you have taken all the steps to complete your electrical education.

Mike Holt

MikeHolt.com/NextStep

LET'S GET YOU TO THAT NEXT LEVEL!
Call 888.632.2633 or visit MikeHolt.com/NextStep

Notes

ABOUT THE AUTHOR

Mike Holt
Founder and President
Mike Holt Enterprises
Groveland, Florida

Mike Holt is an author, businessman, educator, speaker, publisher and *National Electrical Code* expert. He has written hundreds of electrical training books and articles, founded three successful businesses, and has taught thousands of electrical *Code* seminars across the U.S. and internationally. His dynamic presentation style, deep understanding of the trade, and ability to connect with students are some of the reasons that he is one of the most sought-after speakers in the industry.

His company, Mike Holt Enterprises, has been serving the electrical industry for almost 50 years, with a commitment to creating and publishing books, videos, online training, and curriculum support for electrical trainers, students, organizations, and electrical professionals. His devotion to the trade, coupled with the lessons he learned at the University of Miami's MBA program, have helped him build one of the largest electrical training and publishing companies in the United States.

Mike is committed to changing lives and helping people take their careers to the next level. He has always felt a responsibility to provide education beyond the scope of just passing an exam. He draws on his previous experience as an electrician, inspector, contractor and instructor, to guide him in developing powerful training solutions that electricians understand and enjoy. He is always mindful of how hard learning can be for students who are intimidated by school, by their feelings towards learning, or by the complexity of the *NEC*. He's mastered the art of simplifying and clarifying complicated technical concepts and his extensive use of illustrations helps students apply the content and relate the material to their work in the field. His ability to take the intimidation out of learning is reflected in the successful careers of his students.

Mike's commitment to pushing boundaries and setting high standards extends into his personal life as well. He's an eight-time Overall National Barefoot Waterski Champion. Mike has more than 20 gold medals, many national records, and has competed in three World Barefoot Tournaments. In 2015, at the tender age of 64, he started a new adventure—competitive mountain bike racing and at 65 began downhill mountain biking. Every day he continues to find ways to motivate himself, both mentally and physically.

Mike and his wife, Linda, reside in New Mexico and Florida, and are the parents of seven children and seven grandchildren. As his life has changed over the years, a few things have remained constant: his commitment to God, his love for his family, and doing what he can to change the lives of others through his products and seminars.

Special Acknowledgments

My Family. First, I want to thank God for my godly wife who's always by my side and for my children.

My Staff. A personal thank you goes to my team at Mike Holt Enterprises for all the work they do to help me with my mission of changing peoples' lives through education. They work tirelessly to ensure that, in addition to our products meeting and exceeding the educational needs of our customers, we stay committed to building life-long relationships throughout their electrical careers.

The National Fire Protection Association. A special thank you must be given to the staff at the National Fire Protection Association (NFPA), publishers of the *NEC*—in particular, Jeff Sargent for his assistance in answering my many *Code* questions over the years. Jeff, you're a "first class" guy, and I admire your dedication and commitment to helping others understand the *NEC*.

ABOUT THE ILLUSTRATOR

Mike Culbreath—Illustrator

Mike Culbreath
Graphic Illustrator
Alden, Michigan

Mike Culbreath has devoted his career to the electrical industry and worked his way up from apprentice electrician to master electrician. He started working in the electrical field doing residential and light commercial construction, and later did service work and custom electrical installations. While working as a journeyman electrician, he suffered a serious on-the-job knee injury. As part of his rehabilitation, Mike completed courses at Mike Holt Enterprises, and then passed the exam to receive his Master Electrician's license. In 1986, with a keen interest in continuing education for electricians, he joined the staff to update material and began illustrating Mike Holt's textbooks and magazine articles.

Mike started with simple hand-drawn diagrams and cut-and-paste graphics. Frustrated by the limitations of that style of illustrating, he took a company computer home to learn how to operate some basic computer graphics software. Realizing that computer graphics offered a lot of flexibility for creating illustrations, Mike took every computer graphics class and seminar he could to help develop his skills. He's worked as an illustrator and editor with the company for over 30 years and, as Mike Holt has proudly acknowledged, has helped to transform his words and visions into lifelike graphics.

Originally from South Florida, Mike now lives in northern lower Michigan where he enjoys hiking, kayaking, photography, gardening, and cooking; but his real passion is his horses. He also loves spending time with his children Dawn and Mac and his grandchildren Jonah, Kieley, and Scarlet.

ABOUT THE MIKE HOLT TEAM

There are many people who play a role in the production of Mike Holt books. Their efforts are reflected in the quality and organization of the information contained in the books, and in their technical accuracy, completeness, and usability.

Technical Writing

Mario Valdes is the Technical Content Editor and works directly with Mike to ensure that content is technically accurate, relatable, and valuable to all electrical professionals. He plays an important role in gathering research, analyzing data, and assisting Mike in the writing of the textbooks. He reworks content into different formats to improve the flow of information and ensure expectations are being met in terms of message, tone, and quality. He edits illustrations and proofreads content to "fact-check" each sentence, title, and image structure.

Mario is licensed as an Electrical Contractor, most recently having worked as an electrical inspector and plans examiner for an engineering firm in South Florida. Additionally, he was an Electrical Instructor for a technical college, teaching students pursuing an associate degree in electricity. He taught subjects such as ac/dc fundamentals, residential and commercial wiring, blueprint reading, and electrical estimating. He brings to the Mike Holt team a wealth of knowledge and devotion for the *NEC*.

Editorial and Production

Brian House is Vice President of Digital and Technical Training at Mike Holt Enterprises. He leads the apprenticeship and digital product teams, creating cutting-edge training tools, and partnering with in-house and apprenticeship training programs nationwide. He is part of the content team that helps Mike bring his products to market, assisting in the editing of textbooks, coordinating content and illustrations, and assuring technical accuracy and flow of information.

Brian is a licensed unlimited electrical contractor in multiple states, and ran an electrical contracting firm for nearly two decades. His work covered service and new construction for residential, commercial and industrial sites to designing and installing energy-efficient lighting retrofits, "green" biomass generators, and Solar PV systems. Brian is also a Certified Mike Holt Instructor and travels across the country to teach Mike Holt seminars. He's a permanent member of Mike Holt's video panel for the videos that accompany Mike Holt textbooks.

Toni Culbreath works tirelessly to proofread and edit the publications. Her attention to detail and her dedication is irreplaceable. A very special thank you goes out to Toni (Mary Poppins) Culbreath for her many years of dedicated service.

Cathleen Kwas handled the design, layout, and typesetting of this book. Her desire to create the best possible product for our customers is greatly appreciated, and she constantly pushes the design envelope to make the product experience just a little bit better.

Vinny Perez and **Eddie Anacleto** have been a dynamic team. They have taken the best instructional graphics in the industry to the next level. Both Eddie and Vinny bring years of graphic art experience to the pages of this book and have been a huge help updating and improving the content, look, and style our graphics.

Dan Haruch is an integral part of the video recording process for all of the textbooks, and spends much of his time making sure that the instructor resources created from those products are the best in the business. His dedication to the instructor and student experience is much appreciated.

Notes

INVEST IN YOURSELF

Save 25% On One Of These Best-Selling Libraries

Comprehensive Exam Preparation Video Library

A complete course designed for your success, in-depth instruction for electrical theory and Code, with step-by-step instructions for solving electrical calculations.

PROGRAM INCLUDES:

Understanding Electrical Theory Textbook
• Electrical Theory videos

Understanding the NEC® Volume 1 Textbook
• Understanding The NEC® Volume 1 videos

Bonding and Grounding Textbook
• Bonding and Grounding videos

Understanding the NEC® Volume 2 Textbook
• Understanding The NEC® Volume 2 videos

Electrical Exam Preparation Textbook
• Electrical Calculations videos

Master or Journeyman Electrician Practice Exam
NEC® Online Quiz
Digital answer keys

Plus! A digital version of each book

Master Library [23MACOMM]
Journeyman Library [23JRCOMM]

6 Textbooks | 6 Digital Books | 130+ Video Streaming Hours | Streaming Audio

---

Life Skills Video Program

This program explores the core skills of success. It will help you create a personal program to help you improve your ability to reach your goals in your professional and everyday life. This life skills primer gives you the roadmap to build the life you want and reach all of your goals. Learn with Mike as he shares his wisdom and experiences that have made him successful in business for over 40 years.

PROGRAM INCLUDES:

Life Skills Textbook
• Life Skills videos
• Life Skills streaming audio
Plus! A digital version of the book

Product Code: [LIFEMM]

Electrical Estimating Video Program

It's important to understand how to price your jobs to run your business profitably. Mike's Electrical Estimating Program teaches you what's involved in costing a job (materials, labor, overhead) in order to maximize profit; it also explains how to complete the bid by determining material costs, labor costs, and the calculation of direct job costs and overhead. You'll learn how to be competitive, and when necessary, say "no" to a job.

PROGRAM INCLUDES:

Electrical Estimating Textbook
• Electrical Estimating videos
Digital answer key
Plus! A digital version of the book

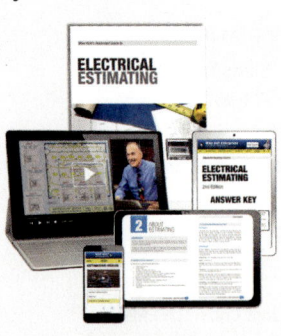

Product Code: [EST2MM]

Call Now 888.632.2633
Discount code: B23UN1WB25
or Order Online at MikeHolt.com/Products

Mike Holt Enterprises

INVEST IN YOURSELF

Save 25% On One Of These Best-Selling Libraries

Comprehensive Exam Preparation Video Library

A complete course designed for your success, in-depth instruction for electrical theory and Code, with step-by-step instructions for solving electrical calculations.

PROGRAM INCLUDES:

Understanding Electrical Theory Textbook
- *Electrical Theory videos*

Understanding the NEC° Volume 1 Textbook
- *Understanding The NEC° Volume 1 videos*

Bonding and Grounding Textbook
- *Bonding and Grounding videos*

Understanding the NEC° Volume 2 Textbook
- *Understanding The NEC° Volume 2 videos*

Electrical Exam Preparation Textbook
- *Electrical Calculations videos*

Master or Journeyman Electrician Practice Exam
NEC° Online Quiz
Digital answer keys

Plus! A digital version of each book

Master Library [23MACOMM]
Journeyman Library [23JRCOMM]

6 Textbooks | 6 Digital Books | 130+ Video Streaming Hours | Streaming Audio

Life Skills Video Program

This program explores the core skills of success. It will help you create a personal program to help you improve your ability to reach your goals in your professional and everyday life. This life skills primer gives you the roadmap to build the life you want and reach all of your goals. Learn with Mike as he shares his wisdom and experiences that have made him successful in business for over 40 years.

PROGRAM INCLUDES:
Life Skills Textbook
- *Life Skills videos*
- *Life Skills streaming audio*

Plus! A digital version of the book

Product Code: [LIFEMM]

Electrical Estimating Video Program

It's important to understand how to price your jobs to run your business profitably. Mike's Electrical Estimating Program teaches you what's involved in costing a job (materials, labor, overhead) in order to maximize profit; it also explains how to complete the bid by determining material costs, labor costs, and the calculation of direct job costs and overhead. You'll learn how to be competitive, and when necessary, say "no" to a job.

PROGRAM INCLUDES:
Electrical Estimating Textbook
- *Electrical Estimating videos*
Digital answer key

Plus! A digital version of the book

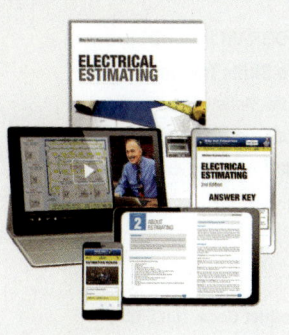

Product Code: [EST2MM]

Call Now 888.632.2633
Discount code: B23UN1WB25
or Order Online at MikeHolt.com/Products

Mike Holt Enterprises